Nowhere Countries: Exclusion of Non-Citizens from Rights through Extra-Territoriality at Home

Nowhere Countries: Exclusion of Non-Citizens from Rights through Extra-Territoriality at Home

By

Pauline Maillet

BRILL
NIJHOFF

LEIDEN | BOSTON

Cover illustration: Nowhere country. Copyright Rafael Moreno.

Library of Congress Cataloging-in-Publication Data

Names: Maillet, Pauline, author.
Title: Nowhere countries : exclusion of non-citizens from rights through extra-territoriality at home / Pauline Maillet.
Description: Boston : BRILL, 2020. | Includes bibliographical references and index. | Summary: "What do the international airports of France and Morocco, the Australian islands of Cocos and Christmas and Canada's Vancouver Island have in common? At first sight, this is nothing but a collection of dispersed geographical sites whose names may evoke distant exotic or refined lands and the associated delights of travels far away from home. These travel promises may well materialize for the holders of a passport delivered by a wealthy country, who experience the pleasures and convenience of international mobility"– Provided by publisher.
Identifiers: LCCN 2019043814 | ISBN 9789004383494 (hardback) | ISBN 9789004383500 (ebook)
Subjects: LCSH: Exterritoriality. | Freedom of movement. | Emigration and immigration law. | Emigration and immigration–Government policy. | Aliens. | Minorities–Legal status, laws, etc. | International law and human rights.
Classification: LCC KZ3678 .M35 2020 | DDC 342.08/3–dc23
LC record available at https://lccn.loc.gov/2019043814

Typeface for the Latin, Greek, and Cyrillic scripts: "Brill". See and download: brill.com/brill-typeface.

ISBN 978-90-04-38349-4 (hardback)
ISBN 978-90-04-38350-0 (e-book)

This book is printed on acid-free paper and produced in a sustainable manner.

Tis strange -but true; for Truth is always strange;
Stranger than fiction.

LORD BYRON, Canto XIV, Don Juan (1823)

Contents

Acknowledgments

This book could not have been written without considerable support from many people. It was truly a privilege to be part of the Balsillie School of International Affairs' diverse and dynamic community. I could not have dreamed of a more stimulating, international, interdisciplinary and supportive research environment. Special gratitude is owed to my doctoral committee from the Balsillie School of International Affairs (Canada), Wilfrid Laurier University (Canada) and the University of North Carolina (United States). Alison Mountz was a great mentor, providing me with intellectual support and guidance. She made my work much richer, encouraging me to pursue ethnography and helping me navigate the challenges of data collection in a highly politicized field. I am also indebted to Rhoda E. Howard-Hassmann for her rigorous intellectual guidance and sound advice. She strengthened my work, encouraging me to make my research more accessible to a wider audience and to publish it as a book. I owe many thanks to Kim Rygiel, who took the time to provide me with detailed and constructive feedback and who was always very supportive; her knowledge of the French context was very precious. I would like to thank Mark Gibney, whose legal expertise was highly appreciated. I am also very grateful for the generous financial support of the Balsillie School of International Affairs, Wilfrid Laurier University and the Province of Ontario.

Special thanks go to my good friends and colleagues Shani Hormozi, Taguhi Dallakyan and Tracey Wagner-Rivzi for their collegiality and unfaltering support. It has been great to learn from and count on each other. This work owes much to their enduring friendship.

I also owe thanks to Jean-Marie Fardeau, former director of the Paris Office of Human Rights Watch, for his trust and for putting me in touch with the relevant individuals in the organization. It was a pleasure to do research at Charles de Gaulle and Orly airports with Alice Farmer and Laura Schülke. I am grateful to Emeritus Law professor Danièle Lochak for opening her archives, thereby enabling me to fine-tune my understanding of the history of the waiting zone. I would also like to express my appreciation to Rafaël Moreno, who took pictures to illustrate this book. His professionalism and patience were very valuable.

Research participants deserve recognition and thanks for their trust. Many interviewees were very generous with their time and eager to share their expertise. I have been truly humbled and inspired by some of the people I interviewed, particularly activists. I must, of course, acknowledge all the individuals I met while engaging in participant observation, and particularly those placed under the waiting zone framework. This book is dedicated to the latter and to all non-citizens stranded in nowhere countries in general.

My final and most heartfelt thanks are to my family. I have been very lucky to be able to count on my two brothers, Emile and Hadrien Maillet, and on my sister in law, Ezaline De Faget de Casteljau. Their hospitality, kindness and encouragements throughout this endeavor were very precious. I am most grateful to my parents, Janguy and Maryse Maillet, for their unwavering support and belief in this project. I continue, to this day, to be inspired by their generosity, strength of character and personal integrity..

Illustrations

Figures

Map

Charts

Tables

Abbreviations

Anafé	*Association nationale d'assistance aux frontières pour les étrangers* (National Organization for Assistance to Foreign Nationals at Borders)
CDG	Charles de Gaulle. The full name of the airport is Roissy-Charles de Gaulle.
CESEDA	*Code de l'entrée et du séjour des étrangers et du droit d'asile* (Code on the Entry and Residency of Foreign Nationals and the Right to Asylum)
CFDT	*Confédération française démocratique du travail* (Democratic French Work Confederation)
CIC	Citizenship and Immigration Canada
Cimade	*Comité Inter-Mouvements Auprès des Evacués* (Inter-Faith Committee for Evacuees)
CNDA	*Cour nationale du droit d'asile* (National Court of Asylum)
DCPAF	*Direction Centrale de la Police aux Frontières* (Central Border Police Department)
DIMIA	Department of Immigration and Multicultural and Indigenous Affairs
EC	European Commission
ECRE	European Council on Refugees and Exiles
EMN	European Migration Network
GASAI	*Groupe d'analyse et de suivi des affaires d'immigration* (Immigration Affairs Review and Monitoring Group of French Border Police)
Gisti	*Groupe d'information et de soutien des immigrés* (Group providing information and support to immigrants)
HRW	Human Rights Watch
IATA	International Air Transport Association
ICAO	International Civil Aviation Organization
IGC	Intergovernmental consultations on migration, asylum and refugees
INAD	Inadmissible person
ITF	International Transport Workers' Federation
NGO	Non-governmental organization
OFPRA	*Office Français de Protection des Réfugiés et Apatrides* (French Office for Protection of Refugees and Stateless persons)
UNESI	*Unité nationale d'escorte, de soutien et d'intervention* (National escort, support and intervention unit)
ZAPI 3	*Zone d'attente pour personnes en instance* (Waiting zone for persons whose case is pending)

Introduction

What do the international airports of France and Morocco, the Australian islands of Cocos and Christmas and Canada's Vancouver Island have in common? At first sight, this is nothing but a collection of dispersed geographical sites whose names may evoke distant exotic or refined lands and the associated delights of travels far away from home. These travel promises may well materialize for the holders of a passport delivered by a wealthy country, who experience the pleasures and convenience of international mobility. For others, the unwelcome non-citizens (be they refugees, asylum seekers, impoverished tourists -really impecunious or perceived as such- or labour migrants), the experience was, has been, and is different altogether. Upon their physical arrival on certain parts of the sovereign territories of the aforementioned States, they were, have been or are deemed outside of France, Australia, Canada and Morocco for the purposes of immigration law. These *personae non gratae* were, have been or are denied access to certain rights (in part or in total) or subjected to a less advantageous legal framework on account of their presence in an extra-national space, or rather in a space *construed* as extra-national. The term "nowhere countries", coined by French activists, aptly describes these spaces *deemed* extra-territorial for non-citizens categorized as undesirable. Neither in nor out the country, those rejected at the aiport border or arriving by boat have arrived to "Not-France", "Not-Australia", "Not-Canada", or "Not-Morocco" and have been denied the rights normally accrued upon arrival on sovereign territory.

This book traces some of the past -and sometimes actual- practices, policies and legal mechanisms developed by France, Australia, Canada and Morroco to exclude undesired non-citizens from rights through extra-territoriality. In other words, it demonstrates how these countries have managed to claim that the non-citizens in question are somehow located outside of their territories to avoid conferring them the domestic and international rights associated with sovereign soil. Disguised as highly technical and abstract issues, the exclusionary strategies presented here directly impact a significant number of human lives, changing people's fate.

1 Terminology: What Do I Mean by "extra-territoriality"?

I need to clarify my usage of the term "extra-territoriality", which differs from that of many authors. When using the noun "extra-territoriality" or the

 DOI:10.1163/9789004383500_002

adjective "extra-territorial", I do not refer to States acting outside of their territorial boundaries.[1] In today's globalized world, States engage in conduct that significantly affects the individual's human rights beyond their borders (Coomans and MT Kamminga 2004). States police irregular migration beyond their territorial limits, on other States' territories or on international areas (such as the high seas) (Ryan and Mitsilegas 2010). An important literature has developed to argue that States' obligations under international human rights and refugee law do not stop at their borders (see Langford et al 2013; Gibney and Skogly 2002 and 2010; De Schutter et al 2012; Salomon and Seiderman 2012; King 2009; Coomans and MT Kamminga 2004; Gondek 2009). Gammeltoft-Hansen (2011) has demonstrated that States retain some responsibilities under refugee and international human rights law when they exercise migration controls well outside of their borders, as for example in international waters or in areas under foreign territorial jurisdiction. Such obligations extending beyond geographical boundaries have been called "extraterritorial obligations" (without a hyphen).

By contrast, in this book, I use the term "extra-territoriality" (with a hyphen) to refer to exclusionary pratices taking place within States' territories. More precisely, this term refers to the designation, by a State, of a piece of its territory as "not national territory", for certain categories of people: non-citizens *depicted* as undesirable. I argue that exclusion from rights through extra-territoriality may take two main forms. Under the first configuration, State authorities refuse to accord the (full) protection of human, refugee and domestic legal rights to some non-citizens who are physically located in spaces labeled "extra-territorial". This reasoning is premised on the argument that the non-citizens in question are simply not located on the State's territory. Since they do not encounter themselves in national space, they cannot benefit from the protection afforded by domestic or international law. Under this first configuration, non-citizens are placed in a legal limbo: they are left outside of applicable legal frameworks, both at the domestic and international levels. State authorities exclude non-citizens from the applicable legal regime by refusing to apply it.

Scholars and activists alike have referred to the process of designating national spaces as extra-territorial as "legal fictions" (Gammeltoft-Hansen 2011) or as "extraterritorial legal fictions" (Del Valle Galvez 2005- *Ficción jurídica*

---

1 I am aware that some scholars use the term "extraterritoriality" more broadly. For example, Weizman (2005) also uses the noun to refer to "sites that are within the body of the state but over which it has lost control". He observes that such extraterritorial sites can become "quasi-utopian spaces".

extraterritorial in Spanish). Such legal fictions are particularly dangerous for those who are caught in their nets: they establish an internal no man's land and raise issues of legal insecurity and the absence of legality. They result in the non-application, or at least incomplete application, of the domestic and international norms regarding immigration and asylum that bind States (Del Valle Galvez 2005). A regional human rights court, the European Court of Human Rights, found such practices illegal in the landmark case *Amuur v. France* in 1996. The establishment of extra-territorial spaces within national territory as devices for States to *openly* deflect from domestic and international obligations was *formally* rejected. This (partly) explains why States have turned to another, subtler, type of exclusion through extra-territoriality.

The second configuration is less manifest; non-citizens who physically encounter themselves in spaces labeled "extra-territorial" are not straightforwardly denied legal protection. Rather, they are accorded a less protective regime compared to that granted to non-citizens who are *not* located in spaces *designated* as extra-territorial. Under this second configuration, non-citizens are not left outside of the reach of the law, but are subjected to an alternate legal framework that provides diminished protection. Parallel -and less protective- legal frameworks build on the premise that unwelcome non-citizens at the border find themselves at the threshold of, but not having yet entered sovereign territory. They find themselves, instead, in territorial border zones where the State establishes the distinction between physical and legal entry: physical presence proves insufficient and only lawful admission amounts to entry into the territory (Basaran 2011). Although physically on national soil, rejected non-citizens at the border are not present from a legal standpoint, for they have not crossed yet "law's admission gate" (Shachar 2007). The first and the second configurations of extra-territoriality are not necessarily mutually exclusive, as a study of the French case of the airport's international zone and waiting zone will reveal. This second form of extra-territoriality enables States to appear engaged in the global refugee protection regime, while severely undermining the latter. This book aims to present some of the legal mechanisms, enforcement practices and mental landscapes that have upheld various extra-territorial spaces of exclusion worldwide. The terms "extra-territorial", "extra-national" and "non national" will be used interchangeably. In these times of seemingly unending migration crisis, scholarship that documents violations of non-citizens' rights by State authorities abound. Yet, insufficient attention has been accorded to extra-territorial spaces as mechanisms of exclusion from rights. Since the 1996 *Amuur* case, several scholars and practitioners have dismissed such exclusionary mechanisms as belonging to the past (cf. chapter 3). I propose to demonstrate that, on the contrary, they are very much in use today and should be studied in their own right.

2 Liberal Democracies and Extra-Territorial Exclusion

Importantly, the exclusionary devices presented in this book were all designed and exported by liberal democracies (France, Australia and Canada). The latter are parties to human rights and refugee conventions at the regional and international levels. In France and Australia, elected Parliaments actively contributed to and validated the creation of extra-territorial spaces of exclusion. Findings validate Hindess' (2001, 94), observation that liberal government and authoritarian practices are not mutually exclusive, but rather two sides of the same coin. Liberal discourse and the discourse of exception (Agamben 1998, 2005; Butler 2004) associate deprivation of rights with exception, extra-legality or emphasis on executive powers. By contrast, research findings illustrate Basaran's (2011, 109) observation: "The challenge of liberties is inherent to liberal rule and the rule of law, which always contain within themselves the possibility for limiting liberties, for creating new legal exclusions". I intend to trace and expose the extra-territorial mechanisms that have been mobilized to produce rejection, illegality, and deprivation of rights within liberal democracies. I do not mean to drive the reader into despair but rather to offer a counterpoint to the dominant discourse that there is "no other way" to deal with non-citizens attempting to enter liberal democracies. The mistreatment of non-citizens on the move, including people seeking refuge, has become so normalized today, that it is hard to recall that a few decades ago, not only did liberal democracies such as France and Australia let non-citizens enter their borders fluidly, but also actively recruited them. By going back to the origin of these exclusionary devices, by showing how they were constructed, I hope to convey the message that there is nothing "natural" about the exclusion of non-citizens through extra-territoriality.

3 Extra-Territorial Exclusion as a *Non-Entrée* Mechanism

Wealthy countries began to erect (literal and figurative) fences between people in need of international protection and themselves in the hope of curtailing the number of asylum claimants reaching their territories in the 1980s. Hathaway (1992) first referred to such fences as *non-entrée* practices in 1992. The latter include, but are not limited to, excision of zones of arrival, airport transit visas, carrier sanctions, maritime interception on the high seas, immigration liaison officers at departure points, safe third countries agreements. The extra-territorial exclusionary mechanisms described in this book have to be situated within a wider network of measures designed to prevent asylum seekers' arrival. In other terms, nowhere countries are but one of the many devices developed by States to stop unwanted non-citizens from reaching their gates. They are actually the last mechanism to hold back claimants, when all the previous ones have failed. They constitute a *non-entrée* tool in their own right. Nowhere countries can be established and thrive on any part of a State territory, but international zones at airports have been spaces of choice for these extra-territorial zones of exclusion.

4 The Status of the International Zone at International Airports

International airports are interesting sites where legal and cartographic borders do not map onto one another (Lochak 1992). There, borders are created at the heart of States' territories, without a territorial delimitation between States. This creation of borders *ex nihilo,* or what Del Valle Galvez (2005) refers to as the "legal fiction of the interior border", is permissible under international law, as there is no human right to enter a country, except one's own.[2] The admission of an individual to a country is a State's discretionary act. However, as Del Valle Galvez (2005) explains, this "legal fiction of the interior border" can easily lead to an "extra-territorial legal fiction" (hyphen added). France implemented this extra-territorial legal fiction in the 1980s and early 1990s.

The French government considered individuals in international zones to be *not* on French territory for they had not gone through police control and customs. Thus, France transformed the legal distinction between *de facto* entry and formal entry (that characterizes the "legal fiction of the interior border") into the dichotomy formal entry/no formal entry. This manoeuvre allowed the French government to circumvent domestic and international laws. When these events unfolded, France, like other Council of Europe States, was witnessing a surge in the number of asylum seekers arriving at its gates (Parliamentary Assembly of the Council of Europe, 1988). France used the international zone as a buffer zone to keep undesirable non-citizens, and asylum seekers in their midst, at bay.

2 Cf. the Universal Declaration of Human Rights, article 13 (2): "Everyone has the right to leave any country, including his own, and to return to his country".

The Convention on International Civil Aviation (hereafter "Chicago Convention") came into being on December 7, 1944 so that "international civil aviation may be developed in a safe and orderly manner" (Chicago Convention 1944, preamble). Annex 9 to the Chicago Convention uses the term "direct transit area". This international legal instrument (July 2005, Twelfth Edition, Chapter 1.A)[3] defines such space as "a special area established in an international airport approved by the public authorities concerned and under their direct supervision or control, where passengers can stay during transit or transfer without applying for entry to the State". However, Annex 9 does not specify the perimeter of the "direct transit area". Kpatinde (1995) explains that the transit area "usually stretches from the runway to the first police checkpoint". The international zone in airports is also called "sterile zone" or "transit zone" in other countries. Under international law, international zones are not extra-territorial spaces. As soon as legal scholars, international human rights courts and treaty monitoring bodies turned to the matter of the international or transit zone, they clearly stated that this space was integrally part of the State's territory.

5 Research Scope and Methodology

This interdisciplinary research endeavor was originally confined to the international and waiting zones of Paris Roissy-Charles de Gaulle (CDG) airport in France. I collected, analyzed and organized data on the legal and geographic spaces of exclusion at the French international airport over the course of four years. As it became clear that such exclusionary legal techniques, practices and mental landscapes were not circumscribed to the French site, it seemed fit to signal that other countries were similarly resorting to extra-territoriality to stop non-citizens depicted as undesirable from reaching their soil. Strikingly similar exclusionary mechanisms appeared to be at work in France, Morocco, Canada and Australia, in spite of the (significant) geographical distance separating these countries from one another. This book does not ambition to offer the reader the same level of information on the four geographical sites but rather to point to the similarities amongst these extra-territorial exclusionary devices. Before detailing the research methods that were used, I need to explain what French waiting zones are and why I first chose to study CDG airport's waiting zone.

3 The first page of Annex 9 reads: "This edition incorporates all amendments adopted by the Council prior to 8 March 2005 and supersedes, on November 2005, all previous editions of Annex 9".

In the 1980s and early 1990s, the French government argued that the international zone of Paris' airports was not French territory, refusing to provide those confined there with domestic and international rights. When the Law on the Waiting Zone came into existence in 1992, non-citizens at the border ceased to be detained in a legal vacuum premised on extra-territoriality. Since this time, designation of the term "waiting zone" has assigned both legal and geographical dimensions to this place. The Law on the Waiting Zone establishes a particular legal regime for non-citizens (French: "*étranger*") denied entry into French or Schengen territory or claiming asylum at a French border arriving by train, boat or airplane (CESEDA 2016 articles L221-1 to L224-4).[4] Individuals located in the waiting zone are not governed by ordinary laws, but instead subjected to its particular legal regime. The regular refugee determination procedures do not apply to asylum seekers at the border. Unaccompanied minors are denied due process rights that children in France enjoy (HRW April 8, 2014).

This parallel legal regime created a "legal space of lesser rights" (Basaran 2011) for rejected non-citizens and asylum seekers at the border, whom have been considered outside of the country from a legal standpoint. Since the implementation of the Law on the Waiting Zone, foreign nationals arriving at the border have been subjected to a watered-down legal framework compared to the one applicable to their counterparts already deemed on French soil—who are either applying for asylum or are to be removed after being caught for residing illegally in the country.

Individuals falling under the purview of the waiting zone framework are detained during the time necessary for them to be returned or, if they are claiming asylum, to determine whether or not their claim is inadmissible or "manifestly unfounded". As a rule, only asylum seekers passing this initial screening will be entitled to enter French territory where claims will be examined on their merits. Since the new law that passed on July 29, 2015, asylum seekers may also be admitted to the territory when deemed particularly vulnerable by the refugee agency. When not considered as such, unaccompanied minors seeking asylum still have to pass the "manifestly unfounded test", save in a very few cases.

4 The French legal document "CESEDA" (*Code de l'entrée et du séjour des étrangers et du droit d'asile*) gathers all laws and policies applicable to the entry and residency of non-citizens (including asylum seekers) in the country. It is available at: http://www.legifrance.gouv.fr/affichCode.do?cidTexte=LEGITEXT000006070158. The original Law on the Waiting zone and its subsequent updates and extensions can all be found in this online document.

I chose to focus on CDG's waiting zone. The international airport of Paris CDG is France's main and Europe's second largest airport (HRW, 2009). The airport serves more than 60 million passengers every year, and CDG's waiting zone detains the greatest number of individuals in France; in 2011, 6013 individuals were denied entry (Paris' Airports 2012, 7; Anafé January 2013, 18) and more than 88 percent of asylum applications at French borders were made there (OFPRA April 11, 2012, 34). CDG is also the only waiting zone to feature a built-in detention center (called "ZAPI 3").

This work called for several research methods. Firstly, I engaged in discourse analysis of a variety of sources. I studied laws, minutes of parliamentary debates, domestic legal and administrative documents, reports written by parliamentarians, documents produced by activists, court judgments at the domestic and European level, government's response to reports by the Council of Europe and by Human Rights Treaty-based bodies (such as the Committee against torture or the Committee on the Rights of the Child). This analysis shed light on how some ideas become common sense and set aside different interpretations (Waitt, 2010).

Secondly, I carried out 35 semi-structured expert interviews. The politicized nature of the issue of the waiting zone rendered participants wary of researchers. The former were reassured by my university affiliation in North America and the fact that research findings would be written in English. Participants were invited to answer questions regarding their perception of the legal framework applying to the border zone, their role and actions therein. I interviewed many different actors who were interacting with or governing foreign nationals placed in CDG's waiting zone: civil servants; volunteers and employees of domestic civil society organizations; employees of regional and international organizations; legal and religious practitioners; interpreters; members of Parliament. Interviews showed the gaps between how policies and laws are written and how they are put into daily practice (Mountz, 2010). Unless otherwise specified, interviews were carried out in person between August 2013 and August 2014. Interviewees were identified through the snowball method described by Babbie and Benaquisto (2009), participant-observation at courts and information publicly available on the Internet. Those confined in the waiting zone were not interviewed.

Thirdly, I used the participant observation method. As Coutin and Fortin (2015) note, ethnographies

> provide insight into the workings of law on the ground, the consciousnesses of legal actors, the routine practices of legal institutions, the impacts of law in the lives of marginalized groups, the nature of legal

> advocacy and the differences between law's claims and its realities, all of which have been key to seeing law as a social phenomenon rather than merely as doctrine.

I observed court proceedings before the Court of First Instance, the Appeal Court and the Administrative Court. Those placed under the waiting zone regime are presented to a liberty and custody judge at the Court of First Instance after four and 12 days of detention. The role of this judge is to review the legality of the foreign national's detention. The liberty and custody judge assesses whether authorities respected the "fundamental rights" of the persons subjected to the waiting zone framework. Should this not be the case, the liberty and custody judge has the power to release the non-citizen from the waiting zone, *de facto* admitting the person to the territory. At the time of research, non-citizens placed in CDG's waiting zone were brought to the Bobigny Court of First Instance, located 17 kilometers away from the airport. Since October 2017, hearings before the liberty and custody judge take place at the airport, in a building designated as an "annex" to the Bobigny Court. This new court, whose existence and operation has raised tremendous indignation amongst non-citizens' rights advocates, is located next to the detention center, on airport compounds (cf. figure 1).

As for the judge at the Appeal Court, he or she hears appeals against the liberty and custody judges' rulings. Finally, the administrative judge adjudicates appeals launched by asylum claimants against the Ministry of the Interior's decision refusing them entry to the country on asylum grounds (cf. charts 1 and 2). Court hearings are public and I did not need to seek permission to observe them. I had the opportunity of observing the work of a state-paid lawyer at the Court of First Instance at Bobigny.

I also engaged in participant observation at CDG, visiting the places where rejected travelers and asylum seekers are detained: small cells -that can be found in almost every terminal- and CDG's administrative detention center. I had sought the permission from the Ministry of the Interior to visit these places with the NGO (non-governmental organization) Human Rights Watch (HRW). Permission was granted at the end of January 2014. I carried out eight visits from January to March 2014. I also visited Paris Orly airport's waiting zone twice within this time frame: the room at the airport where people are confined during the day and the rooms at the hotel Ibis where they spend the night. This observational research was invaluable to study the interactions of non-governmental workers and civil servants with persons placed in the waiting zone. As Herbert (2000) remarks, participant observation is a method that allows one to observe not only how people narrate their work, but how

FIGURE 1 Court of First Instance next to the detention center (June 2019). Copyright Rafael Moreno.

they actually go about doing it. All data on detainees were collected through participant observation. I engaged in this method mindful of the fact that the researcher is not an omniscient observer but part of the social relations under study (Herbert 2000; Hyndman 2001). Paradoxically, my gender and age helped me with data collection during fieldwork. As a young woman, many authorities did not take me seriously. As a result, they felt that they could talk to me.

Many years of antagonism between authorities and activists rendered the concurrent use of interviews and participant-observation at CDG impossible. Yet, volunteering with an NGO was the only way of entering the waiting zone, as members of the public and journalists were banned from this space.[5] Sites that are difficult to access force researchers to take a role in the social

5 Since a 2016 law (Law of March 7, 2016), journalists in possession of a valid press card may be authorized access to French waiting zones. However, the wording of the law makes journalists' access to the waiting zone highly uncertain. The law states that journalists "may be authorized access" to the waiting zone provided that they do not infringe on detainees' integrity, that they do not interfere with the functioning of the waiting zone and do not represent a threat to its security.

interactions they study (Makaremi 2008). I therefore attempted to interview as many officials as possible before visiting the airport's spaces of confinement with HRW. Wilfrid Laurier University's Research Ethics Board approved the research methods. Most participants were assigned pseudonyms in order to protect their identities. Real names were only used in four instances, when consent was explicitly given to disclose identity and when it could not be foreseen that such disclosure would be detrimental to the interviewee.

On and at CDG airport, data was collected in French. This proved to be challenging, as it entailed translating highly technical and specific terms into English. Yet, this also constituted an opportunity to reflect on vocabulary and seek conceptual precision. For example, the French term *"étranger"* was translated as "non-citizen" or "foreign national" (the two terms being used interchangeably), as these expressions trigger a less negative emotional response than "foreigner" or "alien". Data collection from research participants ended in August 2014.

6 Chapter Outline

Part 1. The creation and expansion of nowhere countries through the law or lack thereof

The book is structured to develop the argument that extra-territorial spaces have served to curtail access to domestic legal rights as well as access to human and refugee rights granted by international law. Part 1. is concerned about the creation and expansion of nowhere countries from a legal and political standpoint. Court judgments, laws and government regulations are analyzed to highlight congruent patterns.

In chapter 1, I will demonstrate how the French government established the international zones of Paris' airports in the 1980s and early 1990s as non-French, extra-territorial spaces to circumvent domestic and international laws. I will show how the international zone was an "abject space" (Isin and Rygiel 2007) where people, deprived of the ability to enact rights, were rendered non-existent. This chapter will illustrate how governments create extra-territorial legal fictions and the danger they pose to individuals who find themselves in these spaces. It will show that the international zone functioned as a *non-entrée* mechanism (Hathaway 1992), designed to reduce the number of asylum seekers reaching sovereign territory.

Chapter 2 will trace how the Law on the Waiting Zone, a parallel and less protective legal framework premised on extra-territoriality, was established through regular democratic processes. Before the Law on the Waiting Zone came into existence, the same legislative provisions applied to all foreign nationals detained for immigration control purposes: the law did not establish any distinction between those at French borders and those already deemed on French territory. Non-citizens all benefited from the same rights. This equality before the law ended in 1992, with the Law on the Waiting Zone. As I will demonstrate, this less advantageous legal regime was premised precisely on the idea that international zones, renamed "transit zones" and then "waiting zones", were somehow extra-territorial spaces.

Chapters 3 and 4 will further explore the notion of extra-territoriality. In chapter 3, I will argue that the initial construction of the international zone as an extra-territorial space has endured in both mindsets and practices. Amongst individuals working in or on the waiting zone can be found the deeply ingrained idea that the waiting zone is not French territory (at least) for non-citizen populations. This argument, just like in the 1980s and early 1990s, has been used to exclude non-citizens from rights. In other words, some individuals have been denied the protection of international law based on their presence in excised, non-French territory.

In chapter 4, I will contend that the Law on the Waiting Zone has reinvented exclusion through another form of extra-territoriality, premised on the non-citizen's legal status at the border. Although physically in France, rejected non-citizens and asylum seekers at the border are not present from a legal standpoint, for they have not crossed yet "law's admission gate" (Shachar 2007). In this chapter, I will detail how the Law on the Waiting Zone excludes particularly vulnerable groups from the protection they are entitled to under international law. Since 2011, authorities may enforce this exclusionary legal regime anywhere on French territory: *ad hoc* waiting zones can be created when a group of 10 non-citizens (or more) arrives in France outside of a border crossing (for example on a beach). Finally, it will be shown how the Law on the Waiting Zone was exported to the North-African country of Morocco.

As for chapter 5, it will present the extra-territorial mechanism deployed by Australia to curtail access to domestic and international rights, the Australian legal technique of exclusion being strikingly similar to its French counterpart. Excision, or the removal of Australian territory from the "migration zone", i.e. from the space earmarked for visa applications, has consisted in making Australian territory legally disappear for foreign nationals having reached the country shores spontaneously. Barred from applying for asylum in Australia, claimants have been taken to detention facilities far away from the mainland, where they have experienced isolation and deprivation of liberty. There, on the remote Australian territory of Christmas Island and on the islands of Manus (Papua New Guinea) and Nauru, asylum claimants have been denied access to

Australia's refugee status determination system. It is my argument that Australian governments have used excision like a magic wand, to turn the country's asylum obligations into resettlement generosity. This chapter will describe how successive Australian leaders from varied political obedience have subverted the Refugee Convention while claiming to honor the country's obligations under this international instrument.

Part 2. Inside nowhere countries: enforcement practices and mental landscapes

Now that part 1 has built the conceptual framework, part 2 proposes an embedded description of a nowhere country. It will immerse the reader into the materiality and daily functioning of the waiting zone. Chapters 6 and 7 will share ethnographic findings, unveiling practices and mental landscapes in spaces inaccessible to the general public or journalists.

Chapter 6 will focus on airport terminals while the next one will turn to the detention center, "ZAPI 3". ZAPI 3 stands for *zone d'attente pour personnes en instance,* which can be translated as "waiting zone for persons in process". In chapter 6, I will argue that airport terminals are truly the border police's realms. Third parties rarely venture into these spaces. There, asymmetrical power relations prevail and both detainees and researcher experience arbitrariness. Airport terminals constitute the less visible part of CDG's waiting zone. Some passengers may have difficulties reaching the waiting zone status, deprived of the "right to have rights" (Arendt 1968) in the international zone. Some authorities' mindsets towards non-citizens and their border enforcement jobs may be conducive to ill treatment.

Chapter 7 will study the other part of CDG's waiting zone, where NGO presence is unique. Anafé and the Red Cross work at the detention center respectively two (or three) days a week and seven days a week, twenty-four hours a day. I observed that liberty and custody judges at Bobigny often told non-citizens that they could find these organizations at ZAPI 3, as if NGO presence made confinement acceptable and ensured the respect of rights. Yet, the presence of visitors or third parties does not guarantee satisfactory access to rights in ZAPI 3. In this space, the issues are not so much material conditions of detention but rather confinement *per se* as well as access to rights. ZAPI 3 very much remains a place of deprivation of liberty characterized by limited visibility and police omnipresence. There, abuse and tension transpire, in contradiction with euphemistic discourses presenting it as a hotel or place of recreation. Nowhere countries such as "Not-France" and "Not-Australia" constitute "vanishing points", "where national security is prioritised over human security and where the protection of human rights and human life disappear" (Mountz 2013). In nowhere countries border control takes precedence over rights.

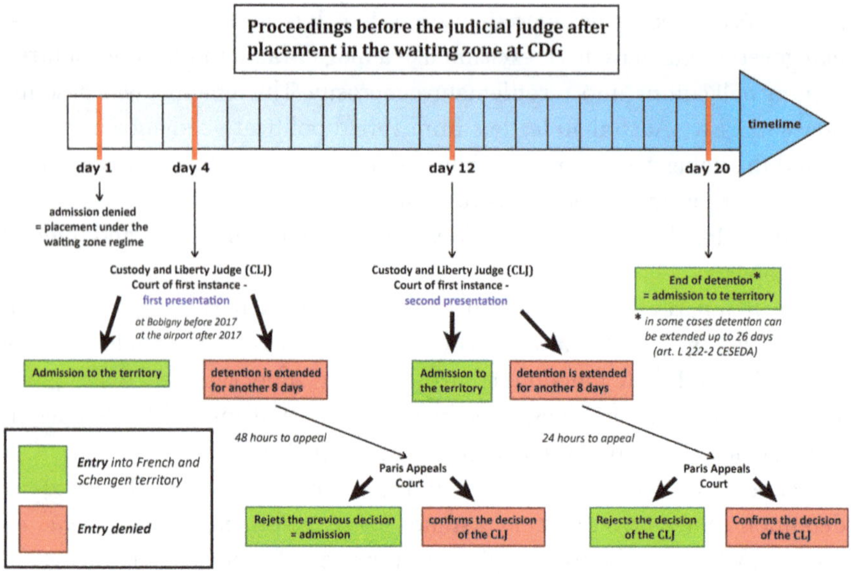

CHART 1 Proceedings before the judicial judge after placement in the waiting zone at Charles de Gaulle (based on Anafé, August 2015)

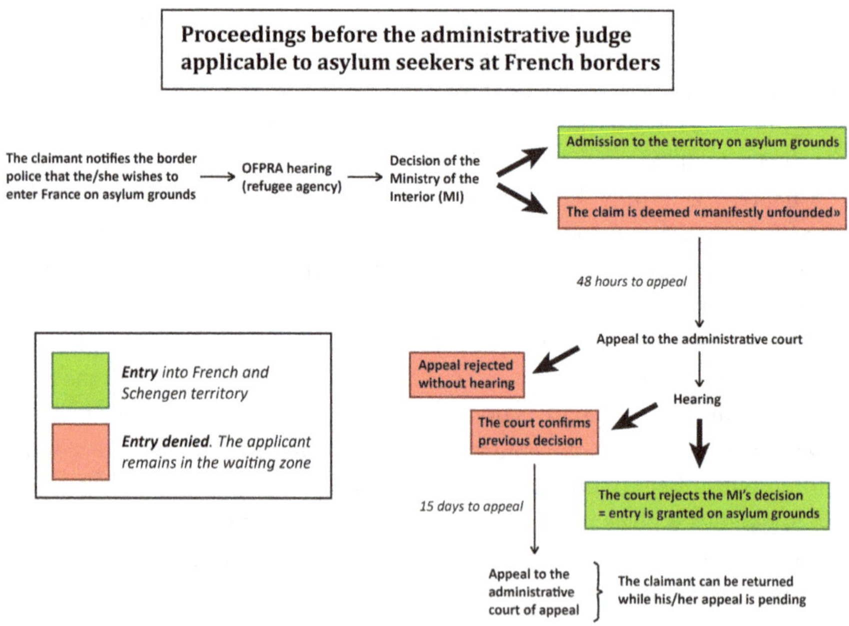

CHART 2 Proceedings before the administrative judge applicable to asylum seekers at French borders (based on Anafé, August 2015)

Part 3. Nowhere countries or one *non-entrée* mechanism amongst many

Chapter 8 will examine a *non-entrée* mechanism (Hathaway 1992) that may come into play thousands of kilometers away from French and Schengen territory: carrier sanctions. In this chapter, I will unveil the symbiotic relations between carrier sanctions and the institution of the waiting zone, showing how the former finance the latter, making its very existence possible. Finally, chapter 9's findings will buttress the argument developed throughout this book: nowhere countries constitute *non-entrée* mechanisms *per se*. I will present evidence supporting the claim that the waiting zone *in itself* constitutes the ultimate gate that asylum seekers need to pass before finally reaching the regular refugee status determination system. The waiting zone serves the same purpose as its predecessor, the international zone. It is one of many devices crafted by States to keep asylum claimants away from their territory and constitutes the last *non-entrée* mechanism when all the upstream ones have failed.

PART 1

The Creation and Expansion of Nowhere Countries through the Law or Lack Thereof

CHAPTER 1

The Establishment of the International Zone at French Airports as an Abject, Extra-Territorial Space

How did the French government establish the international zone in airports as an extra-territorial space? What was the role of activism inside and outside the international zone? A short presentation of the historical and political context is in order to situate these developments.

1 Refugee Policies in Council of Europe Member States in the 1980s and 1990s

In the early 1980s, Council of Europe member States[1] began to witness a tremendous increase in the number of asylum seekers arriving at their gates (Parliamentary Assembly of the Council of Europe 1988). For example, the number of individuals seeking international protection in France rose significantly over the 1980s, from 20,000 applications per year in the early 1980s, to 61,000 in 1989 (Intergovernmental Consultations on Migration, Asylum and Refugees (IGC) December 2012, 183). As Agier (2010) observes, the image of the refugee underwent a profound transformation over the course of this decade and the following. In the 1930s, 1940s or 1950s political exiles from Spain, Poland or Hungary were admitted. They embodied strong personal honor and ideological meaning: the refugee was then a noble figure. Agier (2010) notes that the shift in the public perception of refugees occurred in the 1980s and 1990s, when massive population displacement took place in Africa and where ethnicized and de-personalized crowds received refugee status collectively as they crossed borders under the *prima facie* procedure. This is how Dr Felix Schnyder, a former United Nations High Commissioner for Refugees, explained the difference between individual and *prima facie* group determination:

1 The Council of Europe describes itself as "the continent's leading human rights organization". It counts 47 member States (Council of Europe, April 15, 2019). It is not to be confused with the Council of the European Union.

 | DOI:10.1163/9789004383500_003

> In the case of group determination we are confronted with a mass of people who flee the consequences of political events in which they have not necessarily participated. In the case of individual determination a person claims to have been individually the victim of, or threatened personally by, persecution.
>
> quoted in JACKSON 1999, 3

As refugees came to be seen as undesirable and vulnerable victims, political and intellectual solidarity gave way to fears. Tending to the biological needs of these populations became the priority, relegating moral and ontological questioning aside. Personal stories became obscured; exiles lost their singularity (Agier 2010). Johnson (2011, 1016) concurs with Agier's analysis. As she explains, "over the past 60 years, the image of the refugee has been reframed: from the heroic, political individual to a nameless flood of poverty-stricken women and children". As the Cold War ended, public perception viewed refugees' testimonies as suspicious. The refugee figure was transformed into that of a migrant (Agier 2010). The refugee was no longer useful to the West in its ideological war and became depoliticized, stripped of political agency (Johnson 2011). Crépeau (1995) and Johnson (2011) also note that by the 1980s, the image of the refugee from the global South had replaced that of the European refugee in public imagination. Barnett (2002, 254) shares this analysis: "Alleged differences in race and culture have made refugees a source of suspicion and hostility since the developing world became the source of significant refugee flows to the West in the 1970s".

International and European law and policies reflected this shift: on November 30, 1992, member States of the European Union adopted the London resolutions. One of these three resolutions was concerned with "manifestly unfounded applications for asylum". A significant number of asylum claimants were premised *not* to be genuine applicants. The resolution opened with the following words:

> Aware that a rising number of applicants for asylum in the member States are not in genuine need of protection within the member States within the terms of the Geneva Convention, and concerned that such manifestly unfounded applications overload asylum determination procedures, delay the recognition of refugees in genuine need of protection and jeopardize the integrity of the institution of asylum [...].

The resolution identified unfounded applications and agreed to treat them under accelerated procedures. Article 1 defined manifestly unfounded applications:

> An application for asylum shall be regarded as manifestly unfounded if it is clear that it meets none of the substantive criteria under the Geneva Convention and New York Protocol for one of the following reasons:
> - there is clearly no substance to the applicant's claim to fear persecution in his own country; or
> - the claim is based on deliberate deception or is an abuse of asylum procedures.

The two other London resolutions laid down the concepts of "host third countries" and of "countries in which there is in general terms no serious risk of persecution". Under the former, member States of the European institutions agreed to send asylum claimants to third countries (i.e. not member States) when claimants had been granted protection or could have sought protection there. Under the latter, member States agreed to treat applicants coming from countries deemed safe according to accelerated procedures. In short, EU countries found ways of delegating the responsibilities for asylum seekers to other countries and of expediting their claims. At the international level, the facilitation division of the Chicago Convention introduced the possibility of fining carriers at the 1988 meeting. The Schengen Convention transformed this possibility into a legal requirement, imposing penalties on carriers transporting third country nationals lacking appropriate travel documents (article 26).[2] While article 26 explicitly stated that signatories had to honor their obligations under the Refugee Convention (1951) and its Optional Protocol (1967), in practice it forced companies to refuse passengers inappropriately documented, refugees or not (cf. chapter 8).

2 France in the 1980s: the Rise of Xenophobia and Restrictive Migration Laws in the Midst of Economic Difficulties

A clear correlation can be established between the rise of economic troubles and the development of laws restricting the entry and residency of foreign nationals in France. Like those of other industrialized and capitalist countries,

2 The official name of the Schengen Convention is "Convention implementing the Schengen Agreement of 14 June 1985 between the Governments of the States of the Benelux Economic Union, the Federal Republic of Germany and the French Republic on the gradual abolition of checks at their common borders, 19 June 1990". Hereafter the term "Schengen Convention" will be used.

France's economic struggles began in 1973–1974. The two oil shocks (1973–1974 and 1979–1980) fueled the country's economic difficulties, putting a sudden end to low prices on raw materials and hampering growth (Eck 2004). As Fernandez (2001 107) explains, when the first oil shock took place, more than 70 percent of French energy resources relied on oil imports. A weak internal demand in France is also believed to have played a significant part in the economic crisis, as households stopped consuming as much as during the 1960s (Eck, 2004). As a result, unemployment rose dramatically: while 2.6 percent of the working population was unemployed in 1973 (Eck 2004, 45), this number rose to 8.9 percent in 1991 and 9.9 percent in February 1992 (Duhamel and Forcade 2005, 114).

Prior to the crisis, France, whose prosperity was largely due to foreign workers, was a relatively open country (Gueslin 1992). This changed with the first oil shock. While criteria for granting French citizenship were broadened in 1973, an array of restrictive measures appeared as early as 1974. France decided to stop recruiting foreign workers, issuing an administrative document (on July 5, 1974) putting "temporarily" an end to immigration (Gueslin 1992, 226). As the 1970s drew to a close, the State developed a policy of assisted voluntary returns. The government even tried to force return by not renewing work and residence permits (Gueslin 1992); in 1978 it attempted to forcibly return 500,000 nonnationals over five years but encountered resistance from the States of origin, particularly Algeria and Morocco (Colombani and Portelli 1995, 133).

Eck (2004) clearly rejects any causal link between the presence of foreign workers and the rise of unemployment. French workers were not interested in foreign workers' jobs. Furthermore, non-French workers and their families positively impacted economic activity through consumption. Besides, assisted voluntary returns and the curtailment of migration did not curb unemployment. Yet, as Guiraudon (2006 a) explains, since the 1970s, hostility towards non-French citizens has grown in all the electorate, from the Right to the Left. Eurobarometer polls show that French public opinion disapproved of reforms bringing benefits to migrants. In 1989, 24 percent of the French population polled considered that rights granted to migrants should be curtailed (Guiraudon 2006 a, 274). Another poll, asked the following question: "Would you prefer, over the next years, to prioritize the integration of migrants currently living in France or the departure of a significant number of migrants currently living in France?" Public opinion in the 1990s favored the latter over the former (Balme 2006, 400–401).

The National Front appeared on the French political scene in 1983 when it made inroads in local elections. Since this date, the far-right, anti-migrant party has influenced the debate on migration at the local, regional and national levels

(Guiraudon 2006 a). The National Front was chosen by 11 percent of voters in the 1984 European elections (Grunberg 2006, 461). It became gradually known as the authoritarian, nationalistic, xenophobic and "anti-establishment" party (Grunberg 2006). During the first round of the 1988 presidential election Jean-Marie Le Pen, leader of the National Front, made a significant score, gathering 14.39 percent of votes (Duhamel and Forcade 2005, 107). Guiraudon (2006 a) explains how immigrants' place in French society has been constructed as a "public issue". Immigrants from former colonies have been designated as far right political parties' scapegoats.

Public opinion has seemed hostile or indifferent regarding immigrants. The latter tend not to vote and, in general, face limited access to decision-making centers.[3] Ruling parties therefore refrain from taking measures benefiting immigrants (Guiraudon 2006 a). For example, the Socialist party's stance on migration evolved to espouse anti-migrant sentiments amongst the population. During his presidential campaign, in January 1981, François Mitterrand had promised to grant the right to vote to non-citizens at local elections (after five years of presence on French territory).[4] Facing hostile public opinion, he went back on such an electoral promise as early as August 1981 (Gueslin 1992, 226). As for Charles Pasqua, Minister of the Interior from 1986 to 1988 under the conservative government of Jacques Chirac and the presidency of Mitterrand, he sought to attract National Front voters by embracing the same discourse on nationalism and immigration.[5] He declared: "Overall, the majority and the National Front have the same values" (Colombani and Portelli 1995, 301). His 1986 law made entry into France subject to proof of financial resources and facilitated immigrant expulsion (Gueslin 1992, 226). When Socialists returned to power in 1988, the Pasqua law was partly abrogated but a strict policy of border control was maintained (Gueslin 1992, 227).

3 Until 1981, foreign nationals had to wait for five years to vote or to be elected after acquiring French citizenship (Guiraudon 2000).

4 Cf. point 80 of the election manifesto of the Socialist Party for the presidential election of 1981, available at: http://discours.vie-publique.fr/notices/083001601.html. Today, citizens of countries that are not members of the European Union still do not have the right to vote at local elections, even after five years of presence on French territory.

5 French political institutions allow for a peculiar configuration: the president and the parliamentary majority can be from different political parties. This situation is captured by the French word *cohabitation*, which can be translated in English as coexistence. A *cohabitation* took place from 1986 to 1988 when a parliamentary majority hostile to the President was elected on March 16, 1986 (Cohendet 1993, 24 and 33). Out of the 577 seats at the National Assembly, the Left won 251, the Right 291 and the National Front 35 (Cohendet 1993, 34).

3 Long-Term Confinement in the International Zone in Inhumane Conditions

Lochak (1992 680) describes the legal framework in place for non-citizens (*étrangers* was the official terminology) willing to enter French territory in the years preceding the Law on the Waiting Zone (July 6, 1992). At the time, the conditions of entry were set out by article 5 of the Ordinance from November 2, 1945 (hereafter: "the 1945 Ordinance") and specified by the decree of May 27, 1982 and modified and completed by the decrees of July 30, 1987 and August 30, 1991. In order to enter France, a non-citizen had to carry the documents and visas required by the international conventions and domestic laws in force. Access to French territory could be denied to anyone, even those who were in possession of the requested documents, whose presence would be deemed a threat to public order, or who had been banned from the territory or against whom a deportation order had been taken.

In the 1980s, numerous non-citizens were deprived of liberty in Paris' airports' international zones for extended periods of time. In these buffer zones, authorities kept those denied admission to the country or waiting on an admission decision. Dominique Monget-Sarrail, lawyer at the time and counsel in the *Amuur v. France* (1996) case, recalls:

> The French government told us: "no, they have not arrived in France yet since they did not exit the airport". Some people arriving at Orly and Roissy airports were kept in the international zone, prevented by authorities from going beyond checkpoints-you know of admission to the territory- and people were kept like that, sometimes during months. There was an Iranian who lived there six months, I do not remember if it was [at] Orly or Roissy. So at night he slept in boarding rooms on benches, he would wash [in airports' lavatories] ... So, at the time the situation of several groups of non-citizens like this had caught our attention. We had been told either by airline trade unions or by cleaners working at airports who were surprised to see the same kids play and sleep there for weeks. A certain number of [persons] were blocked like this. Even families. Not only isolated persons like the Iranian but also entire families (Interview, August 2014).

Employees working for Paris' Airports or airline companies were distressed by the plight of these people. In the 1980s and early 1990s, some of these travelers turned away at Paris' airports were detained in small holding rooms in the airport's international zone and/or in nearby hotels, which were construed as an extension of the international zone. Airport and airline employees were confronted first hand with distressed non-citizens crammed in holding rooms at airport terminals, as they were tasked with guarding them. Some of these employees, like Christophe, Jean and Aurélien belonged to the CFDT trade union. The latter stands for *Confédération française démocratique du travail* (Democratic French Work Confederation). It is a trade union gathering employees that belong to different professions and work in different structures, ranging from public to private. CFDT claims to be free from any political affiliation.[6] At the time, Christophe occupied an important position in the Air France CFDT trade union. He recalls that CFDT trade unionists employed by Paris' Airports, Air France and even the border police gathered to discuss the role that they were forced to play with respect to rejected passengers:

> … We started discussions on this theme: we are confronted to things that are not our job; it is not our job to hold families. Why should we stay at the door and prevent people from leaving?
>
> RESEARCHER: It was not even the police?
> CHRISTOPHE: Oh no, often it was employees; they (non-citizens) were put in rooms and employees were in their office. And they were told "careful that they do not leave!"
> RESEARCHER: Employees that were working for?
> CHRISTOPHE: Air France or Paris'Airports; who were on site
> RESEARCHER: What was these employees' occupation?
> CHRISTOPHE: Station agents
> RESEARCHER: In the plane?
> CHRISTOPHE: No, not in the plane, at the counters. Basically people who are here when you enter the airport. Before you board the plane. They are in contact with passengers (Interview, February 2014).

Conditions of detention were inhumane and unhygienic: no provisions were made to provide the stranded travelers with food, water or basic hygienic supplies. In an attempt to mitigate this unbearable situation, airline and airport

6 Cf. CFDT's website: https://www.cfdt.fr/portail/nous-connaitre/la-cfdt-en-10-points-asp_5025 Accessed July 9, 2016.

employees asked border policemen to bring these supplies themselves. Christophe went on:

> We also had issues with meals, -I mean sandwiches- and sanitary supplies for babies and women. We were asking officers to bring (these things) for the next day, as people did not have anything
>
> RESEARCHER: But agents brought these things from where?
>
> CHRISTOPHE: From their home! Or went to buy it, we had to be resourceful (*c'était le système D*) because people were in rooms like that, imagine that you are left here (Interview, February 2014).

According to these trade unionists, people could be detained for days in these small holding rooms where they lacked adequate access to toilet or shower facilities (Interview, February 2014).[7]

4 Detention in the International Zone in a Legal Limbo Premised on Extra-Territoriality

In addition to being detained in unsanitary and inhumane conditions, most non-citizens denied entry at airport borders experienced confinement in international zones in a legal void. Yet, domestic law at the time provided for the detention of passengers turned away at the border and equipped them with legal safeguards. The 1945 Ordinance (article 35 bis) allowed detention of non-admitted individuals in administrative facilities for a maximum of seven days, time period deemed necessary for them to be returned.[8] However, detention was to take place "in case of absolute necessity" during "the time strictly necessary for the departure" of the foreign national. While the decision to detain was taken by an administrative agent (*préfet*), detainees had to be presented to a liberty and custody judge (*juge des libertés et de la detention*) after 24 hours. On an exceptional basis, the judge could extend the duration of detention to six more days, bringing the maximum amount of time spent in confinement to seven days in total. After this time, if return had not occured, the non-citizen

---

7 At the time of interview (February 2014), Aurélien and Christophe were still affiliated with the airline section of the CFDT trade union, while Jean had just left.

8 Ordinance from November 2, 1945 (hereafter: "the 1945 Ordinance").

had to be set free. The judge's decision could be appealed and the public prosecutor (immediately informed of the detention decision) always had the possibility of checking detention conditions. Important rights were attached to article 35 bis, including the rights to see a doctor and a counsel and to communicate with the consulate or any person of the detainee's choosing. The non-citizen had to be notified of the aforementioned rights by an interpreter if he or she did not know French. This legislative provision also applied to those already considered on the territory that were to be removed. The law provided all foreign nationals detained for immigration control purposes with the same guarantees, whether they sought to enter France or were forced to leave the country.

According to the newspaper *Le Monde* (Bernard January 21, 1992), 10,000 travelers per year were denied entry into France due to missing or improper travel documents. Less than one percent of these travelers were placed in administrative detention under the legal rules applicable at the time. Therefore, in the 1980s and the early 1990s, the bulk of non-citizens rejected at the border were held in the international zone in a legal vacuum. Detention outside of the 1945 Ordinance allowed the border police to keep non-admitted foreign nationals for more than seven days and, generally, to deny them the safeguards provided by article 35 bis of the same Ordinance.

The government left rejected passengers outside of the protective reach of domestic laws. The case of asylum seekers was different: French legislation did not permit their detention. Indeed, the 1945 Ordinance authorized detention *only once a non-admission decision was made, not before.* At the time, a decree (May 27, 1982) stated that only the Ministry of the Interior could decide to deny entry to asylum seekers, after consulting with the Ministry of Foreign Affairs. From September 1991 refugee agency representatives were delegated to the borders to hear claimants and advise the Ministry of Foreign Affairs before it offered its opinion to the Ministry of the Interior (Lochak 1992, 680). Importantly, France was already a party to the 1951 Refugee Convention and to its 1967 Protocol. As such, the French State had to honor its *non-refoulement* obligation and could not impose criminal sanctions against refugees for illegal entry (respectively articles 33 and 31 of the Refugee Convention). The duty of *non-refoulement* is the cornerstone of refugee law: it "prohibits States from exposing a refugee 'in any manner whatsoever' to the risk of being persecuted for a Convention reason" (Hathaway and Gammeltoft 2015, 238). *Non-refoulement* "prohibits a State from returning a refugee or asylum seeker to territories where there is a risk that his or her life or freedom would be threatened on account of race, religion, nationality, membership of a particular social group, or political opinion" (Lauterpacht and Bethlehem 2003). Domestic legislation acknowledged the obligation to take international conventions into account in entry decisions (article 5 of the 1945 Ordinance). Under domestic and international law, asylum seekers could not be denied entry for lack of travel documents. They could only be refused access for security reasons, under article 5 of the 1945 Ordinance: threat to the public order, previous banishment from territory or deportation order.

In practice, those seeking international protection could be confined for days or weeks in the international zone while the refugee agency, the Ministry of Foreign Affairs and the Ministry of the Interior decided on their cases. Some claimants also experienced *refoulement* (cf. section VI). To justify these practices, the French government argued that the international zone had extra-territorial status. As a result, domestic laws (including laws that incorporated international obligations) did not apply to populations held in this space. As explained by Hoop de Scheffer, Council of Europe rapporteur, who visited Roissy-Charles de Gaulle airport on November 20, 1989:

> Asylum-seekers are detained in a so-called international zone at the airport, which means that they are not yet on French territory and the French authorities are therefore not under a legal obligation to examine the request as they would be if a request was made by someone already on French territory. The international zone has no legal background and must be considered as a device to avoid obligations [...]. No legal basis for detention exists and a maximum term is not prescribed by law.
>
> LORD MACKIE of Benshie September 12, 1991, 7

French authorities at CDG assumed that they were under no legal obligation to examine asylum seekers' requests in international zones, on the basis that they were not on French territory yet. French authorities insisted that the duration of detention was limited to a week. However, some asylum claimants told the Council of Europe Rapporteur that they had been waiting for six weeks in the international zone (Benshie September 12, 1991, 7).

In short, non-citizens denied admission or waiting on an admission decision at French airport borders were deprived of liberty in a legal limbo. The French government established the international zone as an "abject space". There, non-citizens were stripped of the possibility of exercising rights (Isin and Rygiel 2007). Isin and Rygiel explain:

> ... abject spaces-extraterritorial spaces where international and national laws are suspended-have spread throughout the world in the past decade as spaces for holding refugees, asylum seekers, deportees, combatants,

> insurgents, and others caught in the new global policing and policies net. These spaces include various frontiers controlled by State authorities, zones where special rules and laws apply, and camps where laws are suspended (2007, 181).

They note that Agamben's logic of exception (1998) cannot capture the essence of abject spaces. In internment camps conceptualized by Agamben (i.e. "spaces of abjection") undesirables were eliminated. By contrast, "abject spaces" render people invisible and inaudible. Although Isin and Rygiel envision "abject spaces" as relatively new, their concept applies well to the situation of non-citizens in French airports' international zones at the time. In these zones resistance was possible: non-citizens challenged their confinement with the assistance of lawyers, and a series of legal proceedings led to the birth of the *Waiting Zone* legislation in July 1992. International zones were spaces of politics.

5 The Coalescence of Activism inside and outside of the International Zone

Distressed by the plight of detainees, trade unionists decided to contact NGOs defending human and foreign nationals' rights. Informal meetings led to the creation of the NGO Anafé in 1989. "Anafé" stands for *Association nationale d'assistance aux frontières pour les étrangers* (National Organization for Assistance to Foreign Nationals at Borders). The NGO was created "to provide legal and humanitarian assistance to foreign nationals in difficulty at French borders" (Anafé 2010, 5). Anafé employees Lise and Anne explain that one of the first demands of the organization was to access international zones (Interview, December 2013). This original structure gathered diverse trade unions, NGOs, and lawyers representing foreign nationals. Aurélien, Christophe and Jean were all very active in the CFDT, some of them occupying key positions in the trade union's airline section. As such, they were instrumental in the creation of Anafé. Jean and Christophe recount how the NGO was born:

> CHRISTOPHE: People stayed in this room for two, three, four, five or six days. It was inhuman ... People called us, trade unions, it fell on the CFDT. I suppose that others [trade unions] were called too but they said: "We cannot do anything". Well I do not know, I do not know what they said.

JEAN: There were many families going back and forth: inadmissible in France and inadmissible in [other countries] … they were doing ping-pong. These are anecdotes but it contributed [to the flight attendants' trade union joining Anafé].

CHRISTOPHE: So this adventure began like this. We met the main NGOs: Amnesty International, the Cimade,[9] France Terre d'Asile. These contacts translated into a meeting that Jean organized at Roissy. Then we had a second and then a third meeting and quickly lawyers came, lawyers who were working on the case, who were defending foreign nationals. They came to these meetings and quickly the idea of creating an NGO appeared. It was original as Anafé was an NGO made of NGOs, and also of trade unions (Interview, February 2014).

Interestingly, even the CFDT police trade union was affiliated with Anafé at first:

RESEARCHER: The police trade union was a member of Anafé?

CHRISTOPHE: Yes, at first. Then they left because it brought them too many problems. I think that, we can say it; at some point they provided an internal note that went into the press.

JEAN: It was when someone died.

CHRISTOPHE: It was the case of the guy who had been suffocated; he had been forcibly put on the plane, the policeman had seated on him a bit too hard, he had squashed his rib cage and the guy died. There was an internal report. Of course it was confidential. We got it through them and obviously … they were not upset when they left but said it was not possible: "it is no longer possible for us to be both inside and outside".

RESEARCHER: of course. And how long did they stay?

CHRISTOPHE: Two years.

9 Cimade stands for *Comité Inter-Mouvements Auprès des Evacués* (Inter-Faith Committee for Evacuees).

JEAN: It was very small. At the time the police CFDT was very small (Interview, February 2014).

Activist lawyers who were close to Gisti (*Groupe d'information et de soutien des immigrés*), a group providing information and support to immigrants and one of Anafé's member organizations, launched a series of trials at the end of the 1980s against the French government. They challenged the detention of their clients (of different origins and nationalities but all caught in similar situations) in the international zone on the basis that it amounted to an arbitrary deprivation of liberty. At the time, there were few lawyers specializing in foreign nationals' rights in Paris. They were all activists and knew each other well. They were also at the forefront of legal fights in other fields such as labor law or the right to housing. Dominique Monget-Sarrail was one of them. She recalls:

> They said there was no law, because we [lawyers] said "there is one, it is the one applicable to people to be removed". Either there is no law and they have to be set free because you do not have the right to keep them since there is no law, or there is a law and you have to apply it, so they have to be set free. You have been keeping them long enough and not in decent conditions. So this translated into a series of trials organized by a group of friends. We all knew each other; we all had the same professional activity. At the time in the Paris area we must have been about twenty lawyers specialized in foreign nationals' rights (Interview, August 2014).

6 Legal Activism: the Use of the "Legal Fiction" Argument to Challenge the Extra-Territoriality Thesis

Lawyers used the term "legal fiction" as a weapon to challenge the government's arbitrary practices in the international zone. They coined the term to debunk the French government's extra-territorial theory according to which non-nationals present in the international zone were deemed outside of France (Interview with Serge Slama, law professor, Paris, July 2014). It is not a legal term and therefore cannot be found in legal textbooks (Interview with Danièle Lochak, law professor, Paris, July 2014). Activist lawyers using the term "legal fiction" did not define it. According to the Oxford online English dictionary (accessed December 7, 2014), a fiction is "an invention or fabrication as opposed to fact". The expression "legal fiction" was precisely meant to convey the idea that the government fabricated the international zone as a lawless area. Activists found it useful to denounce the exclusion of individuals located in the international zone from the guarantees offered by French law and international human rights and refugee law. In Del Valle Galvez's (2005) terminology, they fought the government's creation of an extra-territorial legal fiction: they refused to consider that individuals in the international zone encountered themselves in an extra-territorial space.

Lawyer Christian Bourguet explains that the term originated from a visit to Orly's police station, which he made with fellow activist Patrick Mony (Israel 2002). The policemen told them that the international zone was the fiction according to which they were able to deprive people of liberty. Bourguet seized this idea: he argued before the Courts of First Instance that the international zone was a legal fiction. As of 1988, he started to litigate against the Ministry of the Interior on behalf of people held at airports (Israel 2002). From this date onward, many lawsuits were introduced against the Ministry of the Interior. The goal was to obtain a ruling that would release the asylum seekers in question from the international zone on the grounds that detention in this space was tantamount to arbitrary sequestration and therefore resulted in severe infringement upon a fundamental liberty (Lochak 1992, 682). The newspaper *Le Monde*, dated November 21, 1989, described one of these trials (Peyrot 1989).

Isabelle arrived at CDG from Zaire on November 4, 1989. She had fled her country where she had been imprisoned, beaten, and raped by soldiers on account of her religious opinions. In spite of presenting a regular passport, visa and financial means, she was denied entry at the border and detained at the Arcade hotel at CDG. Bourguet paid her a visit on November 11 and made her sign a refugee status request, which he forwarded immediately to the director of OFPRA (*Office français de protection des réfugiés et apatrides*), the refugee agency. A photocopy of the request was also forwarded to the border police. As his client remained deprived of liberty, Bourguet sued the Ministry of the Interior before the Paris Court of First Instance.[10] He pleaded that his client's arbitrary detention had severely infringed upon her fundamental rights (*voie de fait*). But Isabelle was released just before the judge heard her case. The judge could not rule on "a situation that had ended". As the newspaper notes, the government had already resorted to the same manoeuvre several times. The Ministry of the Interior had consistently made sure that the non-citizen was no longer held in the international zone at the date of the hearing. Since the foreign national had either been sent back to his or her country of departure or admitted to French territory, the point of contention had disappeared

10 The Harrap's dictionary (2007) translates *Tribunal de Grande Instance* as "Court of First Instance" (cf. chart 3).

(Bourguet 1992). Therefore, the judge had no other option but to declare that he lacked jurisdiction. This strategy on the part of the government endured for a few years after Isabelle's case.

The Paris Court of First Instance finally put an end to it by issuing a very unusual ruling. On November 22, 1991, the Court allowed a Haitian asylum seeker to sue the Ministry of the Interior for "arbitrary sequestration" and monetary compensation even if he had been admitted to France in the meantime. The plaintiff had landed in CDG on November 6, 1991. He had been refused entry and confined for two days in the international zone and six days at the Arcade Hotel, which was construed as an extension of the international zone. He had been informed that he was to be put in the next available plane to Port-au Prince. The court hearing took place on February 26, 1992 and also dealt with the similar cases of four other asylum seekers (three Haitians and one Zairian) who had landed in Roissy on November 19, 1991 (Bernard January 21, 1992). Their lawyers had also been authorized by the same Court of First Instance on November 26, 1991 to pursue the cases on their merits. At the hearing, the Ministry of the Interior acknowledged the following: their deprivation of liberty was not based on any legal document, a legal framework existed but was not applied and lastly, *the order was expressly given to civil servants not to detain foreign nationals at the border under the existing legal framework* (Paris Court of First Instance, hearing, February 26, 1992). The Court ruled on March 25, 1992.

The hearing revealed that the plaintiffs' right to seek asylum (guaranteed by the French Constitution as well as by international instruments) had been severely violated. Hathaway (2005) clearly explains that States cannot escape from their international obligations under the Refugee Convention by resorting to a "legal ruse". As he points out, the *non-refoulement* provision of the Refugee Convention (article 33) can be breached when States avoid acknowledging formally the arrival of a refugee by changing their domestic law. International zones, excised territory, and territorial sea are all part of the State's territory. This is a fact that cannot be changed by domestic law. Therefore, under international law there is no difference between refusing to examine the asylum claim of individuals located in international zones or excised territory and refusing to examine the claim of those considered by the State to be on its territory (Hathaway 2005). Yet, France did not uphold its *non-refoulement* obligation, as decisions were made to return the asylum seekers in question to Kinshasa and Port-au-Prince. Their return was stopped *in extremis* when the Court heard their case. The asylum seekers also faced obstacles when filing their claim: only two plaintiffs could have their claim registered while the other two were treated as regular migrants failing to fulfill entry conditions.

The Court ruled on March 25, 1992. It rejected the government's extra-territoriality thesis. Asylum seekers' lawyers (Stéphane Maugendre, Simon Foreman and Christian Bourguet) argued that the "international zone" was a "police fiction" (*fiction policière*) designed to dispense with judicial oversight after 24 hours of detention. The Court concurred with the plaintiffs' counsels' analysis: it explicitly stated that the international zone constituted a "legal fiction" and could not be exempt from fundamental principles of individual liberty. It found that there was no domestic or international document giving extra-territorial status to all or part of the Arcade hotel where asylum seekers had been held.[11] It rejected the Ministry of the Interior's arguments and found that holding at the Arcade hotel constituted a deprivation of liberty. Interestingly, the centerpiece of the lawyers' argumentation -the legal fiction thesis-originally began as an arbitrary, informal response fabricated by civil servants. It proved to be a powerful tool as it was endorsed by the Paris Court of First Instance and used to justify its ruling. But how did the French government develop the extra-territoriality thesis in the first place? I would now like to offer some possible explanations.

7 Factors that Contributed to the Establishment of the International Zone as an Abject Space

International zones suddenly became the center of attention in the 1980s, when the number of people seeking international protection in Europe soared. The Parliamentary Assembly of the Council of Europe (recommendation 1088, 1988) expressed concerns regarding the restrictive measures adopted by member States to limit the arrivals. Lord Mackie of Benshie (September 12, 1991, 5) pointed out that some asylum claimants may be "only admitted at the airport in so-called international zones, where their legal status is unclear". France managed to keep non-citizens categorized as undesirable (and asylum seekers in their midst) at bay by declaring that the international zone was not France.

11 These are the precise words of the court: "*Attendu que le défendeur n'est pas fondé à soutenir pour écarter le grief d'atteinte à la liberté individuelle, que l'étranger serait seulement empêché d'entrer en France, en étant retenu dans un lieu devant être considéré comme une "extension" de la zone internationale de l'aéroport; qu'en effet, il n'est pas justifié de l'existence d'un texte, national ou international, conférant une quelconque extra-territorialité à tout ou partie des locaux de l'hôtel* ARCADE*, situé au demeurant hors de l'enceinte de l'aéroport et de la zone "sous douane" de celui-ci. Attendu qu'en l'état cette zone, qui constitue une fiction juridique, ne saurait être soustraite aux principes fondamentaux de la liberté individuelle*".

At the time, the status of the international zone, also called "transit zone", was not well defined. Legal scholars had not given much thought to the status of this space and domestic courts had issued contradictory rulings. The French government seized this opportunity to pursue political aims, taking advantage of the discrepancy between legal and cartographic borders at airports.

When events unfolded, international law did not directly address the status of the transit zone. International law did not explicitly state whether or not transit zones were part of a State's territory or what laws applied to passengers located in these spaces. Originally, Annex 9 to the Chicago Convention's definition of a "direct transit area" (1st edition, 1950) did not include passengers. At first, it was "a special area established in connection with an international airport, approved by the public authorities concerned and under their direct supervision for accommodation of traffic which is pausing briefly in its passage through the Contracting State". In 2004 the Facilitation Division of the International Civil Aviation Organization proposed to broaden this definition to mention that "passengers can stay during transit or transfer without being submitted to border control" in the direct transit area (FAL/12-WP/6, 12/11/03). This international legal instrument did not, and still does not, specify the perimeter of the direct transit area. There are no indications as to what is encompassed by the direct transit area. It became apparent in 1993, at a conference gathering lawyers and activists from Europe and North America, that countries delineated airport transit zones' perimeter differently (Anafé 1993). This lack of consensus allowed the French government to claim that the international zone included hotels. Even today, the reader of an international law textbook looking for the "transit zone" entry in the table of contents will be disappointed: there is no such thing.

Nevertheless, it does not mean that airports' transit zones were not covered by international law in the 1980s. As previously mentioned, Annex 9 to the Chicago Convention established that the transit zone *was directly supervised or controlled by the public authorities of the State concerned*. This meant that the State in question exercised its territorial sovereignty over the transit zone. As Labayle (1993, 48) explains, a State exercising its sovereignty over a territory is competent both to create and implement rules. As soon as international legal scholars, international human rights courts and treaty monitoring bodies turned to the matter of the international or transit zone, they clearly stated that this space was integrally part of the State's territory. Under international law, airports' transit zones are not extra-territorial spaces.

French domestic courts' lack of consensus regarding the status of the international zone may have also created a climate conducive to the development of the extra-territoriality thesis. The highest judicial and administrative courts of the country came to some contradictory conclusions during the 1980s. The former (*Cour de Cassation*) found that the international zone was a part of French territory while the latter (*Conseil d'Etat*) found precisely the opposite. These domestic debates left the door open for the government to use the international zone as a device to deflect from its international obligations. charts 3-5 below provide some background on the French legal system and help understand the significance of these rulings.

In the case *Youssef*, the Final Court of Appeal (*Cour de Cassation*) held that the international zone was part of national territory on October 28, 1987. The Court explicitly stated that the entirety of Roissy airport was a part of French territory, therefore agreeing with the ruling made earlier (June 12, 1984) by the Appeal Court. The latter had found that "[...] the entirety of Roissy-Charles de Gaulle airport, upon which French sovereignty applies, is a part of French territory, the legal status of zones called 'international' or 'under customs' has no consequence on the French character of this part of national territory [...]" (quoted in Final Court of Appeal, criminal chamber, public hearing of October 28, 1987-translation is mine).

In this case, a criminal court had sentenced a Jordanian citizen, Youssef Youssef, on January 5, 1984 to leave France (precisely to be "taken back to the border"-*reconduit à la frontière*) for residing irregularly in the country. Invoking political reasons, Youssef refused to board the plane for Amman on January 7, 1984. As a result, further legal action was taken against him. The defendant argued that, having crossed the police and customs border checkpoints, he had left the territory (he was in the international zone) and that therefore he could not be considered as being illegally in France. But the Court rejected his argument and sentenced him again to leave the country since, as of January 7, 1984, he was guilty of being voluntarily present in France without valid documents authorizing his stay. His lawyer, Christian Bourguet, appealed the decision immediately. Youssef was finally forced to board the plane for Jordan on January 20, 1984. He returned to France a few months later and the Paris Appeal Court heard his case. The Court upheld the previous ruling and found on June 12, 1984 that Youssef had indeed breached the law regulating foreign nationals' residency in the country but did not hand down any sentence. The case went all the way up to the Final Court of Appeal (*Cour de Cassation,* cf. charts 3 and 4), which also rejected Youssef's arguments: it stated that even if the defendant had been taken beyond police and customs checks, he had still breached the law as the entirety of the airport was indeed a part of French territory (Lochak 1992, 682).

Interestingly, in this case it was Youssef's lawyer, Bourguet, who developed the extra-territoriality thesis (i.e. the idea that the international zone was not

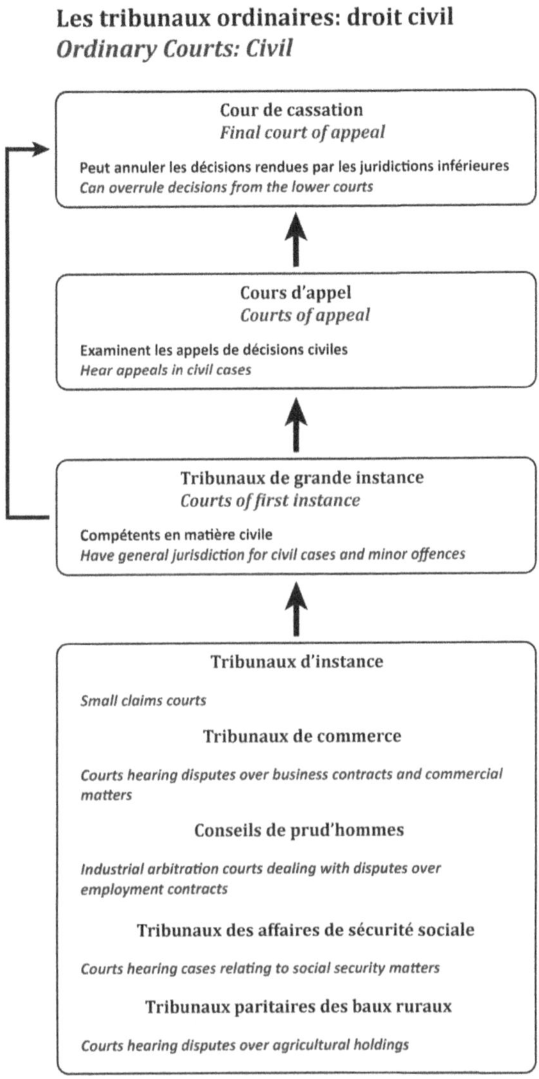

CHART 3 French civil courts (based on Harrap's Unabridged Dictionary, 2007)

a part of French territory). He explains why and how he developed this argument (Bourguet 1992): his client, a Palestinian born in the West Bank, had told him that he was likely to be jailed in Jordan upon his arrival in the country (his fear materialized as he was imprisoned for four months when he was finally forcibly returned to his country of citizenship, Jordan). Therefore Bourguet thought of a way to stall the return: since his client had been sentenced to be "taken back to the border", he questioned the location of the border. He argued

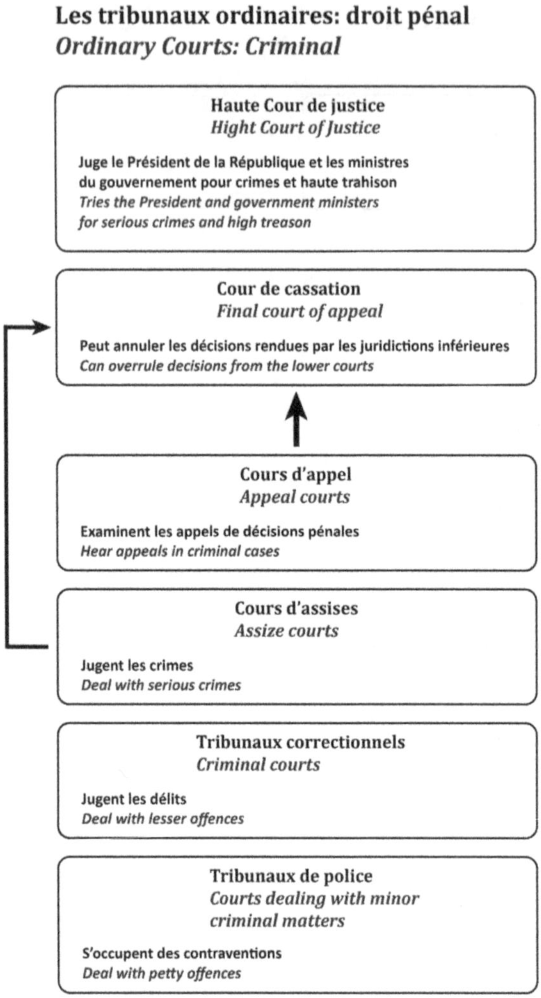

CHART 4 French criminal courts (based on Harrap's Unabridged Dictionary, 2007)

that the border was where police and customs checks took place at the airport, not where the plane exited French air space. The implications of this argument were important: it meant that his client could be taken beyond police and customs checkpoints but not forced to board a plane for a specific country. If the border was indeed materialized by police checkpoints, his client could not be sentenced for staying irregularly in France as he would not be on French territory: French courts would not have jurisdiction. The extra-territoriality thesis was therefore used at the beginning of the 1980s by an activist lawyer in the hope of protecting his client whose asylum claim had been rejected by France.

Shortly after the first level court held that the international zone was part of France in the *Youssef* case, the Council of State (*Conseil d'Etat*, cf. charts 5), the highest administrative court in France, came to a completely opposite conclusion: the international zone was *not* part of France. The *Eksir* case (January 27, 1984) was about whether the implementation of the decision to refuse entry to a foreign national could be deferred. The question boiled down to whether presence in the international zone equaled presence on French territory. The Council of State found the claimants to be in a situation of extra-territoriality, outside of France in the eyes of the law (Lochak 1992, 680).

Bourguet was also the counsel in the *Eksir* case. A few months after the *Youssef* case started, he advised three young Iranians who had fled their country to claim asylum in France. They arrived at Charles de Gaulle in November 1983

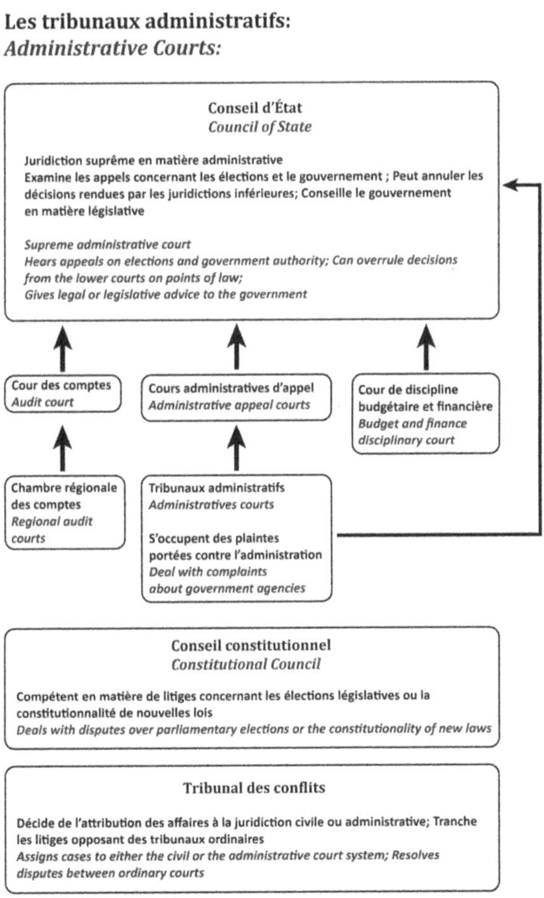

CHART 5 French administrative courts (based on Harrap's Unabridged Dictionary, 2007)

flying from Karachi via London. They were first returned to London after being turned away by the Ministry of the Interior at Charles de Gaulle on November 24, 1983. In London they refused to make the connecting flight to Karachi and were sent back to France. At Charles de Gaulle, they were put on a plane to Karachi on November 28. They finally landed again at Charles de Gaulle on December 2, after authorities at Karachi refused to readmit them (Robert 1984). Bourguet (1992) appealed against the first decision refusing them entry to France. He asked the Paris Administrative Court to defer the implementation of the decision. In French administrative law, a decision's implementation can only be deferred under certain conditions. It has to be proven that if the decision were to be maintained, it would modify (*de facto* or *de jure*) the situation the claimants were experiencing when the decision was made (Lachaume 1985). The Paris Administrative Court refused to defer the decision (on December 7): it found that its implementation would not make a difference to the situation of the claimants either in law or in fact. The Council of State confirmed this interpretation on January 27, 1984, therefore implicitly concluding that the international zone was located outside of France. The highest administrative court must have considered that the claimants were not yet in France as they had not exited the international zone when the border police first refused them entry. Hence the decision's implementation (which maintained them outside of France) could not modify their situation. Interestingly, the three Iranians had been deferred to a criminal court in Bobigny for breaching the law regulating the entry and residency of foreign nationals. The Bobigny Court had authorized them to reside in France temporarily (Robert 1984).

These two contradictory rulings worked to the State's advantage: the international zone was both France and not France at the same time, according to the direction of the border crossing. When it came to returning someone to a country of origin or a third country, the international zone was France, and foreign nationals refusing to embark could be subject to criminal prosecution for illegally staying in the country while in the international zone. However, for foreign nationals arriving from another country and landing in Charles de Gaulle, the international zone was not France yet. This interpretation allowed the French government to argue that non-citizens were not to be subjected to the regular legal provisions (Gisti January 1989). Article 35 bis of the 1945 Ordinance could not apply to them since the international zone was located outside of France and French laws only applied to French territory (Lochak 1992, 681–682). Such an absurd situation led Bourguet (1992) to refer to the detention spaces at the airport and at the Arcade hotel as the "nowhere country".

The history of French airports' international zones illustrates how governments create extra-territorial legal fictions and the danger they pose to individuals who find themselves in these spaces. It corroborates Del Valle Galvez's (2005) observations: extra-territorial legal fictions establish an internal no man's land and raise issues of legal insecurity and absence of legality. They result in the non-application, or at least incomplete application, of the domestic and international norms regarding immigration and asylum that bind States. French airport international zones were declared outside of sovereign territory for immigration control purposes. These pieces of land were knowingly placed outside of the reach of the law: border authorities used to detain individuals at airports in a legal limbo, in spite of applicable laws. In the 1980s, foreign nationals stranded at French borders were rendered without rights by French authorities. As Arendt (1968) demonstrated, human beings who are stripped of their status of legal subjects no longer belong to a political community and lose their dignity along with their very place in the world (Caloz-Tschopp 1993). In the next chapter, I will trace how the Law on the Waiting Zone, a parallel and less protective legal framework premised on extra-territoriality, was established through regular democratic processes.

CHAPTER 2

The Birth of French Waiting Zones or the Manufacturing of an Illiberal Law through Regular Democratic Mechanisms

Non-citizens in the international zone ceased to be detained in a legal void as of July 6, 1992, when the Law on the Waiting Zone was finally passed. The Socialist government presented this new legislation as significant progress: France was setting a fine example in terms of rights protection. Yet, the Law on the Waiting Zone offered a less advantageous legal framework to non-citizens compared to the one previously in place (i.e. article 35 bis of the 1945 Ordinance). Under this new law, detainees were to be presented to a judge after four days in the waiting zone (compared to one day previously) and could not spend more than 20 days in the waiting zone (confinement was limited to seven days previously). Furthermore, the Law on the Waiting Zone established a parallel and less protective system of rights based on the distinction between physical and legal entry. Before the Law on the Waiting Zone came into existence, the same legislative provisions applied to all foreign nationals detained for immigration control purposes: the law did not establish any distinction between those at French borders and those already deemed to be on French territory. Non-citizens all benefited from the same rights. This equality before the law ended in 1992, with the Law on the Waiting Zone. Since this time, foreign nationals arriving at the border have been subjected to a watered-down legal framework compared to the one applicable to their counterparts already deemed to be on French soil (who are either applying for asylum or are to be removed after being caught for staying illegally in the country). This less advantageous legal regime was precisely premised on the idea that international zones, renamed "transit zones" and then "waiting zones", were somehow extra-territorial spaces. The Law on the Waiting Zone did not dispel the ambiguity surrounding the status of this space in stakeholders' minds.

How could a parallel system of rights be established in a liberal democracy bound by international human rights and refugee conventions? This chapter will pay heed to the observation made by some scholars that liberal government and authoritarian practices are not mutually exclusive, but rather two sides of the same coin (Hindess 2001, 94). As Dean (2002, 38) writes,

 | DOI:10.1163/9789004383500_004

> (...) governing liberally does not necessarily entail governing through freedom or even governing in a manner that respects individual liberty. It might mean, in ways quite compatible with a liberal rationality of government, overriding the exercise of specific freedoms in order to enforce obligations on members of the population.

These observations have translated into concrete lines of enquiry: European scholars have identified illiberal practices in EU member States and offered recommendations to end them (Bigo et al September 2009). I will trace how the framework of the waiting zone was made possible through regular democratic mechanisms (Basaran 2011). Both Parliament chambers approved the government bill, in spite of some parliamentarians and civil society actors vigorously protesting against both procedure and content of the legislative provision. The Constitutional Council, a domestic moral authority, approved the government's extra-territoriality thesis indirectly. This court found that non-citizens confined at the border did not experience the same degree of constraint as those confined on the territory. The former were therefore considered less in need of protection than the latter. Ironically, this less protective framework based on the concept of extra-territorial presence in the waiting zone was the direct product of activism that sought to oppose detention in a legal void. The history of the birth of the waiting zone illustrates the dangers (or ambiguities at best) of activism using "the tools and grammar of law" (Makaremi 2009 a, 428) and proves Belcher and Martin's (2013) point: law is not always liberal. In fact, as Basaran (2011) demonstrates, law is a technique of government that can be used to take away fundamental rights from certain populations. She explains:

> The government of populations called migrants develops its effectiveness, precisely by embedding the limitation of liberties within the legal framework. Migrants are not outside the law, but embedded and produced through it, similar to previous segregation and exclusion policies that provided a specific legal framework for particular populations (2011, 105).

This chapter will highlight the political nature of the law. I will first describe the context and content of the Marchand amendment. Although this legislative provision was partly censored by the Constitutional Council, its history is worth studying. Indeed, the Marchand amendment is truly the ancestor of the 1992 Law on the Waiting Zone: the latter derives its main features and philosophy precisely from the former. Both are premised on the idea that non-citizens arriving at the border do not need the same rights as their counterparts who are already considered on French territory. The ambiguous status of the transit zone persisted with the Marchand amendment and the subsequent Law on the Waiting Zone. The government's justifications for the amendment will be analyzed. It will be my contention that the Constitutional Council played a significant role in the manufacturing of this illiberal law. Finally, how did litigation crises result in the broadening of the definition of the waiting zone?

1 Context of the Marchand Amendment

As explained in chapter 1, activist lawyers started to sue the Ministry of the Interior from 1988 for arbitrary detention of foreign nationals in the international zone. The judge who heard the cases had a limited mandate: putting a stop to an illegal administrative practice resulting in a severe violation of fundamental rights. The judge could therefore only order the government to put an end to confinement in the international zone. Until November 1991, these trials did not affect the government, who always instructed border authorities to return or admit to the territory the foreign national in question before the hearing took place. The situation finally changed when the Paris Court of First Instance issued a very unusual ruling. On November 22, 1991, the Court allowed a Haitian asylum seeker to sue the Ministry of the Interior for "arbitrary sequestration" and monetary compensation even if he had been admitted to France in the meantime. Faced with challenging upcoming litigation, Philippe Marchand, the Socialist Minister of the Interior at the time, decided to draft a legal provision ("the Marchand amendment") addressing the situation of non-admitted foreign nationals in the international zone, which he renamed "transit zone" (cf. section IV). While laws cannot apply retroactively, he hoped that this legislation would shield the Ministry from further legal troubles. As I will demonstrate throughout this book, the French government has always passed laws regulating the status of persons held in the international (and then waiting) zone as a result of legal action. The Marchand amendment was an *ad hoc* response to a legal crisis.

As the parliamentary session drew to a close, Marchand hastily introduced this new legal provision as an additional article (7 bis) to a bill under discussion at the National Assembly. MPs were debating a government bill whose purpose was to modify domestic law in order to align it with the requirements of the Schengen Convention (signed by France on June 1990 and ratified on July 1991) pertaining to the entry and deportation of unauthorized foreign nationals and to the carriers' responsibility framework. The Schengen

Convention had significantly redefined borders of contracting parties. States had pledged to abolish borders internal to the territory to which the Schengen Convention applied, and to tighten external ones: they had committed to shift border control from internal to external borders to create an internal area of free movement (article 2 and 4). With the Schengen Convention, each State party had become responsible for guarding other parties' borders (article 4). Importantly, the Schengen Convention had also established the carrier responsibility framework (cf. chapter 8 for extended discussion). Under article 26, States had agreed to inflict financial penalties on carriers bringing inadequately documented individuals to their gates. Carriers had also been obliged to return non-admitted passengers. As the numbering "bis" indicates, the Marchand amendment was grafted onto an already existing provision (article 7). This provision's purpose was to incorporate some elements of the carrier responsibility framework into national law.[1]

The bill under discussion also aimed to introduce non-Schengen related provisions to curb immigration. The goal was to increase the effectiveness of the measures in place to remove those staying irregularly on French territory. The government had declared the fight against illegal immigration an important objective during a Ministers' meeting in July 1991. The bill proposed to penalize foreign nationals staying on French territory after their tourist visas had expired and to deport those who overstayed their residence permit for more than a month (French National Assembly debates, December 19, 1991). The history of the Marchand amendment, and of the subsequent Law on the Waiting Zone, is intertwined with the construction of the Schengen area's external borders and restrictive domestic migration laws.

The Minister of the Interior introduced the legislative provision on the transit zone at the end of the parliamentary session, after a declaration of emergency. This way of proceeding allowed the government to minimize preliminary checks. The domestic human rights commission, which was scheduled to examine the provision the following day, had not had the time to issue recommendations (French National Assembly debates December 19, 1991, 8268). MPs were therefore forced to ponder the amendment in the absence of the commission's report. Furthermore, introducing the bill as an amendment allowed Marchand to dispense with debates at the Council of Minister and with consultation at the Council of State. MPs from the right-wing opposition disapproved of the way the government introduced the transit zone provision

1 Article 3 of the bill under discussion sought to incorporate financial sanctions against carriers into domestic law while article 7 aimed at obligating companies to transport back the non-admitted passengers and to pay for their living expenses before return.

(French National Assembly debates December 19, 1991, 8266 and 8268). More significantly, Socialist senators, i.e. from the same political party as the government, also protested. They lamented that the human rights commission could not express its opinion on the matter (French Senate debates January 16, 1992, 206). Senator Guy Allouche observed that the government bill should have been submitted to the Council of State. According to Allouche, careful consideration should have prevailed as the bill touched upon the fate of thousands of human beings hoping to enter France or Schengen area countries (French Senate debates January 16, 1992, 207). Michel Dreyfus-Schmidt, another Socialist senator, regretted such hastiness, which prevented careful consideration of the bill (French Senate debates January 16, 1992, 233).

As for NGOs and counsel representing foreign nationals, they considered the amendment procedure a ploy to shield the government's legal proposal from ordinary scrutiny. While they acknowledged that the amendment was related to the bill under discussion (in the sense that both aimed to modify the 1945 Ordinance) they argued that the modifications and additions brought by article 7 bis exceeded by far the limits inherent to the government's right of amendment, as defined by the Constitutional Council jurisprudence. Resorting to the amendment procedure allowed the government to skip the Council of Ministers' debate as well as the Council of State's consultation (Anafé et al January 28, 1992, 1–2).[2] The plaintiffs' lawyers, who were suing the Ministry of the Interior for arbitrary sequestration, vigorously denounced the government's arguments. They wrote a letter to Parliamentarians on January 21, 1992 in which they remarked that the hearing date of the case (i.e. January 26, 1992) had been known since November 1991. The government could have, therefore, included the transit zone provision into its bill from the beginning. The provision would have then been examined under normal conditions and it would have been possible to have a serious democratic debate. Yet, the Ministry of the Interior waited for December 18, 1991, the day before the National Assembly was due to debate the proposed bill, to introduce the provision via an amendment.

In spite of this discontent, the bill went through the law-making machinery unusually quickly. The amendment was submitted to the National Assembly for debate and adoption on December 19, 1991. The National Assembly law committee (*Commission des lois de l'Assemblée Nationale*) had revised it the day before. The National Assembly adopted the text after the first reading. It

2 The following organizations wrote to the President of the Constitutional Council: Anafé, Cimade, France Terre d'Asile, Gisti and the Ligue des Droits de l'Homme.

then made its way to the Senate on January 16, 1992; the high chamber also adopted it after the first reading. Then, both chambers worked together on improving the text. They both agreed on the updated version (which was adopted by the National Assembly on January 21 and by the Senate on January 22). The Constitutional Council declared the Marchand amendment partly incompatible with the Constitution on February 25, 1992. The government bill, expunged of the Marchand amendment, became the law of February 26, 1992. As for the provision on the transit zone, it finally came to being through the Law on the Waiting Zone of July 6, 1992. Table 1 helps situate these developments chronologically.

I will now discuss the content of the Marchand amendment.

2 The Marchand Amendment: a Less Protective Provision Premised on Extra-Territoriality

Article 7 bis intended to legally regulate (yet again) the detention of foreign nationals and asylum seekers in the international zone, which was renamed "transit zone". The proposed legal provision applied to non-citizens, who were turned away at a French air or sea border (9,044 individuals in 1990) as well as to individuals claiming asylum at these borders (690 asylum seekers had gone through the international zone at airports in 1990 during the review of their claim).[3] It also applied to passengers who found themselves stranded in transit zones after having been sent back to France by their country of destination or who were refused boarding to another destination by the carrier. The transit zone was broadly defined as encompassing the space between boarding or landing and border control. It could also encompass one or several accommodations located on the airport or seaport compounds. The task of precisely delineating the transit zone was left to an administrative authority, (the prefect -*préfet*) which was granted tremendous leeway as no specific distance or radius was specified for the accommodation. The non-citizen detained in the waiting zone could ask for the assistance of an interpreter or a doctor and communicate with any person of his or her choosing. The public prosecutor (immediately informed of the decision to detain) could check the detention conditions at any time.

3 These numbers were given by the Minister of the Interior to MPs (French National Assembly debates December 19, 1991, 8255–8256).

TABLE 1 The Law on the Waiting Zone in context

Date	Event
1974	First oil shock
5 July 1974	The French government decides to stop recruiting foreign workers.
1980s	Significant increase in the number of individuals seeking international protection in Council of Europe member States. Confinement of non-citizens denied entry into French territory and of asylum seekers for extended periods of time in the international zone of Paris' airports in a legal limbo.
1983	The National Front appears on the French political scene: makes inroads in local elections
1984	The Council of State rules that the international zone is not French territory. Case of Eksir.
1987	The Final Court of Appeal rules that the international zone is a part of French territory. Case of Youssef
1988	The Parliamentary Assembly of the Council of Europe expresses concerns regarding the measures adopted by member States to limit the arrivals of asylum seekers
1989	Activist lawyers start suing the Ministry of the Interior (MI) for arbitrary detention of foreign nationals in the international zone. The judge has a limited mandate and can only order the government to put an end to confinement in the international zone. These trials do not affect the MI, who always instructs border authorities to return or admit to the territory the non-citizen in question by the date of the trial. The point of contention therefore always disappears by the hearing date.
June 1990	France signs the Schengen Convention
July 1991	France ratifies the Schengen Convention
22 November 1991	The Paris Court of First Instance allows a Haitian asylum seeker to sue the MI for arbitrary sequestration and monetary compensation, even if he has been admitted to France in the meantime.
19 December 1991	The Marchand amendment is submitted to the National Assembly for debate and adoption.
25 February 1992	The Constitutional Council declares the Marchand amendment partly incompatible with the Constitution

TABLE 1 The Law on the Waiting Zone in context (*cont.*)

Date	Event
26 February 1992	The Paris court hears the arbitrary sequestration case
25 March 1992	The Paris court hands down its decision: the international zone is not an extra-territorial space
6 July 1992	Creation of waiting zones: the Law on the Waiting Zone is passed
30 November 1992	European Union member States adopt the London resolutions, including the resolution on "manifestly unfounded applications for asylum". This resolution is premised on the idea that a significant number of claimants are not genuine applicants.

Compared to article 35 bis in force at the time (cf. chapter 1), the Marchand amendment provided significantly fewer guarantees to foreign nationals confined in the transit zone. This was particularly striking on two points. The amendment did not set any time limits to detention in the transit zone (compared to a seven day maximum under article 35 bis). A non-admitted foreign national and asylum seeker could be detained "for the time strictly necessary for his departure or for the examination of his asylum claim" (French National Assembly debates December 19, 1991, 8279). Under article 35 bis, detainees had to be presented to a liberty and custody judge after one day of confinement. By contrast, the Marchand amendment did not provide for any judicial oversight.

The National Assembly Law Committee suggested several significant modifications. Michel Pezet, rapporteur of the law committee, observed that under the Marchand provision asylum seekers could spend months in the transit zone while the refugee agency determined their status. Indeed, under the amendment, asylum seekers "claimed asylum at the border". On behalf of the law committee, he suggested that asylum seekers should instead seek permission from the Ministry of the Interior to enter France in order to file an asylum claim on French territory. This would shorten their wait in the transit zone to a few days. The law committee also suggested that the duration of detention be capped at 20 days. Importantly, only an administrative judge could then decide to prolong the detention for ten more days. This brought the maximum time in the transit zone to 30 days. The law committee also suggested that the hearing before the administrative judge took place in the transit zone where the non-citizen was held. The government agreed to these modifications and the updated bill arrived before MPs on December 19, 1991.

According to activist and law professor Lochak (1992, 682), the Marchand amendment (i.e. the ancestor of the Law on the Waiting Zone) reflected a significant shift in the government's approach to the international zone: this space was finally considered a part of French territory. Before the amendment, the government clung to the following argument: article 35 bis could not apply to the international zone due to the extra-territorial status of this space (Lochak 1992, 681). In other words, French laws could only apply to French territory and the international zone was not French territory. Foreign nationals stranded in the international zone encountered themselves in an indeterminate space, literally outside of the law, excluded from its protective reach. Makaremi (2009 a) concurs with this analysis. In fact, most actors working today in and on the waiting zone consider the extra-territoriality issue to have been solved a long time ago, precisely when the Law on the Waiting Zone came to force (cf. chapter 3). The Marchand amendment can be read as the French government's acknowledgment of its sovereignty over the transit zone. By bringing back the individuals held in the international zone under the purview of the law, the government implicitly recognized that the transit zone was in France.

Yet, it is my argument that the initial construction of the international zone (renamed "transit zone") as an extra-territorial space persisted with the Marchand amendment and the subsequent Law on the Waiting Zone, albeit in a different form. Prior to the Marchand amendment, the law provided foreign nationals detained for immigration control purposes with the same guarantees, be they located on French territory or at its borders. The Marchand amendment put a stop to this, differentiating between non-citizens already on French territory and those arriving to France, providing the latter with significantly fewer guarantees. This less protective legal framework was precisely built on the premise that non-citizens and asylum seekers who were rejected at the border found themselves at the threshold of, but not having yet entered, French sovereign territory. Marchand's entire argumentation in defense of his legal provision was based on the idea that individuals in transit zones had not yet arrived in France. Before the National Assembly he argued that foreign nationals in the waiting zone were not detained since they were not on French territory (French National Assembly debates, December 19, 1991, 8256). Contrary to those detained on French territory, non-citizens in transit zones were free to move and therefore did not need the same guarantees as those confined on French territory. He said that, although public opinion saw the transit zone as French territory, it was actually an airport zone (*zone aéroportuaire*).

Marchand refused to use the same vocabulary to describe confinement on the territory under article 35 bis and in the transit zone. While article 35 bis talked about *rétention* ("detention" in English), Marchand insisted that the term *maintien* (holding) should be used regarding the transit zone. This different vocabulary was meant to convey the idea that foreign nationals in transit zones experienced a greater degree of freedom than their counterparts detained on French territory under article 35 bis of the 1945 Ordinance. Marchand claimed that non-citizens only faced one closed door in transit zones: that leading to French territory (French Senate debates January 16 1992, 235). As the argument went, foreign nationals were free to leave the transit zone at any time for any other destination of their choosing. Lochak (1992, 687) debunked the government's argumentation: as she pointed out, under the *rétention* regime the foreign national was also free to leave at any time for any other destination. Furthermore, she remarked that for this freedom to be exercised, the non-citizen had to find a willing host country as well as a means of transport, which made it quite hypothetical. To convey the idea that the distinction between confinement under article 35 bis and confinement in the transit zone remains unjustified, I use the English term "detention" to refer to both situations. This differentiation was created by the government and legitimized by the Constitutional Council to grant fewer rights to non-citizens at the border than to those already considered on French territory.

Arguing that the transit zone configuration was fundamentally different made sense for the government for numerous reasons. It justified the assertion that there was indeed a legal vacuum; foreign nationals could not be detained under article 35 bis of the 1945 Ordinance since their situation was completely different. A new law, especially tailored to them, was therefore necessary. The bill also proposed to abrogate article 35 bis. Along the lines of this logic, since foreign nationals in transit zones experienced deprivation of liberty to a much lesser extent, there was no reason why they would benefit from the same guarantees as those in *rétention*. Marchand misled parliamentarians, insisting that the transit zone was an accommodation zone without any prison-like character. One MP from the right-wing Opposition, Francis Delattre (French National Assembly debates December 19, 1991, 8259), disagreed with this assessment and did not hesitate to call transit zones "internment camps" (*camps d'internement*). The response he received from Pezet, the National Assembly law committee rapporteur (i.e. himself an MP), revealed that parliamentarians had received erroneous and biased information from the government. Based on information provided by the Ministry of the Interior, the rapporteur replied that hotels could be found in transit zones. He explained that the domestic refugee agency, healthcare providers, consulates and embassies all had offices in these hotels. In addition, interpreters and lawyers could be consulted on site (French National Assembly debates December 19, 1991, 8259). This idyllic vision did not match reality as the aforementioned trial before the Paris Court of First Instance revealed. Likewise, the government's contention that non-citizens could freely circulate in the transit zone was debunked at the trial where it became clear that asylum seekers were locked up in hotel rooms and subject to constant police surveillance (Paris Court of First Instance, hearing, February 26, 1992). Allouche, a Socialist senator, was amazed to discover that non-citizens were detained in transit zones when watching a TV documentary (French Senate debates January 22, 1992, 392).

Some parliamentarians agreed with the government's argumentation while others refused its logic. Paul Masson, rapporteur at the Senate (French Senate debates January 16, 1992, 212) claimed that, unlike in *rétention*, the non-citizen was not locked up in transit zones, as he "freely circulated in a large perimeter defined by the administrative authority". Gérard Gouzes (French National Assembly debates January 21, 1992, 63) a Socialist MP, also argued that there was a fundamental difference between detention in the transit zone and under article 35 bis: in the transit zone the "migrant" (his term) was free to go to his country of origin at any time. The two situations could not be compared. Charles Lederman (a Communist senator) protested against the proposed duration of detention in the transit zone (French Senate debates January 16, 1992, 232). He referred to the opinion expressed by the Constitutional Council on September 3, 1986: the Council had found that systematically detaining foreign nationals in *rétention* for an additional three-day period (i.e. on top of the seven days already provided for by the law) ran against the Constitution. The Council had concluded that, should it be difficult to deport the foreign national, extending the detention for three extra days, even under judicial oversight, infringed upon individual liberty guaranteed by the Constitution. Exceptions could only be tolerated in cases of absolute emergency or in the presence of a particularly significant threat against public order (Lochak 1992, 686). Masson dismissed Lederman's point by arguing that the Council's opinion was not applicable to the matter at hand: once again, being in the transit zone was different from being in *rétention* (French Senate debates January 16, 1992, 232). Stakeholders' different understandings of the status of the transit zone proved that the Marchand amendment did not clarify the status of this space.

3 Persisting Ambiguity Regarding the Status of the Transit Zone

The status of the international zone was anything but clear in the 1980s, when the highest courts of the country ruled that this space was both inside and outside of France (cf. chapter 1). Minutes from the parliamentary debates reveal that the Marchand amendment did not put an end to the transit zone's ambiguous status. MPs and senators grappled with this notion and had diametrically opposed understandings. For example, Pezet (French National Assembly debates December 19, 1991, 8259), the French National Assembly law committee rapporteur, wondered in which part of the territory individuals found themselves after disembarking from the plane and before crossing border checkpoints. He highlighted that they were not in France under financial provisions; the entire body of French law was not meant to apply to individuals just because they landed on French territory. However, French criminal laws did apply. He concluded by noting the complexity of the transit zone. In contrast to Pezet, Socialist senator Allouche observed that the government wanted to transform a rightless zone into a zone where national law applied, "even though we do not really know if it is French territory!" (French Senate debates January 22, 1992, 391).

In contrast to both these positions, François Colcombet, an MP, comprehended the transit zone as a part of French territory. He said:

> The new article 35 quater of the 1945 Ordinance gives a legal framework to the situation of foreign nationals who, arriving by air or sea, are not admitted to enter French territory, or, more precisely, are not allowed to leave the transit zone, because they are indeed on French territory and not in an intermediary zone, like characters from *Orphée's testament* who dwell between life and death. If a woman were to give birth in the transit zone, the child would be registered in France. Likewise, if an offence were committed, French police and judiciary would be competent.
>
> FRENCH NATIONAL ASSEMBLY DEBATES, January 21, 1992, 67

NGOs noted that the amendment did not solve the extra-territoriality question. Several organizations promoting human and non-citizens' rights wrote to Robert Badinter, then president of the Constitutional Council.[4] They denounced the amendment's inconsistencies by observing that there were only

---

4 The following organizations signed the letter: Anafé, Cimade, France Terre d'Asile, Gisti, and the Ligue des droits de l'homme.

two possible scenarios; either the transit zone was geographically part of French territory as ruled by the Final Court of Appeal in 1987 (*Youssef*) or it was not, as ruled by the Council of State in the *Eksir* decision in 1984. If lawmakers decided to abide by the *Youssef* ruling and therefore to exercise their competence over this space, then what was the rationale for subjecting foreign nationals in the transit zone to a different law than that applicable to those on the rest of French territory? Why would they be governed by a law, which would be less protective of their liberties? The implications of the second scenario were also far-reaching: acknowledging that the transit zone was not a part of French territory meant that article 7 bis was contrary to the constitution as lawmakers were not competent to adopt it. Indeed neither lawmakers nor administrative authorities have the competence to pass a law that applies beyond national territory or take individual decisions implementing such law (NGO letter to the President of the Constitutional Council January 28, 1992, 5).

4 The Government's Justification for the Amendment: Emphasis on Progress, Security and the Upcoming Litigation's Danger

The government presented the amendment as necessary for striking a balance between individual liberties and border control and security (French Senate debates January 16, 1992, 229). Marchand portrayed France as an exemplary, progressive country in Europe in this regard: France would be the first country to provide a legal status and safeguards to individuals held in transit zones, promising that they would not spend more than 30 days in these spaces (French National Assembly debates January 21, 1992, 71 and December 19, 1991, 8256). Gouzes, president of the National Assembly Law committee, described the situation of non-admitted travelers in other countries' transit zones. According to him, non-admitted passengers could be detained in prison in Ireland, Denmark and the United Kingdom, while in Germany and the Netherlands they could be detained in police premises at the airport (French National Assembly debates December 19, 1991, 8271). Marchand insisted that his legal provision would place France far ahead of its neighbors in terms of legal protection in the transit zone. He explained that the government had decided to give a legal basis to what was currently an administrative practice (French National Assembly debates December 19, 1991, 8256). The Paris Court of First Instance, that heard the arbitrary sequestration case, expressed outrage precisely at the government's efforts to give a legal base to an illegal administrative practice harmful to individual liberties (Paris Court of First Instance February 26, 1992). Appalled by the procedure, the Court declared the Ministry of the

Interior's attempt to turn an illegal administrative practice into an acceptable one through law making as incompatible with the rule of law.

Security loomed large in the Minister of the Interior's discourse: he was adamant that freedom of movement neither could nor should run against the State's security. Freedom of movement should not mean the loosening of migration controls. He emphasized that some non-admitted foreign nationals were undesirable (i.e. individuals whose presence would be a threat to public order, or who had been banned from the territory or against whom a deportation order had been taken). The Minister of the Interior used the upcoming legal proceedings to his advantage, referring to them to create a sense of urgency. He warned senators that State practices could be found illegal. He argued that, should this possibility materialize, discarding the transit zone's legal provision would be tantamount to suppressing border control. Indeed, if article 7 bis was not adopted and the plaintiffs won the case, no foreign national could be detained in the transit zone. As a consequence, all non-admitted passengers and asylum seekers would have to be granted entry even if they did not fulfill the criteria. Marchand raised the specter of invasion: a familiar trope associated with calls to increase border control. He claimed that the disappearance of French borders would translate into several thousands of individuals coming to France each year. These people would swell the ranks of illegal workers residing in the country without authorization. This uncalled for situation would be against the State's interest (French Senate debates January 16, 1992, 229–230).

Prime Minister Edith Cresson reiterated that the transit zone provision resulted from a legal crisis. When the president of the human rights commission wrote her a letter expressing his dissatisfaction about the commission not being able to offer its opinion to parliamentarians, Cresson replied that the government could not wait for the commission's report due to the looming trial date (letter of the Prime Minister to the president of the domestic human rights commission, January 16, 1992). She clearly stated that the government's decision to legislate on the transit zone was triggered by the Court of First Instance's November ruling allowing the plaintiffs to sue the Ministry of the Interior on the merits of their case. As she openly admitted, initially the government had no intention to pass a law on the transit zone: the situation had not been challenged before national courts or the European Court of Human Rights. She argued that it was a government leader's responsibility to make sure civil servants did not have to act illegally for extended periods of time. Therefore, the government could not wait for the spring parliamentary session. This unsettling admission on the part of the French government -*that it did not care about respecting the rights of foreign nationals as long as there were no legal proceedings involved*- will be found over and over again in the history of the Law on the Waiting Zone. It is now time to examine the role played by the Constitutional Council in the birth of the Law on the Waiting Zone.

5 The Role of the Constitutional Council in the Manufacturing of an Illiberal Law

Interestingly, while Socialist Party MPs adopted the government's bill at the first reading in December 1992, Socialist senators refused to support the text when it came to the Senate for the first and second readings on January 16 and January 22, 1992. Other political groups cast a positive vote and the bill was approved in spite of the Socialist Party senators' opposition. Yet, the minutes from the parliamentary debates reveal that Socialist senators supported the gist of the transit zone provision: they agreed it was necessary to control borders. As such, they opposed the Communist group's request to delete article 7 bis, as they agreed with the spirit of the bill (French Senate debates January 22, 1992, 230). The Socialist senators were uncomfortable with the maximum length of time spent in the transit zone (thought to be excessive) and favored the intervention of a liberty and custody judge rather than an administrative judge to extend the duration of detention. During the first reading, Allouche, speaking on behalf of the Socialist group, explained that the Socialist senators would back the amendment only if the government promised to refer it to the Constitutional Council (French Senate debates January 16, 1992, 207). Allouche requested a clear answer from Marchand, but was not given one. He reiterated his request at the second reading, making it very clear that the Socialist group's vote depended on the government's favorable response.

According to French law, two different actors are entitled to refer a legislative text to the Constitutional Council: the Prime Minister and a group of 60 parliamentarians -either MPs or senators- (French Constitutional Council website, accessed January 2015).[5] The Socialist group at the Senate counted enough members to fulfill the requirements: Why did the senators not refer the bill to the Constitutional Council? Allouche explained that he preferred the former option, arguing that it was in the government's interest: by referring the bill to the Constitutional Council itself, the government would shield itself from any criticism (French Senate debates January 22, 1991, 392). The bill

5 http://www.conseil-constitutionnel.fr.

was passed without the Socialist senators' blessing and became a law. However, confronted with significant opposition both inside and outside of Parliament, the government decided to refer the Marchand provision to the Constitutional Council.

The French Constitutional Council (*Conseil Constitutionnel*), established in 1958, "is a court vested with various powers, including in particular the review of the constitutionality of legislation" (French Constitutional Court website, accessed January 19, 2015). The circumstances under which the Constitutional Council was tasked to review the constitutionality of the proposed legislation on the transit zone were unheard of. Until now, opponents to legislation had introduced referrals (Genevois 1992). In stark contrast, Cresson, Socialist Prime Minister, who therefore belonged to the same government that introduced the Marchand amendment, referred the amendment to the Constitutional Council on February 25, 1992. The Council released its decision on the same day.

The Constitutional Council examined the Marchand amendment under two aspects: the right to liberty and the right to seek asylum (both protected under the French Constitution). *The Council endorsed the government's contention that detention in the transit zone and in* rétention *were of a different nature.* It found that foreign nationals detained (the word used by the Constitutional Council is not detention but holding -*maintien*) in the transit zone under the proposed article 35 quater were not subject to the same degree of constraint as those placed in administrative detention under article 35 bis of the 1945 Ordinance. Nevertheless, the Council found that the amendment infringed upon the right to liberty because the responsibility to extend the duration of detention rested on the administrative judge, not the liberty and custody judge. Indeed, the French Constitution of 1958 (article 66, still in force today) tasked the latter with upholding individual liberties, not the former. As for the right to asylum, the Council found that the Marchand amendment was compatible with this constitutional right, provided that the asylum seeker's detention in the transit zone only occurred for the time necessary for the claimant to be returned, if the claim appeared to be "manifestly unfounded". The Council censored part of the Marchand amendment but legitimized its very rationale, thus contributing to creating an exceptional legal framework for individuals detained in the transit zone. The Council gave legitimacy to the government's bill, thereby soothing the conscience of parliamentarians who were unsettled by the Marchand provision. It therefore played a significant part in the birth of the subsequent Law on the Waiting Zone. It is now interesting to study how the scope of the waiting zone has been significantly extended following litigation "crises".

6 The Law on the Waiting Zone from 1992 to 2016: Successive Extensions of the Definition of the Waiting Zone Following Litigation "Crises"

In March 1992, the Paris Court strongly condemned the government's efforts to turn an illegal administrative practice, harmful to individual liberties, into a law. Yet, this is precisely what happened. Partly censored by the Constitutional Council, the Marchand amendment was modified and became the Law on the Waiting Zone of July 6, 1992. Such a law gave a legal framework to the administrative practices of detention outside of article 35 bis of the 1945 Ordinance and abolished the provisions of article 35 bis pertaining to the detention of foreign nationals turned away at borders. Although the final version of the waiting zone provision was more protective than the initial Marchand amendment, it still granted significantly less protection to individuals than article 35 bis. The Law on the Waiting Zone gave fewer rights to non-citizens arriving at the border than to those already considered on French soil.

Today, the Law on the Waiting Zone governs foreign nationals denied admission into French or Schengen territory or claiming asylum at a French border arriving by train, boat or airplane (CESEDA 2016 articles L221-1 to L224-4). Individuals subjected to the waiting zone's particular legal regime are not granted access to regular refugee determination procedures. This parallel—and less protective—legal framework builds on the premise that rejected non-citizens and asylum seekers at the border find themselves at the threshold of, but not having yet entered French sovereign territory. They find themselves, instead, in territorial border zones where the State establishes the distinction between physical and legal entry: physical presence proves insufficient and only lawful admission amounts to entry into the territory (Basaran 2011). Those assigned the waiting zone status are detained during the time necessary for them to be returned or, if they are claiming asylum, to determine whether or not their claim is inadmissible or "manifestly unfounded". Generally, only asylum seekers passing through this initial sieve will be entitled to enter French territory where claims will be examined on their merits. The Law of July 29, 2015 was adopted to incorporate two European directives of June 2013 pertaining to asylum: the Asylum Procedures Directive (2013/32/EU) and the Reception Conditions Directive (2013/33/EU). Since this law, asylum seekers may also be admitted to the territory when deemed particularly vulnerable by the refugee agency (CESEDA 2018, article L.221-1).

Since July 1992, the scope of the Law on the Waiting zone has been extended significantly, following litigation "crises"(cf. table 2). Initially (in the early 1990s), those denied entry were geographically circumscribed by an administrative authority (*le préfet*) to waiting zones, which ran between points of boarding or disembarkation and border checkpoints. These zones could include accommodation located on or nearby the airport, port, or train station. In 2003, the definition of the waiting zone was widened to include accommodation "nearby the place of disembarkation" (article 50 of the Law of November 26, 2003). The definition was also expanded to include any place where an entering non-citizen goes for administrative or medical reasons (Law of November 26, 2003). As a result, the waiting zone status now accompanies the individual, even kilometers from the point of arrival. For example, individuals turned away at the border at Charles de Gaulle (CDG) airport were deemed outside of France under immigration law when presented to a judge at the Bobigny Court—located 17 kilometers from the airport—after four days of detention. Trapped by the waiting zone framework, foreign nationals "are not expelled by the border, they are forced to *be* the border" (Khosravi 2010, 99). Thus the term "waiting zone" refers both to a geographical and legal space.

The 2003 extension of the definition of the waiting zone was prompted by the arrival of 910 refugees (mostly Kurds of Syrian citizenship, who first said they were from Iraq) on the beach of Boulouris on the French Riviera during the night of February 17-18, 2001 (Rotman April 23, 2001). The secretary of the relevant administrative authority created an *ad hoc* waiting zone, that run from the point of disembarkation on the beach to the Fréjus military compound where the refugees were detained. At the time, the law did not sanction the creation of a waiting zone outside of a port, airport or international train station. Law professor Serge Slama explains that the government, led by Lionel Jospin,[6] decided to admit all refugees into the territory before the liberty and custody judges handed down their ruling. This decision appears to have been motivated by a conversation with Dominique Simonnot, journalist at *Libération:*

> They create a waiting zone of several dozens of kilometers to transport people to the camp. Then all the activist lawyers arrive: Jean-Eric Malabre, Stéphane Maugendre, Dominique Monget-Sarrail, it was the same crowd ... they were often somehow related to Anafé, but mostly to Gisti. They go down there, they try to release everybody by appealing to principles. And the case was solved, -I do not know if this story is

6 Lionel Jospin was Prime Minister from June 1997 to May 2002 when Jacques Chirac was President (from 1995 to 2007). Jospin and Chirac were from different political parties (the former was left-wing while the latter was right-wing). Jospin therefore led the government during times of *cohabitation* (cf chapter 1).

> really well-known: Dominique Simonnot, who was journalist at *Libération,* starts to write articles on this [*Libération* is a respected newspaper in France]. She speaks on the phone with someone from the Ministry and lets him know that she is going to publish in *Libération* [an article saying] that lawyers will manage to release all refugees.
>
> They get scared and I think it is Matignon [official home to the Prime Minister, this term refers to the Primer Minister in common language], so Jospin, who decides to release them. Anafé had contested the act creating the waiting zone and four years afterwards, years afterwards, the Administrative Court cancelled it.
>
> Interview with SERGE SLAMA, July 2014

All refugees were released from the waiting zone, except for a dozen, who were believed to be Palestinians (Simonnot and Hassoux February 21, 2001). Anafé and six other NGOs defending non-citizens' rights sued the government before the Administrative Court of Nice for the creation of an illegal waiting zone. The Court condemned the government in 2005 and cancelled this *ad hoc* waiting zone (Administrative Court of Nice, December 9, 2005). Meanwhile, the government, anticipating a legal defeat, had managed to expand the definition of the waiting zone with the Law of November 26, 2003. Initiated by Nicolas Sarkozy, then Minister of the Interior, this law aimed at cracking down on illegal immigration.

On paper, there are 67 waiting zones in France, all located in ports, airports and train stations open to international passengers (Anafé November 2015, 13). Most are not significant crossings and therefore used infrequently. Since 2011 (Law of June 16, 2011), *ad hoc* waiting zones can also be created when a group of 10 non-citizens arrives in France outside of a border crossing (for example on a beach). In this case, the waiting zone will run between places where authorities have found the non-citizens and the closest border checkpoint. Once again, this change in legislation was triggered by a (perceived) immigration crisis: a boat dropped off 123 refugees—mostly Kurds from Syria—in Corsica in January 2010 (Jamet January 22, 2010). After being placed in detention centers all over the country (in *rétention*), these non-citizens were released by judges. The latter found that the government had not respected legal procedures. Eric Besson, then Minister of Immigration,[7] spearheaded the Law of June 16, 2011, whose goal was to enhance both control over immigration and integration of migrants.

7 There was a Ministry of Immigration from May 2007 to November 2010. Aside from this time period, the Ministry of the Interior has been handling matters pertaining to immigration.

Referring to the Corsican case, Besson argued that it was necessary for administrative authorities to be able to create temporary waiting zones so that irregular migrants would not abscond and wander around the Schengen area freely (Law commission of the French National Assembly September 8, 2010). Table 2 below presents the successive extensions of the definition of the waiting zone.

TABLE 2 The Law on the Waiting Zone from 1992 to 2011

Date	Event
6 July 1992	Creation of waiting zones: the Law on the Waiting Zone is passed. Waiting zones run between points of boarding or disembarkation and border checkpoints. They can include accommodation located on or nearby the airport or port. The task of demarcating waiting zones is left to an administrative authority.
Night between the 17 and 18 of February 2001	The boat East Sea carrying 910 refugees (mostly Kurds of Syrian citizenship) runs aground near the beach of Boulouris, on the French Riviera. The secretary of the competent administrative authority creates a waiting zone that runs between the point of disembarkation on the beach to a military compound, where the refugees are detained. The government decides to release them all before the liberty and custody judges hand down their decision.
26 November 2003	Extension of the definition of the waiting zone to include accommodation "nearby the place of disembarkation" as well as any place where an entering non-citizen goes for administrative or medical reasons.
22 January 2010	A boat drops off 123 refugees (mostly Kurds from Syria) in Corsica. After being placed in detention centers all over the country, they are all released by custody and liberty judges, for the government had not respected legal procedures.
16 June 2011	Extension of the definition of the waiting zone: ad hoc waiting zones can also be created when a group of 10 non-citizens arrives in France outside of a border crossing (for example on a beach).

This chapter traced how a parallel and less protective legal framework, one premised on extra-territoriality, was established through regular democratic processes. The history of the birth of the waiting zone and of its subsequent extensions highlight the difficulties of legal activism. Paradoxically, defending non-citizens through litigation has resulted in significant extensions of the scope of the waiting zone. Each time, the government managed to turn the illegal administrative practice in question into a law. As scholars such as Basaran (2011) note, the infringement of liberties is not an anomaly in liberal democracies or a discontinuity with liberal rule. In the following chapters, I will further explore the extra-territoriality notion and argue that the initial construction of the international zone as an extra-territorial space has endured in both mindsets and practices.

CHAPTER 3

Non-Citizens in French Airports' Waiting Zones Today: the Endurance of Exclusion through Extra-Territoriality

Since the birth of the Law on the Waiting Zone in 1992, international treaty monitoring bodies, legal scholars and the European Court of Human Rights (*Amuur v. France* 1996) have explicitly stated that international zones, or transit zones, are integrally part of the territory of the State on which they are located. Under international law, airports' transit zones are not extra-territorial spaces. Many people working on or in Charles De Gaulle's waiting zone think that the legal issues attached to "extra-territorial legal fictions" (Del Valle Galvez 2005) in the 1980s and early 1990s disappeared when the Law on the Waiting Zone came into being in 1992. To them, the Law on the Waiting Zone represents a striking shift from the previous era, when asylum claimants and rejected travelers were excluded from legal guarantees based on their presence in geographical spaces construed as extra-territorial. Rémi Rouquette, a lawyer and former lecturer in public law, rejects the use of the term "extra-territoriality" to describe today's situation (i.e. at the time of data collection in 2013–2014), pointing out that waiting zones are not-extra-territorial zones but places where a different set of rights apply (Interview, February 25, 2014). Christian is a lawyer specializing in the defense of non-citizens in administrative detention (at the border and on the territory). He affirms that courts are no longer wondering whether those in waiting zones are *de facto* on French territory. All ambiguity on this matter has been dispelled (Interview, December 10, 2013). As for Jeanne, who works at the Ministry of the Interior in the department tasked with reviewing asylum seekers' applications to enter French territory, she argued that the French government adequately responded to the critiques mounted against its practices at the borders by creating the Law on the Waiting Zone (Interview, November 2013). To my question "How does the Ministry of the Interior interpret the European Court of Human Rights ruling *Amuur v. France*?" Jeanne replied:

> We do not pay attention to it. It is a ruling from 1996, but events took place in 1992. The waiting zone was created in 1992. We saw that there was a small issue at the time. As usual, the Court took its time, but it does not mean that the State did not react. The waiting zones were created in 1992. This is the reason why the law came into existence (Interview, November 2013).

 | DOI:10.1163/9789004383500_005

I agree that the establishment of extra-territorial international zones as devices to deflect from domestic and international obligations has been *formally* rejected in July 1992. When MPs passed the Law on the Waiting Zone, they implicitly acknowledged French sovereignty over the international zone, renamed "transit zone" and then "waiting zone". From the moment the Law on the Waiting Zone came to force (and was applied) non-citizens stopped being deprived of "the right to have rights" (Arendt 1968). Furthermore, the excision of airports' international zones was clearly condemned by the Court of Human Rights in 1996. But was the Law on the Waiting Zone really a cause for celebration and a resolution to a problem? Is the term "extra-territoriality" in fact inappropriate to describe the current situation?

In answering these questions, I will make the following arguments. *Firstly, the initial phase of extra-territoriality has endured in mindsets and practices.* Amongst individuals working in or on the waiting zone can be found the deeply ingrained idea that the waiting zone is not French territory (at least) for non-citizen populations. This argument, just like in the 1980s and early 1990s, has been used to exclude non-citizens from rights. In other words, some individuals have been denied the protection of international law based on their presence in excised, non-French territory. *Secondly, the Law on the Waiting Zone has reinvented exclusion through another form of extra-territoriality, premised on the non-citizen's legal status at the border.* Although physically in France, rejected non-citizens and asylum seekers at the border are not present from a legal standpoint, for they have not crossed yet "law's admission gate" (Shachar 2007). The first argument will be developed in this chapter but the second one will be saved for chapter 4.

This chapter will first review how international law explicitly addressed the status of the international or transit zone at airports. It will then highlight how the international zone may still be a lawless space for those denied access to the waiting zone status. Evidence will be provided to demonstrate that the excision issues attached to the international zone have been transferred to the waiting zone. A possible explanation regarding the causes of this transfer will be offered.

1 The Case of *Amuur v. France* (1996): Airports' International Zones Are not Extra-Territorial Spaces

When the French government established the airports' international zones as non-French spaces, international law had not directly addressed the status of the international zone yet. Legal scholars had not given much thought to the status of this space (cf. chapter 1). This changed when the European Court of Human Rights specifically ruled on June 25, 1996 in the *Amuur* case that the international zone at Orly airport did not have extra-territorial status. The Court found that the Somali asylum claimants had been illegally deprived of liberty: no appropriate law had authorized their detention.

The *Amuur* case started at the domestic level when Dominique Monget-Sarrail and her associates Laurence Roques and Pascale Taelman first brought the case to the Créteil Court of First Instance on March 26, 1992. The day before, the Paris Court of First Instance had rejected the government's extra-territoriality thesis, according to which the government argued that the Arcade hotel at CDG airport was part of the international zone and as such had extra-territorial status (cf. chapter 1, the plaintiffs were four Haitian and one Zairian asylum seekers). It was also about a month after the Constitutional Council had upheld the French government's contention that confinement in the international zone and on French territory differed on the grounds that the former was less detrimental to individual liberty than the latter (cf. chapter 2). The Law on the Waiting Zone came to force a few months after the *Amuur* case began. The *Amuur* case has to be understood as part of a series of trials that activist lawyers launched against the French government from the late 1980s (cf. chapters 1 and 2).

When these events unfolded, the European Commission of Human Rights was tasked with filtering the requests to determine their admissibility. The facts of the *Amuur* case are therefore described in both the Commission's decision *Barir and Amuur against France* of October 18, 1993 and in the Court's ruling *Amuur v. France* of June 25, 1996. The information given by Monget-Sarrail, one of the plaintiffs' lawyers, complements that provided in these legal accounts. The *Amuur* case highlights the plight of asylum seekers detained in international zones, caught in the extra-territorial legal fiction designed by the French government. It reveals that those seeking international protection were particularly at risk of *refoulement* when arriving at Parisian airport borders.

Four Somali siblings arrived on March 9, 1992 at Paris Orly airport from Syria where they had spent two months after fleeing from Somalia via Kenya. They alleged their lives were at risk in Somalia after the fall of President Siyad Barre. The border police refused them entry on the basis that their passports were forged. They were placed at the Arcade hotel, which was construed as an extension of the international zone (cf. chapter 1). On March 12 the Ministry of the Interior examined their request to enter France to claim asylum. By March 14, 18 other Somali nationals (among which 11 children) had arrived at Orly from Syria and Egypt. Of these 18 Somali citizens, five were cousins of the Amuur brothers and sister. They were all members of the Darob Marhan tribe, which was in power during the regime of President Mohamed Siyad Barre. They explained that several members of their family had been murdered. On March 24 they obtained legal aid after the NGO Cimade (i.e. one of the founding members of Anafé) put them in touch with a lawyer. On March 25, they wrote a letter to the refugee agency (OFPRA) requesting refugee status according to the Geneva Convention of 1951. On March 26, their case was referred to the Court of First Instance at Créteil on the grounds that their deprivation of liberty was arbitrary.

Lawyers Monget-Sarrail, Roques and Taelman referred the case of the 22 plaintiffs to the European Commission of Human Rights on March 27, 1992. In spite of the President of the European Commission indicating to the French government on March 27 "that it was desirable, in the interest of the parties and the proper conduct of the proceedings, to refrain from sending the applicants back to Somalia before 4 April 1992" (European Court of Human Rights 1996, 18), the four Amuur siblings were forcibly returned on March 29. The Minister of the Interior had refused them entry. The government bypassed the Commission's request by returning the applicants to their country of transit, Syria -which was not a party to the 1951 Refugee Convention- instead of Somalia. At the time of their return (March 29), the Somali claimants had not yet received the answer from the refugee agency. Their case before the Court at Créteil was still pending. The government insisted that the French ambassador in Syria had obtained diplomatic assurances from Syrian authorities that the country would take the Somali nationals.

On March 29 Monget-Sarrail and her associate Taelman were at a conference on asylum. They received a phone call letting them know that the four young Somali (the Amuur siblings were young adults of 22, 21, 19 and 17) were no longer at Orly airport. Monget-Sarrail recounts:

> On Friday the European Commission had invited France not to return them to Somalia, but on Saturday morning they were put on the plane anyway. So we came back from the conference, Pascale [Taelman] went to Orly to see the families that were still there. They were terribly upset as they had been forced on the plane, they did not want to go, they were put in the plane on a hoist. So she went to the airport and I came back to find someone to stop the return. So we called Mrs. Mitterrand who, at the time, was head of *France Libertés* when [François] Mitterrand was president of the Republic.[1] We explained to her the situation: there were

1 *France Libertés* is an NGO that was created in 1986 to defend human rights and ethnic minorities. The organization's website explains that the NGO has been active in defending the right of peoples and individuals to self-determination. Cf. http://www.france-libertes.org/Notre-histoire,2217.html.

> only women and children left. She made him promise not to try to return the others before the [Court of First Instance at Créteil's] decision on Monday. We also told the European Court that France had not respected its invitation to postpone [return]. [France] bypassed this requirement quite cleverly, since the European Court was saying that they should not be returned to Somalia, and they were sent back to Syria where they had transited.
>
> Interview with MONGET-SARRAIL, August 2014

Yet, in spite of Monget-Sarrail securing a non-return commitment from the President's wife, the 18 remaining asylum seekers were presented to a plane for Cairo on March 30. They refused to board it. They were then referred to a criminal court for refusing to abide by the decision denying them entry. On the following day, March 31, the refugee agency declared itself incompetent, as the claimants had not yet been admitted to French territory. This same day, the judge of the Court of First Instance at Créteil declared that the detention of the remaining claimants was illegal and ordered the Ministry of the Interior to immediately release them. The 18 Somali nationals were granted refugee status by the refugee agency on June 25, 1992 and withdrew their request before the European Commission of Human Rights.

Monget-Sarrail and her associates were ready to drop the case as the plaintiffs had all left the international zone. But a lawyer from the European Court called them: he was adamant that they press on with the request nonetheless. Monget-Sarrail recalls:

> It was the first time we referred a case to the European Court; we did not know how to proceed, so we explained how unfair it was. When they were set free, the four others had disappeared so we thought: "It is over". And a lawyer from the Court, a Greek, called us. Luckily, he spoke French flawlessly and told us: "Yes, you have to press on, even if they disappeared, because we are looking for a case to rule on these zones where incoming people are placed. There are many countries in Europe where there are no laws and they are waiting for the Court's decision. Press on with your request, we are going to help you, we will explain how it works". So this is how we could file our request. The [European] Commission examined it and then we were referred to the Grand Chamber and invited to come plead (Interview, August 2014).

Most of the proceedings before the European Commission and the European Court took place in the absence of the plaintiffs. Monget-Sarrail explains that for a long period of time, she and her associates completely lost the trace of the Amuur siblings after their return to Syria. The European Court ruling (1996, 2) reads: "The lawyer who had represented the applicants before the Commission stated that she was unable to contact them but that the terms of the authority to act that had been produced before the Commission also covered the proceedings before the Court", confirming her story. According to Monget-Sarrail, the UNHCR had received assurances from the Syrian government that the Somali nationals would not be placed in refugee camps but would instead receive a residency permit. On this basis, the international refugee organization had tried to convince the four Amuur to return to Syria, their country of transit. Yet, as Monget-Sarrail and her associates later learned, the Amuur had landed in Syrian refugee camps where they had "stagnated" (*végéter*) for months before leaving. They then heard that the siblings were in Moscow (Interview, August 2014). The European Commission's opinion (1993) corroborates her story: "The applicants claimed they were arrested upon arrival in Damascus and two of them were forced to leave Syria for Russia".

The Commission finally referred the case of the four Amuur siblings to the European Court on March 1, 1995. The plaintiffs had argued that several articles of the European Convention of Human Rights had been violated (articles 3, 4, 5, 6, 13 and 25) but the Commission rejected all of the alleged violations save the one based on article 5 (right to liberty and security).[2]

Not surprisingly, the arguments of the government in the *Amuur* case (at the domestic and European level) were the same as those fed to parliamentarians to justify the Marchand amendment and used at the trial before the Paris Court of March 25, 1992. In its observations to the European Commission (transmitted on July 7, 1992), the French government claimed that the plaintiffs' "holding" (*maintien*) in the international zone did not amount to deprivation of liberty: they were not arrested or detained. They were instead "staying" (*séjourner*) in the international zone. They were free to leave for any other destination than France (European Commission 1993). The Créteil Court of First Instance came to the same conclusions as its Paris counterpart the day before: the plaintiffs' detention was not provided by any legislation and "detention may not be ordered by the administrative authorities in cases other than those provided for in Article 35 bis of the 1945 Ordinance, which in any event makes such detention subject to supervision by the courts" (Créteil Court's ruling quoted in the European Court of Human Rights' judgment). The Court

2 The full name of the Convention is " Convention for the Protection of Human Rights and Fundamental Freedoms". The Convention was opened for signature in Rome on November 4, 1950. It came to force in 1953. Cf. website of the European Court of Human Rights.

found therefore that the applicants' detention was unlawful and directed that they be released. The European Court concurred with the domestic court's judgment. It ruled that individuals in the international zone were subjected to French law, even though French authorities claimed the opposite. As France exercised sovereignty over this zone, the protections offered by the Refugee Convention had to be granted. This case law highlights that jurisdiction cannot be withdrawn at will. Under international law these situations of extra-territoriality do not exist, despite States' effort to create "legal fictions" through national policies or legislation (Gammeltoft-Hansen 2011).

Hathaway and Gammeltoft-Hansen (2015, 245) explain that the excised zone, "in which some or all of the legal obligations of the territorial State are declared not to apply" constituted a traditional *non-entrée* mechanism (cf. chapter 1). The concept of *non-entrée*, first coined by Hathaway in 1992, is defined as the efforts deployed by wealthy States to ensure refugees never reach their jurisdiction. They argue that traditional *non-entrée* mechanisms, such as international zones, have been successfully challenged both in law and in practice. They write:

> The notion that a State can delimit the geographical scope of its territory for purposes of avoiding legal liability-for example, by excision or the declaration of an international zone in an airport-has simply been rejected.
>
> HATHAWAY and GAMMELTOFT-HANSEN 2015, 246–247

They argue that, in order to keep refugees at bay, powerful States have now turned to a new generation of *non-entrée* mechanisms based on international cooperation, since they can no longer rely on former tools such as excision. The European Court of Human Rights also implied that, had the Law on the Waiting Zone been in force at the time the complaint was lodged, the applicants would have had no grounds for complaint.

I take issue with these positions. As I will now demonstrate, non-citizens have continued to be excluded from rights based on their presence in excised, non-French territory many years after the Law on the Waiting Zone came into force and the *Amuur* ruling was handed down.

2 When History Repeats Itself: Evidence of the Endurance of the Initial Phase of Extra-Territoriality

The legacy of the excision of international zones weighs heavily on contemporary mindsets and practices. In the 1980s, judges from the highest courts issued contradictory rulings, which gave greater regulatory power to the State. The rulings reveal that the international zone was understood to mean different things according to the political usage of the law. The international zone was both France and not France at the same time, according to the direction of the border crossing (cf. chapter 1). When it came to returning someone to a country of origin or a third country, the international zone was France, and non-citizens refusing to embark could be subject to criminal prosecutions for illegally staying in the country while in the international zone (Final Court of Appeal, *Youssef*, 1987). However, for foreign nationals landing in Charles de Gaulle arriving from another country, the international zone was not yet France (Council of State, *Eksir*, 1984).

When the Ministry of the Interior presented the bill that later became the Law on the Waiting Zone, parliamentarians grappled with the status of transit zones (in December 1991 and January 1992). They exhibited confusion regarding the status of this geographic space. Some of them endorsed the government's assertion according to which it was not France (cf. chapter 2). The status of the international zones of Paris' airports was anything but clear.

Years after the *Amuur v. France* judgment, French domestic courts still issued contradictory rulings regarding the status of the waiting zone, coming again to the conclusion that waiting zones were both located outside of and part and parcel of French territory. Some courts espoused the government's 1980s argumentation according to which waiting (previously international) zones were not French territory for certain populations. This argumentation was used in order to circumvent granting rights guaranteed by French and international law. This resulted in an uneven enforcement of rights. It is fascinating to observe that the same court could make diametrically opposed rulings on exactly the same topic. This seemingly permanent, persistent indecision reveals that the status of waiting zones remains unclear in stakeholders' minds.

In France, the children's judge (*juge des enfants*) has jurisdiction whenever there is a threat to a child's health, security or morality or if the child's education or his or her physical, emotional, intellectual and social well-being are severely at risk (Anafé January 2013, 32–33). On December 7, 2004, the Paris Appeal Court ruled that legal provisions pertaining to the protection of minors were applicable to all minors present on French territory, regardless of their nationality. The court therefore found that the children judge's protection extended to minors held under the waiting zone law who, although turned away at the border, were *de facto* on French territory. Yet, the very same Paris Appeal Court ruled exactly the opposite in 2008 (February 21): as the minor placed in the waiting zone was not on French territory, he could not benefit from protection measures that could be implemented only on French territory (cf. Final

Court of Appeal, March 25, 2009). The Court found that the Convention on the Rights of the Child did not apply to children in the waiting zone.

Finally, the Final Court of Appeal (i.e. the highest court in the domestic judicial order, *Cour de Cassation*) rejected the Appeal Court's February 2008's reasoning, stating that "the waiting zone was under national administrative and jurisdictional supervision". The Final Court of Appeal found that a minor (here an Iraqi asylum seeker) placed in Charles de Gaulle airport's waiting zone was *de facto* on French territory. French law pertaining to the protection of childhood was applicable to all minors located on French territory, regardless of their nationality or legal status in France. The Final Court of Appeal found that the inferior court had violated article 20 of the Convention on the Rights of the Child, which states that "a child temporarily or permanently deprived of his or her family environment, or in whose own best interests cannot be allowed to remain in that environment, shall be entitled to special protection and assistance provided by the State" (Final Court of Appeal, March 25, 2009).

It is beyond the scope of this book to study all of the rulings issued by liberty and custody judges and by the Appeal Court. This would constitute not only a tedious but also an impossible task due to their sheer number. Liberty and custody judges, who assess whether detention in Charles de Gaulle waiting zone's facility should be extended after four and 12 days, can work from 11:00 am until 2:00 am, deciding on the cases of dozens of individuals. I have myself observed, at the Bobigny Court of First Instance, days of hearings finishing after midnight. Hearings do not stop during weekends or holidays and the rulings are not available in electronic format. However, more instances of exclusion from rights on the grounds that waiting zones are not French territory could perhaps be found in other rulings.

In practice, the Final Court of Appeal's 2009 ruling pertaining to the status of the waiting zone has not really been followed. Yet, in the French legal order, the judgments of the Final Court constitute a reference. Children's judges have the power to order placement in a group home or with family members, therefore ending detention in the waiting zone. Gérard, an experienced *ad hoc* administrator, explains that in practice children's judges very rarely dare to take a decision that would contradict the administrative decision placing the minor under the waiting zone regime (Interview, December 2013).[3] He

---

3 Minors are subject to the exact same legal regime as adults, except for their appointment of a legal guardian called *ad hoc* administrator (*administrateur ad hoc*). Under French law minors lack the capacity to represent themselves in legal proceedings. Therefore, the *ad hoc* administrator's mission consists in assisting the child during his or her detention in the waiting zone and in ensuring the child's legal representation in all administrative and judicial

argues that the children's judges' jurisdiction over children confined in the waiting zone should be reaffirmed and explicitly written into the law. It was actually Gérard's organization that brought the issue to the Final Court of Appeal in order to obtain a ruling confirming that the children judge had the power to intervene on behalf of children placed under the waiting zone regime. Gérard deplores that the children's judge's jurisdiction over the waiting zone is neither in the culture nor in most people's psyche—including that of the children's judges'-. They are reluctant to intervene in such cases. Gérard recounts:

> As soon as we had the opportunity we went before the Final Court of Appeal, thinking that it could establish the principle. At the end, the Final Court of Appeal confirmed the principle that had been chosen, in another case, by the Appeal Court. But today in practice, the fact that judges are entitled to make these decisions is not in the culture, in people's unconscious, including judges'. So, in spite of jurisprudence from the Final Court of Appeal it remains complicated (Interview, December 2013).

Organizations advocating on behalf of unaccompanied minors in waiting zones have to constantly reiterate that the children's judge has indeed jurisdiction.

3 The Waiting Zone: the Heir of the International Zone

Beyond court judgments, it appears that stakeholders are still unsure as to whether CDG airport's waiting zone is (fully) part of French territory. Actors working in and on CDG's waiting zone have confessed their ignorance regarding the status of waiting zones. Some of them carry the deeply ingrained idea that individuals detained at the legal border find themselves somehow physically outside of the country, in an excised space, justifying a less favorable treatment. Generally, the waiting zones' status remains a vexed issue that triggers negative emotional responses on the part of most interview participants, who belong to different professions. After a few interviews, I realized that the question "Is the waiting zone French territory?" was emotionally charged, and found it was better to ask it when nearing completion of the interview, after

procedures pertaining to his or her detention (law n°2002–305, 2002, article 17). Cf. chapter 4 for an extended discussion of the role of *ad hoc* administrators.

rapport had been established and in order not to jeopardize the rest of the interview.

For example, I asked Jacques, an inspector of places of deprivation of liberty, the following question: "Are you on French territory when you visit CDG's waiting zone"? Jacques first answered: "This is a good question. When I visit I am not on French territory, but you need to ask the question to a lawyer". When I insisted that I valued his perspective, Jacques became wary: "I may say something stupid, I do not know and I do not care. Why do you ask me this question?" After I quoted the *Amuur v. France* ruling, Jacques was openly annoyed:

> I am not able to answer you because I do not know and I can say that I am not interested. It does not matter to me whether or not I am in the international zone when I visit, I do not know and I do not care: not only does the law authorize me, it *instructs* me to go there. What is the status of this zone? I do not know and I do not care.
>
> Interview with JACQUES, August 2013

Jacques' answer is interesting on two accounts: to him, there is no doubt that the international zone is not France, as he equals being located in the international zone with being outside of France. Secondly, it illustrates that one can write detailed reports on the enjoyment of human rights in the waiting zone without having a clear idea of its status.

Why is the status of waiting zones so unclear? Why do some consider waiting zones excised space? I would like to offer two hypotheses. First, years after the *Amuur v. France* ruling, those working in and on CDG's waiting zone still held the view that the geographical area of the international zone (i.e. the zone between the runway and first border checkpoints) was somehow located outside of France. Second, the different stakeholders confuse the international zone and the waiting zone, and therefore envision the waiting zone as excised space. This confusion probably originates in the definition of the waiting zone itself. Initially, when the Law on the Waiting Zone was first passed in July 1992, it read that the waiting zone "runs between the points of embarkation and disembarkation to the border checkpoints", therefore covering the area of the "international zone". The law also specified that the waiting zone could include nearby hotel-like accommodations. The geographical space of the waiting zone therefore mapped onto that of the international zone and onto what the government construed as its extension, i.e. hotels close by. Why, then, would not the waiting zone inherit from the issues attached to international zones? As previously explained, the perimeter of the waiting zone is now larger than that of the international zone, as it also encompasses any place where the person goes for administrative or medical reasons. One can also be located in the international zone without being assigned the waiting zone regime (cf. chapter 6). Interviews with relevant actors indicate that the issues associated with Paris' airports' international zones in the 1980s and early 1990s have been passed onto waiting zones.

In response to the question: "Is the waiting zone French territory?" Jeanne, a civil servant in the Ministry of the Interior's department tasked with reviewing asylum seekers' requests to enter France, forcefully replied: "I think you know the answer? It is an international zone". I explained I was interested in her opinion as rulings from Appeal Courts and the Final Court of Appeal reiterated that the waiting zone was *de facto* French territory. Jeanne disagreed: "Not at all, it is not (*de facto* French territory). For us (at the Ministry of the Interior) it is not; if we start to say it is, it would mean that they have entered France. It is really an international zone, a bubble" (Interview, November 19, 2013). Dominique, a high-ranking border police manager at CDG, explains that individuals turned away at terminals are brought to the detention center through the runways so that they do not enter the country (Interview, September 2013). This way, Dominique argues, when the person is brought to the detention center, he or she remains in the international zone. Dominique therefore believes that airport compounds are not French territory, and that using the regular roads connecting terminals to the detention center would be tantamount to entering the country.

Interestingly, some stakeholders have declared that the waiting zone was non-French territory for both non-citizens and those working there. Conversations with two former Red Cross employees who had accumulated significant experience in CDG's waiting zone proved illuminating. The Red Cross has been offering humanitarian support to detainees in CDG's waiting zone since 2003, after signing a first convention with the Ministry of the Interior on October 6, 2003. Red Cross employees, called "mediators" (*médiateurs*) spend an important amount of time in ZAPI 3, in direct contact with both authorities and detainees (cf. chapter 7). Laura, a former mediator, explains that the waiting zone is located in the international zone. According to her, neither non-citizens nor Red Cross employees are on French territory when situated in ZAPI 3 (Interview, 2013). Paul, also a former mediator in CDG's waiting zone, tells a revealing anecdote transpiring around the time when the smoke-free policy was first implemented in public spaces (i.e. February 2007).[4] Before the policy was

4 Cf Decree n°2006-1386 of November 15, 2006. Available at: http://www.legifrance.gouv.fr/affichTexte.do?cidTexte=JORFTEXT000000818309&categorieLien=id Acessed April 18, 2019.

enforced, it was possible to smoke in one of the detention center's TV rooms. From February 2007 Red Cross employees were instructed to inform smokers that cigarette consumption was no longer permitted within the perimeter of the waiting zone. However, some border policemen resisted, claiming the policy could not apply in, what they argued, was not French territory: "We are not in France, so why enforce the law?" (Interview, August 2013).

The terms "international zone" and "waiting zone" are used interchangeably by legal practitioners themselves. For example, Clémence and Frédéric, who both represent non-citizens in court proceedings, use the word "international zone" to mean "waiting zone" (interviews, respectively December 2013 and October 2013). While observing court hearings at Bobigny, I also noted that a liberty and custody judge used the term "international zone" to refer to the waiting zone (field notes, November 2013). The choice of this term is not innocent. As Bauder (2013, 2) contends, "language matters in public discourse and everyday exchange: terminology can imply causality, generate emotional responses and transmit symbolic meanings". He concurs with Barnett and Duvall (2005) who, in their analysis of productive power, note that discourse produces subjects with associated rights and responsibilities. Such classification has material consequences for people on the ground. For example, assignment to the categories of "civilian" or "combatant" translates into differential protection under international humanitarian law (Barnett and Duvall 2005). The adjective "international" both reflects the various stakeholders' perspective on the waiting zone and plays a role in the constitution of extra-territorial subjects: it triggers the idea that non-citizens do not share the same space as citizens. This logic legitimates granting them differentiated and watered-down rights compared to the rights granted to those who are similarly categorized (as illegal migrants, asylum seekers and unaccompanied minors) but who, like citizens, are located on French territory. As Palmer and Matthews (2006, 26) put it, "While creating migration borders and boundaries, the government is also shaping moral borders and boundaries of the public's imagination".

In summary, the initial extra-territorial fiction still very much informs stakeholders' understanding of the waiting zone. The government's initial attempt to establish the international zone as an excised geographical space for some populations had far-reaching consequences that are still felt today. The geographical dimension of exclusion has endured as the issues attached to international zones were passed onto waiting zones. In the following chapter, I will demonstrate that the Law on the Waiting Zone established another layer of exclusion by creating a "legal space of lesser rights" through the "legal entry doctrine" (Basaran 2011, 49 and 65).

CHAPTER 4

The French Law on the Waiting Zone: the Reinvention of Exclusion through Extra-Territoriality

As previously demonstrated, in the collective imagination of waiting zone practitioners, this space is not French territory (at least) for non-citizen populations. Non-citizens have been excluded from rights on this basis. This chapter will argue that the Law on the Waiting Zone has reinvented exclusion through another form of extra-territoriality, premised on the non-citizen's legal status at the border. Although physically in France, rejected non-citizens and asylum seekers at the border are not present from a legal standpoint, for they have not yet been legally admitted to the country. My findings concur with the observations of the Commissioner for Human Rights of the Council of Europe. During his visit to France in 2005 he remarked that border police at CDG airport still considered waiting zones as not belonging to French territory, and that a separate set of laws applied to people in waiting zones:

> The first thing that struck me when I visited the Arenc and Roissy waiting zones was their status, as the authorities seemed to take the view that they were not part of French territory. Yet, in so far as I could make out, these zones are physically located in France and not floating somewhere in outer space. Furthermore, there are a number of laws which relate specifically to such zones and establish separate rules for them and so French law should apply to them. Yet, according to the officials I talked to, this was not so—a circumstance which gives these zones an uncertain legal status which should be remedied as soon as possible so as to dispel the legal ambiguity with which they are surrounded.
>
> GIL-ROBLES 2006, §187.

The French government brushed aside the Commissioner's remarks, highlighting the creation of a new "accommodation center" at CDG in 2001 and the resulting improvement in material conditions. Before the opening of a detention center specifically designed to house them, non-admitted citizens and asylum seekers arriving at Charles de Gaulle were detained in nearby hotels in rooms specifically earmarked for this purpose, with sealed windows and cleanliness

 | DOI:10.1163/9789004383500_006

issues.[1] The government also pointed out that French law applied to the waiting zone, which was a "clear legal concept". It did not acknowledge that the Law on the Waiting Zone had established a discriminatory and less protective framework (Gil-Robles 2006, appendix §187–203). Finally, the government also insisted on the rights granted to those placed in waiting zones, which included: the right to be assisted by an interpreter and by a doctor; the right to communicate with a legal counsel or any person of one's choosing; the right to be notified of one's rights in a language that one understands, and a maximum length of detention of 20 days following judicial review after four days of confinement. The Law on the Waiting Zone excludes particularly vulnerable groups from the protection they are entitled to under international law. This exclusionary legal regime may be implemented outside of a border crossing since 2011. Part of the waiting zone legislation travelled to the North African country of Morocco.

1 The Law on the Waiting Zone: an Exclusionary Framework Forced Upon the Most Vulnerable

When the Law on the Waiting Zone came into force in July 1992, the *overt* mechanisms of exclusion shifted in the sense that the law itself (and not the absence thereof) created a less protective regime than that applicable to the same groups regarded as being on French territory. Exclusion, in other words, was reinvented: instead of individuals being placed outside of the law, the law *itself organized* exclusion. The waiting zone's exclusionary legal framework builds on the premise that groups at the border find themselves from a legal standpoint at the threshold of, but not yet having entered French sovereign territory. Volpp (2012, 1–2), writing about the law of immigration, remarks: "Whether formal legal doctrine recognizes a human body as inside or outside a nation's territory is deeply consequential". She notes that physical entry can have various meanings:

> Immigration doctrine does not treat everyone inside (or outside) the same way. "Being here" can mean many different things, depending upon

1 For a description of the conditions of detention in hotel rooms located nearby CDG airport (and construed as an extension of the international zone), see Olivier Clochard's thesis, entitled "*Le jeu des frontières dans l'accès au statut de réfugié, une géographie des politiques européennes d'asile et d'immigration*" [Border games in the access to refugee status, a geography of European asylum and immigration policies] 2007, p. 202.

> the initial conditions of a person's presence inside. The same empirical fact—the physical presence of a human body—can be alternatively understood as an entitlement, if the person is a citizen; as a matter of hospitality, if the person is a legal permanent resident, a lawful temporary visitor, or a refugee; as a trespass, if the person is an undocumented immigrant; or as a nullity, if the person is a "parolee", meaning that the person is physically here but is not recognized as having effected an entry. Thus, we can say that physical presence inside the territory is polysemic, in that it does not have the same meaning for everyone.
>
> VOLPP 2012, 1–2

Her observations shed light on the specific "legal space" (Basaran 2011, 50) applicable to those confined under the waiting zone regime. The concept of legal space makes it possible for individuals sharing the same geographical space to have entirely different sets of rights stemming from their different legal statuses. It contradicts Bosniak's (2007) notion of "ethical territoriality", according to which individuals should be granted the same rights by virtue of being located on the same geographical territory of a national State.

France is not the only country where authorities have resorted to the concept of legal space to accord a less favorable treatment to incoming non-citizens. In the United States, the 1996 modification of the US Immigration and Nationality Act (INA) established the distinction between physical entry into the country and lawful admission at a recognized port of entry. The implications are far-reaching for those considered unlawful: "In this way, entry into the territory—the material act of crossing the geographical border and physically being present within the jurisdiction of the United States, does not equate with gaining immigration-related procedural protections that would apply to those who have been admitted" (Shachar 2007, 4).[2]

---

2 Governments use law as a technique to suit their political needs (Basaran 2011). As such, law may be used to keep people who are physically located on a state's territory away from it, but may also serve the opposite purpose: admit people located outside of a state's territory to it. Weber (2006) observes that new immigration rules came into force in the UK in April 2000, changing the moment at which entry to UK territory is officially granted. Under the new rules, entry is officially granted when a consular official issues a visa overseas. This means that "British borders can be conceptualized as fragmented and fully portable, their location defined, not by sites of enforcement action by States officials but in terms of the current whereabouts of certain intending visitors" (Weber 2006, 36). In other words, non-UK citizens receiving a visa outside of the UK are granted entry to the UK while located on other countries' territories.

In the 1980s, exclusion was triggered by geography and legal absence: it started from the moment the non-citizen set foot in the geographical location of airports' international zones. Today, under the Law on the Waiting Zone, exclusion is triggered by a combination of geography and law: an individual is placed under the waiting zone framework when arriving in the border's physical location and when he or she is either refused entry or registered as an asylum seeker. As will be explained in chapter 6, some non-citizens in the international zone never reach the waiting zone status. Presence in territorial border zones alone is insufficient to trigger the waiting zone regime.

As Basaran (2011, 55) points out, "the Law on the Waiting Zone equips detainees with some fundamental rights, but these rights are limited when compared to the ordinary French legal regime". Two groups particularly suffer from the eroded rights attached to the waiting zone status: asylum seekers and minors (especially when unaccompanied). The waiting zone regime has dramatic consequences for these groups that are granted specific rights under international human rights and refugee law on account of their particular vulnerability.

1.1 *Asylum Seekers*

Asylum claimants in waiting zones cannot yet apply for refugee status: they first have to be legally admitted to the country. In waiting zones, their requests are not examined on their merits. Instead, they are evaluated against the "manifestly unfounded" yardstick over an interview carried out by refugee agency's employees.[3] Since the law of July 29, 2015, asylum seekers may also be admitted to the territory when reckoned particularly vulnerable by the refugee agency. CESEDA's (2016) legal provision L.221-1 reads:

> When OFPRA … considers that the asylum seeker, due to his or her minority or to having been the victim of torture, rape or another serious form of sexual, psychological or physical violence, needs particular procedural guarantees that are not compatible with holding in the waiting zone, this holding is put to an end.

The law considers claimants falling within one or more of the aforementioned categories to be in need of "particular procedural guarantees" that are incompatible with confinement in the waiting zone. How was this legal provision translated into practice? The OFPRA reports for the years 2015 and 2017 do not state how many claimants were admitted to the territory on account of being

3 For a discussion of the origins of the term "manifestly unfounded" cf. chapter 1.

found vulnerable (OFPRA May 13, 2016 and April 3, 2018). According to the refugee agency's 2017 report, five claimants were released from the waiting zone in 2016 due to their vulnerability. Since the agency examined the requests of 902 asylum seekers at the border (including that of 38 unaccompanied minors), only 0.55 percent of claimants were released from the waiting zone under article L. 221-1. When they do not fall within the purview of article L.221-1, unaccompanied minors seeking asylum still have to pass the "manifestly unfounded test", save but for a very few cases (cf. section C).

As Basaran (2011) notes, the refugee agency (OFPRA) only has an advisory function, the final decision being left to the Ministry of the Interior's department of asylum at the border. In practice, the Ministry of the Interior follows OFPRA's advisory opinion almost 100 percent of the time. Jeanne, from the Ministry of the Interior's department of asylum at the border, has been reviewing OFPRA's opinions since 2008. Since she entered the department, the Ministry of the Interior rejected OFPRA's recommendations only twice (Interview, November 2013). However, from a symbolic standpoint this organization is not neutral: it signals that the Ministry of the Interior (whose agenda regarding border control necessarily differs from that of the refugee agency) ultimately decides who can enter France to claim asylum, not the refugee agency. Pascal Brice, director of OFPRA from 2012 to 2018, regretted this organization and advocated for a decoupling of OFPRA from the Ministry of the Interior (Faye and Pascual, April 13, 2019). As the Ministry of the Interior decides whether an asylum claimant should be admitted to France, the issue of asylum is subjected to border control. Jeanne insists that I should not use the expression "asylum procedure at the border". She explains:

> These are not asylum claims at the border, but entry procedures to the territory on asylum grounds. It is very important to have this definition, as those allowed to enter the territory will not have obtained any status. They will still have to apply. It is really a request to enter the territory, a police procedure (Interview, November 2013).

The waiting zone therefore functions as a buffer zone where claimants are filtered, with only a fraction of them gaining access to the actual refugee determination procedures. Those who successfully pass the waiting zone barrier are granted leave to enter the country and have eight days to file a claim. Once they reach the regular refugee determination system the Ministry of the Interior has no more say regarding their claim: the decision to grant protection lies entirely with OFPRA in the first instance and with the National Court of Asylum if necessary (CNDA-an administrative court adjudicating appeals against

OFPRA's decisions). In 2011 OFPRA reviewed the cases of 1857 claimants (for all waiting zones) and recommended that 188 be admitted to the territory: about 10 percent of claimants got access to regular refugee determination procedures (OFPRA April 11, 2012). In 2012, this number was 13.1 percent (OFPRA April 24, 2013). In this regard, waiting zones should be understood as part of many areas flourishing at the margins of the European territory that treat human beings like waste to be sorted, stored and thrown away (Caloz-Tschopp 2004). Actors working in and on the waiting zone use the disposal vocabulary; for example, a lawyer representing the border police at the Bobigny Court of First Instance did not hesitate to state: "France is not the garbage can of Europe" (field notes, October 2013).

At the time of research, the law did not define what constituted a "manifestly unfounded" asylum claim. In 2000, the Administrative Court of Paris had noted that a claim was manifestly unfounded when "it is manifestly unlikely to fit the criteria set out by the Geneva Convention of July 28 1951 or other criteria justifying the granting of asylum" (Anafé January 2013, 53). In theory, OFPRA agents were not supposed to go into details: they simply needed to rule out individuals seeking to enter France for work, study or tourism. However, scholars and activists had documented just the opposite (Clochard et al 2003; Anafé December 2012). Basaran (2011, 56–57) writes: "In reality, however, it has become a predetermination procedure for refugee status, including an analysis of refugee narratives, their truth content and their provenance from safe countries". OFPRA agents at Charles de Gaulle admitted that they considered asylum claims to be manifestly unfounded in the following situations: when they had nothing to do with asylum but also when they relied upon deliberate fraud (for example a Lebanese national claiming to be Syrian), when the discourse was not "personalized" (i.e. when the claimant fails to demonstrate that he or she is the specific target of persecution-escaping war is not enough) or when the discourse was incoherent or too vague (Interview, November 2013).[4]

Since July 29, 2015, the law defines what constitutes a "manifestly unfounded claim". Provision L. 213-8-1 reads:

> A claim that is manifestly unfounded is a claim that, considering declarations made by the foreign national and documents produced when applicable, is manifestly devoid of relevance regarding conditions under

4 OFPRA agents reviewing asylum claims at the border are based at Charles de Gaulle's detention center. They review the cases of asylum seekers placed under the waiting zone regime at Charles de Gaulle but also anywhere in the country (in which case the interview takes place over the phone) Cf. chapters 7 and 9.

which asylum is granted or manifestly devoid of credibility regarding risk of persecutions or severe violations.

The law now explicitly states that asylum seekers' stories are assessed on their content at the border. It means that a claimant is expected to provide a detailed and coherent account of the persecutions that he or she experienced. Yet, someone who just travelled a great distance after surviving difficult events is not in the best conditions to narrate his or her story. While claimants on the right side of the legal border can rely on several NGOs to help prepare their application, those in waiting zones do not have access to the same services, due to the scarce NGO presence and urgency that prevails in these spaces (cf. chapter 7). The Law on the Waiting Zone established a dual set of rights: one for the border and one for what is considered the territory. One has to exit the waiting zone regime to access the normal rights regime (Basaran 2011). I will now compare the legal regime and policies applicable to minors (accompanied and unaccompanied) in waiting zones with those applicable in the rest of the territory.

1.2 *Accompanied Children in the Waiting Zones*

Numerous bodies monitoring human rights treaties have stressed that States' obligations apply to all individuals subject to their jurisdiction. For example, the Committee on the Rights of the Child issued the following comment (Report, A/61/41, 2006, 19–20):

> State obligations under the Convention apply to each child within the State's territory and to all children subject to its jurisdiction (art. 2). These State obligations cannot be arbitrarily and unilaterally curtailed either by excluding zones or areas from a State's territory or by defining particular zones or areas as not, or only partly, under the jurisdiction of the State. Moreover, State obligations under the Convention apply within the borders of a State, including with respect to those children who come under the State's jurisdiction while attempting to enter the country's territory.

Yet, children and their families awaiting deportation from France for lack of residence permit receive more favorable treatment than those awaiting return in waiting zones.[5] The former are not routinely detained pending their

5 The French legal term "*éloignement*" is translated as "deportation". It refers to the removal of individuals residing illegally on French territory. It is used by opposition to the French word "*retour*" or "*réacheminement*" ("return" in English), which refers to the removal of

deportation, contrary to the latter. The government's willingness to respect its international and regional obligations under international law does not extend to individuals placed under the waiting zone regime. An internal policy brief from the Ministry of the Interior dated July 2, 2012 (*Circulaire Valls*) instructs local administrative authorities to ensure that families with minors to be deported from France be circumscribed at home (or in a hotel if they do not have a "stable and decent home") rather than be placed in administrative detention facilities.[6] Families under compulsory residence orders have to abide by certain rules, such as checking in from time to time at the closest police station or handing in their identity and travel documents.[7] Overall, this represents a significant shift in deportation policies. The brief specifically refers to the Convention on the Rights of the Child, and to its core "best interest of the child" principle as the rationale for such a change. Under the brief, the detention of families with children under 18 years of age is still possible but constitutes the exception rather than the rule. Detention will happen if the family fails to comply with the deportation order, i.e. in case of the escape of one or several family members, in case of refusal to board the plane or in case of failure to comply with the rules pertaining to compulsory residence.

The brief also speaks of the necessity to comply with the European Court of Human Rights *Popov v. France* judgment (January 19, 2012). In *Popov*, the Court had ruled that France had breached article 3 prohibiting inhuman or degrading treatment by detaining children (aged five months and three years) with their parents in an administrative detention center in unsuitable conditions. The applicants, a Kazakh family, had been arrested at their house in August 2007 after the rejection of both their asylum claim and application for residence permits. They had been sent to CDG airport to be deported to Kazakhstan. However, with their flight having been cancelled, they had been transferred to a detention center in Rouen-Oissel. The Court found that the detention conditions of the children at the facility had amounted to a violation of article 3: although the center was authorized to accommodate families, it did not offer play areas or activities for children. The beds with sharp metal corners and automatic bedroom doors were dangerous for children.

The Court referred to the Council of Europe Commissioner for Human Rights' findings (Gil-Robles 2006): detaining children in administrative

---

individuals who, although physically present on French territory, have not crossed yet French legal borders.

6 The French term "*circulaire*" is translated as "internal policy brief".

7 The French term "*assignation à residence*" is translated as "compulsory residence order" (which is the term used in the European Court of Human Rights' *Popov v. France* judgment).

facilities with their parents was contrary to the Convention on the Rights of the Child. During his visit to France from September 5 to September 21, the Commissioner had noted:

> Very few centres are equipped to receive them. In any event, no children should be detained on the grounds that their parents do not have the necessary papers to remain in France, in places marked by overcrowding, dilapidation, promiscuity and very strong tensions.
>
> GIL-ROBLES 2006, § 257

The Commissioner had remarked that, although French law provided an alternative to detention in the form of compulsory residence orders, those were rarely used. The Court observed: "[…] it is important to bear in mind that the child's extreme vulnerability is the decisive factor and *takes precedence over considerations relating to the status of illegal immigrant*" (§91, emphasis added). It found that the Rouen-Oissel facility was not adapted to the children's age. Moreover, although the length of detention (15 days) was not excessive *per se*, the children could have perceived it as never-ending. In *Popov,* the Court did not go as far as condemning the detention of children in and of itself. Only the length of their detention and conditions of confinement were found illegal. As for the parents, the Court found that their detention conditions did not amount to a violation of article 3 since they had not been separated from their children.

Whether the brief from the Ministry of the Interior has been really implemented is another issue, but, *on principle,* this constitutes a significant shift in deportation policies.[8] It originates in a promise François Hollande, then Socialist candidate running for president, had made to NGOs to abolish the detention of families with children under 18 in administrative facilities (*Le Monde*, March 14, 2012) pending their deportation from French territory.[9]

The commitment to end the detention of children for immigration regulation purposes does not extend to minors placed under the waiting zone regime. Anafé employees, Lise and Anne, raised the issue with the Ministry of the Interior, denouncing blatant discrimination between the waiting zone and the rest of the territory. To justify this difference of treatment, the Ministry of

---

8 Children are still detained pending their deportation from France (Cf. *Journal du droit des jeunes*, 2015).

9 The letter is available on the website of the NGO *France Terre d'Asile* : http://www.france-terre-asile.org/toute-lactualite-choisie/item/6963-francois-hollande-repond-aux-propositions-de-france-terre-dasile Accessed April 26, 2015.

the Interior argued the waiting zone was not French territory, but the external border (Interview, December 2013).

1.3 *Unaccompanied Children in the Waiting Zones*

Not only are children traveling with their families locked up in waiting zones, but so too are all unaccompanied minors who are not asylum claimants. Who falls under the status of "unaccompanied minor"? According to Anafé (January 2013), the border police consider a person under the age of 18 to be unaccompanied when he or she arrives alone at the border. Interviews with different actors (judges, not-for profit employees and volunteers, lawyers, border police agents), visits at CDG and observations of court hearings revealed that minors placed under the waiting zone legal regime have many different motivations for travelling alone to France, where they may or may not have family. It is hard to categorize unaccompanied minors according to their travel motives, as individuals do not fit into clear-cut categories and may be unwilling to disclose their reasons for travelling (French Red Cross, January 2013, 10). Categorization also masks individuality and personal stories.

Keeping this *caveat* in mind, I will quickly explore their rationales for travelling. Some travel with the intent of doing some sightseeing but others encounter themselves in far more precarious situations: some flee war, persecution, abuse or poverty in their country of origin, some are brought in by parents who reside legally in France but could not secure the authorization to bring their child via legal routes. Some do not enlist the assistance of other parties to travel while others are smuggled. Finally, some are trafficked for various exploitative purposes (such as prostitution or forced labor). Asylum claimants at the border do not represent the majority of unaccompanied minors. For example, in 2011, only 8.53 percent of unaccompanied minors at French borders claimed asylum (i.e. in all waiting zones). This number was 19.74 percent for 2012, 12.96 percent for 2013 and 17.34 percent for 2014.[10] As only those seeking asylum may be admitted into the territory (under very limited circumstances), in practice the law provides for the detention of most unaccompanied minors. As for asylum claimants, the law allows for their detention in many cases.

---

10 I obtained these statistics by computing numbers provided by OFPRA and by Anafé. In 2011, 516 unaccompanied minors were detained in all waiting zones. Of this number, 44 applied for leave to enter French territory on asylum grounds (Anafé 2015, 28 and OFPRA 2012, 34). In 2012, they were 416 unaccompanied minors and 81 claimants (Anafé 2015, 28 and OFPRA 2013, 67). In 2013 and 2014, the numbers were respectively 49 claimants out of 378 minors (Anafé 2015, 28 and OFPRA 2014, 69) and 45 claimants out of 259 minors (Anafé 2015, 28 and OFPRA 2015, 65).

The Law of July 29, 2015 is written in such a way so as to suggest that the detention of unaccompanied minors seeking asylum in the waiting zone is the exception, not the rule (CESEDA, 2016, L. 221-1). While the law implies that most unaccompanied minors will be admitted into the territory when they are in search of international protection, it makes it possible for them to remain in the waiting zone under many circumstances. Unaccompanied children may still have to pass the "manifestly unfounded" test if they come from countries that are classified as safe by the refugee agency or if they presented false identity or travel documents.[11] Their claims may also be assessed against the "manifestly unfounded" yardstick if they provided false information or hid information or documents regarding their identity, citizenship or conditions of entry to the country or introduced several asylum claims under different identities (CESEDA, 2016, articles L.723-2). As Anafé pointed out, these grounds for detention are very broad and not well defined, giving significant margin of manoeuvre to OFPRA (Anafé October 2014). Gérard, *ad hoc* administrator at the Red Cross, explains that many unaccompanied children, in an attempt to protect themselves, do not tell their true stories to *ad hoc* administrators, let alone to refugee agency employees: "It is true that a certain number of minors who are brought in by networks come with stereotyped stories, not only with respect to asylum, but about the entirety of their lives, and so they have a sort of armour that even we do not manage to break" (Interview, December 2013).[12] The law provides for the detention of these unaccompanied minors shielding themselves behind fabricated stories at the border.

At the time of research, 500 unaccompanied children were held in French waiting zones each year, contrary to unaccompanied minors who were already depicted as present on French territory (HRW April 8, 2014). Systematic detention at the border is *per se* contrary to international law: it runs against the "best interest principle" (article 3) and article 37 of the Convention on the Rights of the Child (CRC), which clearly states that detention should only take place as a last resort and for the shortest amount of time possible. Section D of the *Statement of Good Practice* established by the Separated Children in Europe

11 As of October 2015, the refugee agency had decided that 16 countries were safe (OFPRA, October 17, 2015).

12 It is interesting to note that most actors (i.e. judges, border police officers, Red Cross employees, lawyers, inspectors of places of deprivation of liberty, etc) do not make the distinction between immigrant smuggling and trafficking rings. Instead they use the word *réseau*, which can literally be translated in English as "network". In the debate surrounding the detention of unaccompanied minors in waiting zones, the term "network" mostly refers to trafficking enterprises.

Programme[13] also specifically reads: "They [separated children] must never be detained for reasons of immigration policy and practice" (2009). The Council of Europe Commissioner for Human Rights also specifies: "Members States should avoid holding unaccompanied minors, pregnant women, mothers with young children, the elderly and people with disabilities in waiting areas" (Gil-Robles 2001, point 6).

At CDG, a separated detention area specifically dedicated to unaccompanied minors opened in July 2011 (hereafter the "minor area"). Yet, conditions of detention sometimes run against international standards as the said area has limited capacity: it can only host six children at a time (it has three bedrooms, each containing two beds). Whenever the number of unaccompanied minors exceeds this capacity, those who are above 13 will be held in the regular part of the center, with unknown adults, in violation of article 37 (c) of the CRC Convention. Children above 13 will also be detained with adults should the number of unaccompanied male and female be uneven (as boys and girls do not share bedrooms).

At CDG, unaccompanied children placed under the waiting zone regime have always been confined in different places according to their age. Before the dedicated space of detention opened, those under 13 were placed in nearby hotels under the supervision of Air France hostesses. Those older than 13 were detained at CDG's detention center (ZAPI 3) with adults. Laura, a former Red Cross mediator, narrates that when the minor area first opened, the border police considered that only those under 13 could be hosted there. The Red Cross obtained that, space allowing, children older than 13 also benefit from the structure (Interview, August 2013).

Authorities seem to believe that separating minors from adults does not constitute a legal requirement but a favor. Dominique, a high-ranking border police agent, insists that having a specific area for minors is not an obligation. Furthermore, he does not seem to pay much attention to the fact that, under French law and the Children Rights Convention, every person under 18 is a child. Dominique minimizes the issue of detention with adults: "If the person is 17—almost an adult- it is less of a problem to detain him or her with adults,

13 The Separated Children in Europe Programme is a consortium of international intergovernmental and nongovernmental organizations. The 2009 Statement of Good Practice reads: "The Separated Children in Europe Programme (SCEP) started as a joint initiative of some members of the International Save the Children Alliance and the United Nations High Commissioner for Refugees (UNHCR). It has grown and evolved and is now comprised of many non-governmental partners throughout Europe who continue to work closely with UNHCR".

especially considering that in some countries they attained majority a long time ago". The law can be dispensed with. According to him, the minor area "in principle preferably hosts minors who are under 13" (Interview, October 2013).

Beyond the issues of illegal deprivation of liberty and detention conditions, confinement in the waiting zone can have dramatic consequences for minors who arrive at the border on their own. Contrary to minors already portrayed as in France, those in waiting zones may potentially be returned at any time (save during the assessment of their application to enter France to seek asylum). They are indeed subject to the exact same legal regime as adults, except for the appointment of a legal guardian called "*ad hoc* administrator" (*administrateur ad hoc*). Under French law, minors lack the capacity to represent themselves in legal proceedings. Therefore, the *ad hoc* administrator's mission consists in assisting the child during his or her detention in the waiting zone and in ensuring the child's legal representation in all administrative and judiciary proceedings pertaining to his or her detention (law n°2002–305, 2002, article 17).[14] *Ad hoc* administrators are based in two organizations: the Red Cross and *Famille Assistance* (Family Aid), a not-for-profit organization. Gérard has been serving as *ad hoc* administrator since the mission was created in 2005. According to Gérard, the return of minors held at Charles de Gaulle's waiting zone constitutes one of the three challenges that his organization has to tackle (Interview, December 2013). Gérard recalls that when he first started, almost three quarters of unaccompanied minors were sent back. Over the years, this number has diminished dramatically, but return still takes place occasionally. In January 2014, Sylvie, mediator in the minor zone, told us that four or five forced returns had taken place over the last two months.[15] Gérard explains:

> When returns do take place it is always in bad conditions. The bad conditions are that the return goes against what we identified to be the best interest of the child. It takes place in situations where the youth declares not having parents, no family, or to be running from a mistreating family in countries that lack proper childcare structure, in situations where the minor is particularly fragile (Interview, December 2013).

Unaccompanied minors seeking asylum face all of the hurdles and diminished guarantees that come with the waiting zone framework. They, just like adults,

14 In French, article 17 reads: "*L'administrateur ad hoc assiste le mineur durant son maintien en zone d'attente et assure sa représentation dans toutes les procédures administratives et juridictionnelles relatives à ce maintien*".

15 "Us" refers to Human Rights Watch researchers and me.

must prove that their claims are not "manifestly unfounded", only to be granted the subsequent right to apply for asylum once on the right side of the legal border. An interview with refugee agency agents at CDG confirmed that the asylum screening process at the border is absolutely the same for unaccompanied children (interview, November 2013). Gérard explains that those applying for leave to enter France to seek asylum very rarely obtain such permission (Interview, December 2013). In 2012, OFPRA considered that 18.5 percent of unaccompanied minors' requests were not manifestly unfounded (OFPRA, April 24, 2013).

Martini (2004, 31) summarizes well the situation of unaccompanied minors placed under the waiting zone regime:

> Deprived of liberty, sometimes the victim of violence, returned forcefully to countries where his or her security is not guaranteed, the minor held in the waiting zone is an undesirable being to be jettisoned. Once past the imaginary line that separates the waiting zone from the rest of French territory, he or she theoretically, is worthy of all attentions (translation from French is mine).

As soon as they cross the legal border, laws and policies prohibit both their detention and return and allow them to access ordinary asylum procedures.

In summary, the notion of extra-territoriality has been reinvented to curtail rights and diminish international obligations. Extra-territoriality is both the origin and the purpose of the waiting zone regime: individuals are assigned the waiting zone status for not yet being in France and precisely to control their access to and keep them outside of the country. In the eyes of the State, detainees in waiting zones are first and foremost individuals whose mobility needs to be controlled, not rights-holders. Revealingly, the function of *ad hoc* administrator was created to safeguard the state's interests, not to protect unaccompanied children. As Martini (2004) explains, the number of unaccompanied minors started to soar in 1998. Liberty and custody judges therefore had to adjudicate numerous unaccompanied minors' cases (according to the law detainees have to be presented to a judge after four days spent in waiting zones-the judge can either prolong the detention or set the detainee free). Many judges decided to release the children from waiting zones on the basis that they lacked legal capacity to represent themselves and were not assigned a legal representative. Once liberated, children disappeared, becoming illegal migrants. In order to fight this jurisprudence, the government first attempted to grant legal capacity to minors above 16. This would have infringed upon established principles of minor protection, and the government was confronted by hostile reactions.

It finally decided that all unaccompanied minors in waiting zones should be assigned a legal representative. The function of *ad hoc* administrator in waiting zones was therefore invented to prevent judges from releasing children arriving alone at the border (Martini 2004).

2 *Ad Hoc* Waiting Zones or the Possibility for Border Authorities to Create Zones of Lesser Rights Anywhere

The Law on the Waiting Zone allows immigration authorities to tailor the border to their needs: as explained in chapter 2, *ad hoc* waiting zones can be created when a group of 10 non-citizens or more arrives in France outside of a border crossing (for example on a beach). The non-citizens can all be found in one place or in different locations separated from one another by 10 kilometers maximum. In this case the waiting zone will run between places where authorities have found the non-citizens and the closest border crossing: the perimeter of this area and the corresponding legal space of lesser rights may be quite large.

How do legal practitioners view *ad hoc* waiting zones, i.e. the possibility for border authorities to create zones of diminished protection anywhere, including on beaches? A former lawyer, Louise, who was serving as senator at the time of the interview, described these waiting zones as "an aberration". However, she did not find the practical consequences of such waiting zones to be dire: lawyers defending non-citizens know how to plead. She trusted them to draw the liberty and custody judge's attention to any weakness or breach to the law (Interview, January 2014). As for Ségolène, a liberty and custody judge at Bobigny, she trusted judges to release individuals should there be any legal irregularity. She explained that she never had to deal with *ad hoc* waiting zones. She did not find the concept particularly shocking, as those placed under the waiting zone regime will always be presented to a judge after four days: they will be able to enforce their rights. She said: "It is true that it is a little disturbing that an administrative authority has the powers to extend the waiting zone to any place where individuals are found but the procedure still has to be respected" (Interview, November 2013). When I observed that it would be challenging for detainees to exercise their rights due to lack of access to legal aid, she agreed but, once again, highlighted immigration authorities' responsibilities: they would have to respect detainees' rights. Should these rights be violated, the judge would release individuals from the waiting zone (Interview, November 2013). I asked Léa, also a liberty and custody judge at Bobigny, whether the creation of *ad hoc* waiting zones itself should be controlled by the judiciary. She sighed: "What type of control would we have? What would we be good for? There is a tendency to put the judiciary at the heart of everything. For me it is an immigration policy issue, an administrative problem, not a judiciary one ... Immigration is a policy" (Interview, November 2013).

France is not the only country where immigration authorities tailor the border to their needs. As Shachar observes, the US and other countries of immigration have managed to create "malleable borders", i.e. borders that can be flexibly redrawn to keep at bay "unwanted untruders". She writes (2007, 2):

> This redesign (of the border) has been accomplished by enforcing the sovereign prerogative to deny or permit access in a whole new way: by redrawing (indeed, redefining) the once fixed and static territorial border, transforming it into something more malleable and movable, which can be placed and replaced—by the words of law—in whatever location that best suits the goal of restricting access.

With the Law on the Waiting Zone, French authorities can create legal spaces of lesser rights pretty much anywhere they see fit. This legal manoeuvre involves shifting "the border of immigration regulation" (Shachar, 2007) to circumvent granting some rights. It is remarkable that the waiting zone legal regime of exclusion through extra-territoriality was exported to the North-African State of Morocco.

3 The Exportation of the Law on the Waiting Zone to Morocco

The present definition of the waiting zone under French law is quite similar to that under Moroccan law. In Morocco, the law n°02-03 (article 38) defines the waiting zone as a zone that "runs between points of boarding or disembarkation and border checkpoints. It can include, at the port or airport, one or several accommodations granting to the non-citizens in question the necessary services". This was the definition of the waiting zone in force in France in January 2003, when the Moroccan government crafted law n°02-03 regulating the entry and stay of non-citizens in Morocco (Belguendouz 2003). As the Moroccan provisions pertaining to the waiting zone seem to have been copy-pasted from the provisions that were in effect in France in January 2003, the Moroccan definition of the waiting zone does not include any place within Moroccan territory where a non-citizen goes for administrative or medical reasons. In France, the expansion of the definition of the waiting zone to the space under the feet of the foreign national occurred in November 2003. Nor does the Moroccan definition include *ad hoc* waiting zones, which French law created in 2011. The waiting zone provisions and their application are not devoid of issues in Morocco.

In France, an administrative authority called the *préfet* (prefect) delineated the perimeter of waiting zones through regulations. By contrast, in Morocco the physical space of the waiting zone has not been defined. This lack of precision could be an issue. The French organization Anafé and the Moroccan NGO Gadem[16] conducted two fact-finding missions at the international airport Mohammed V of Casablanca in 2012 and 2015. According to the testimonies gathered by the NGOs, people placed under the waiting zone regime at Moroccan airports have been held in the transit zone and in police cells at airport terminals. Anafé and Gadem heard of other places of confinement (such as a hotel or the warehouse of the airline company *Royal Air Maroc* situated next to the runway) but could not collect sufficient information to confirm that these places were indeed in use at the time of the mission in 2015.

The French waiting zone provisions adopted by Morocco often remain dead letters, especially those protecting the legal rights of non-citizens. The NGO inquiry revealed significant gaps between the law and its implementation on the ground. For example, under the law, Moroccan border police must hand over a written document to the non-citizen upon placement under the waiting zone regime. This document needs to be dated and motivated: i.e. the decision needs to rest on legal and factual reasons. However, in practice, non-citizens never receive such documents. Without a material proof of their date of entry into the waiting zone regime, they are vulnerable to abuse. According to the law n°02-03, individuals may spend up to 20 days in the waiting zone. Yet, non-citizens have been routinely kept for more than one month in the airport's waiting zone without appearing before a judge.

The law n°02-03 provides for judicial oversight: non-citizens remaining in the waiting zone after four days (and then after 12 days) must be presented to a judge at the Court of First Instance. Authorities need to explain to the judge why the foreign national could not be returned and how an extension of his or her stay in the waiting zone will enable return. Should the authorities' request to extend confinement in the waiting zone for another 8 days be unsubstantiated, the judge has the power to reject it, *de facto* admitting the non-citizen to Moroccan territory. It is also the judge's role to set the non-citizen free if authorities violated his or her rights. These legal provisions remain theoretical: in

16 Gadem stands for "*Groupe antiraciste d'accompagnement et de défense des étrangers et migrants*".

practice, non-citizens undergoing more than four days of confinement in the waiting zone never see a judge.

The French waiting zone provisions were grafted onto a country that does not have the same legal structure as France. The law n°02-03 states that an asylum claimant may be kept in the waiting zone during the time necessary for authorities to assess whether or not his or her request is "manifestly unfounded". Yet, there are no procedures in place to assess requests to enter Moroccan territory on asylum grounds. In Morocco, the UNHCR is in charge of examining asylum claims but the UN agency cannot intervene in waiting zones. The possibility of entering Morocco at the airport to seek asylum therefore only exists on paper. In practice, asylum claimants at Moroccan airport borders have experienced *refoulement* to countries where their safety and liberty have been at risk. According to the data collected by the NGOs, the border police do not register asylum claims. Asylum seekers do not receive any administrative document informing them of their placement under the waiting zone regime. They are not presented to judges and may spend lengthy periods of time in the transit zone; for instance, one claimant from Sri Lanka was held for 39 days before being returned to Colombo (Anafé and Gadem 2017, 36).

Finally, those confined in Moroccan waiting zone have faced material hardships and undignified conditions of detention. Access to food appears to have varied greatly from one place of confinement to the next. People rejected at the airport border have been fed cheese sandwiches by airline companies or the border police twice a day or have had to purchase their meals themselves. They have not had access to a shower and have slept on seats or directly on the floor without being provided with a blanket. They have not had the possibility of accessing their luggages and have had to spend the entirety of their confinement in the waiting zone with the same set of clothes.

To conclude, the Law on the Waiting Zone did not mark a striking shift from the previous era, when asylum claimants and rejected travelers were excluded from legal guarantees based on their presence in international zones construed as extra-territorial. The Law on the Waiting Zone itself forces an exclusionary legal framework on the most vulnerable, premised on their location outside "law's admission gate" (Shachar 2007). The term "extra-territoriality" appropriately captures the situation today. Since 2011, this legal regime of diminished protection can be enforced outside of border crossings, through *ad hoc* waiting zones. Finally, the French exclusionary legal regime travelled to the country of Morocco. The next chapter will gesture towards the similarities between the French and the Australian mechanisms of exclusion.

CHAPTER 5

Excision or the Australian Government's Attempt to Subvert the Refugee Convention through Extra-Territoriality

> Why would boat people jump a queue to nowhere? And if they do make it here, they won't be here anyway. They can't come to Not-Australia. It may just work. Only history will judge how we stopped people coming to Not-Australia and the manner in which they didn't come (Feik November 2, 2012).

∴

This quotation from Nick Feik, editor of the Australian magazine *The Monthly*, illustrates the absurdity of Australia's policy of non-citizen exclusion through extra-territoriality: Australian governments have made Australian territory legally disappear for non-citizens arriving by boat to the country shores. Like France, Australia resorted to extra-territoriality to exclude certain categories of incoming non-citizens from legal and refugee rights. The Australian legal technique of exclusion bears some striking resemblance with the French one. In both countries, the law *itself* organized exclusion and conferred powers to the executive branch to extend the perimeter of exclusion as it saw fit. Both exclusionary policies started in a similar way: the executive managed to turn an illegal practice into a law. In both countries the space of exclusion expanded significantly over the years, following so-called immigration crises. Like their French counterparts, Australian governing parties from the right and the left of the political spectrum have supported exclusion through extra-territoriality.

In Australia, such exclusion began in 2001. It materialized in the form of excision of sovereign territory from the "migration zone". Non-citizens landing on a part of Australian territory that had been excised from the migration zone have been deemed outside of the country from a legal standpoint. They have entered a legal regime characterized by watered-down protection under domestic and international law. Precluded from applying for asylum in Australia, they have been taken to detention facilities far away from Australia's mainland.

 | DOI:10.1163/9789004383500_007

They have experienced isolation and deprivation of liberty on the remote Australian possession of Christmas Island and even on the foreign countries' territory of Nauru and Papua New Guinea (on the country's malarial and remote island of Manus). There, their refugee status determination claims have not been processed according to regular Australian procedures. Having been denied access to the system in place for asylum claimants considered in Australia, they have not benefited from the guarantees attached to the country's refugee determination system. What is the migration zone? A definition of the latter should be provided before going any further. Otherwise it is impossible to grasp the significance of the excision policy.

Under Australian law, any non-citizen must be granted a visa to enter and reside in the national space legally. Non-citizens located outside of the country (such as refugees in camps) need to apply for an "offshore visa" while non-citizens already on Australian soil qualify for an "onshore visa". In the last configuration, foreign nationals need to be considered within Australia's migration zone to launch a visa request. Asylum seekers are not exempt from this requirement. Before the excision policy was put into place, Australia fulfilled its legal obligations towards asylum seekers arriving by boat by granting them "onshore protection visas" when found in need of international protection (Gibney 2004). *The Migration Act 1958* (December 2018)[1] states that the migration zone:

> (…) means the area consisting of the States, the Territories, Australian resource installations and Australian sea installations and, to avoid doubt, includes:
> a) land that is part of a State or Territory at mean low water; and
> b) sea within the limits of both a State or a Territory and a port; and
> c) piers, or similar structures, any part of which is connected to such land or to ground under such sea; but does not include sea within the limits of a State or Territory but not in a port.

While the meaning of the migration zone has remained the same on paper prior to and after 2001, its content -i.e. the actual space of the migration zone- has diminished significantly from 2001 onwards until *de facto* disappearing completely in 2013. The Australian exclusion device has indeed consisted in withdrawing foreign nationals' access to the migration zone by cutting out some parts of Australian territory from the migration zone. Non-Australian citizens

1 https://www.legislation.gov.au/Details/C2019C00004.

landing on Australian territory without obtaining permission prior to their departure have arrived in a piece of land or in territorial waters construed as "Not-Australia" as far as they were concerned. Importantly, under international law, asylum seekers do have the right to arrive in another country in search of international protection. They do *not* need to gather administrative permission prior to travelling. In fact, States that are parties to the 1951 Refugee Convention and to its 1967 Protocol have the obligation not to *refoule* an asylum claimant arriving at their borders to a country where his or her life or liberty may be at risk under conventional grounds. This is why the Australian government's use of the terms "illegal" or "unlawful" to qualify asylum seekers arriving by boat does not hold under international law. I will therefore be careful not to use these terms in regard to spontaneous boat arrivals. The term "unplanned arrival" will be preferred to that of "unauthorised arrival".

Excision has been a defining feature of Australia's migration law and policy since 2001. As Vogl (2015, 115) notes, the policy of excision survived multiple federal elections and government changes: while the consequences of entering an excised zone have changed over the years, the lands in question were never "unexcised". Non-citizens stepping in a piece of land that had been carved out from the migration zone have been entering a legal space marked by legal uncertainty and arbitrariness. Oftentimes excision has translated into human and refugee rights violations. Scholars have written extensively on Australia's migration and refugee policy, which is incredibly complex (Gibney 2004; Johnson 2014; Kneebone 2006, 2010; Mcadam 2013; McNevin 2007, 2014; Mountz 2013; Taylor 2005, 2006; Weber 2007). My goal is not to offer a comprehensive view of the latter. Indeed, I will rather strive to compare and contrast the Australian and French extra-territorial mechanisms of exclusion. The excision's legal and ideational foundation will be detailed. While exclusion has taken different forms over the years, what has not changed is its rationale: extra-territoriality. It will be my argument that excision constitutes the pinnacle of Australia's long-standing policy of preference for resettlement over asylum. The regular refugee protection regime was contaminated by the excision one, and the space of exclusion was extended following perceived immigration crises. This chapter begins by presenting the events and the political context preceding the introduction of the excision policy.

1 The *Tampa* Incident

In general, most non-citizens seeking international protection in Australia arrive by plane legally; they travel on a visa and subsequently claim asylum

(Kneebone 2010, 353). In 2009 (28), the Australian Department of Immigration and Citizenship explained: "the overwhelming majority of around 4,000 people who seek Australia's protection each year arrive lawfully by commercial aircraft". The greatest number of asylum seekers comes from the People's Republic of China (Kneebone 2010, 353). However, in the late 1990s, boat arrivals outnumbered plane arrivals, as a result of the conflicts in Afghanistan and the Middle East (Kneebone 2010, 353). According to official statistics, 921 asylum seekers arrived by boat to Australia in 1998–1999. This number increased to 4,175 the following year (Stratton 2009).

People fleeing this part of the world have attempted to reach Australia by boat from Indonesia after transiting through countries such as Turkey, Syria, Saudi Arabia, Malaysia or South Africa (Kneebone 2010). As Dupont (2002, 13) explained, at the beginning of the 21st century, about 80 percent of all asylum seekers from Iraq and Afghanistan transited through Malaysia on their way to Australia, for Malaysia allowed Muslims to access its territory without a visa. Generally, it has been estimated that 85 percent non-citizens arriving by boat to Australia without a visa had departed from Indonesia (Taylor 2007 quoted in Kneebone 2010, 354). In other words, most people seeking to reach Australia without prior authorization have undertaken the final leg of the journey from Indonesia.

The year 1997 marked a turning point for boat arrivals to Australia. Up to that date, boats aimed to reach mainland Australia. In 1997, boats started targeting Australia's northern islands of Ashmore Reef and Christmas Island (Department of Immigration and Multicultural and Indigenous Affairs -DIMIA 2004). Both territories are located closer to Indonesia than to Australian mainland: Christmas Island is situated 380 kilometers South of Java but 2,600 kilometers northwest of Perth (Kneebone 2010, 354). The 433 passengers of the *Palapa 1*, a small Indonesian fishing boat *en route* to Australia, found themselves in distress in the Indian Ocean in late August 2001 (Vogl 2015, 123). The *Palapa 1* was the 137th boat to have left Indonesia for Australia within a twelve-month period (Kneebone 2010, 357). Yet, *Palapa 1* boat people were not treated according to the procedures that had applied to passengers of the previous 136 boats. The latter had been allowed to land in Australian territory, from which they had been flown to the mainland for their claims to be processed (Kneebone 2010, 357).

Prior to the *Palapa 1*, Australian Department of Immigration (DIMIA) Compliance Officers interviewed asylum seekers on the mainland. Those deemed not to be in need of international protection were sent to "separation detention" on the mainland where they were neither informed of their rights nor provided with lawyers. Those "screened in" were also sent to detention centers on mainland Australia. By contrast, they benefited from free legal advice on their claims (HRW 2002, 13). They were processed according to onshore procedures in Australia (Schloenhardt 2002, 311). Those found to be refugees received an onshore protection visa (called "subclass 785") for three years, as Australia had stopped granting permanent shelter to claimants entering the country without authorization in 1999. Visa recipients were able to work but could not apply for family reunion or long-term stay (Gibney 2004, 188). Nor could they re-enter the country (Schloenhardt 2002, 309). Limitations to protection had been introduced in 1999: asylum seekers who had previously resided but had failed to seek protection in other countries were excluded from visa subclass 785 (Schloenhardt 2002, 308). While this onshore temporary protection visa was certainly no panacea, it enabled access to Australian refugee status determination procedures and temporary protection in the country.

By contrast, passengers of the *Palapa 1* were denied access to the Australian protection system. On August 26, 2001, the captain of the Norwegian freighter the *MV Tampa,* responding to a call from the Australian Coast Watch, rescued the passengers of the overcrowded, sinking ship. Seeking international protection, the 433 rescuees pressured the captain into heading for the Australian territory of Christmas Island (Mathew 2002, 661). The boat people, for the most part, were originally from Afghanistan (HRW 2002, 4).

However, the Australian authorities forbade the ship from entering Australian territorial waters and from disembarking the rescuees. Many of the asylum seekers required urgent medical attention: four were unconscious, three were pregnant and one had a broken leg. On August 27, Arne Rinnan, Captain of the *MV Tampa*, requested food and medical assistance (Mathew 2002, 661). On August 29, the ship entered Australian territorial waters. In response, the Australian military boarded and took control of the ship. The rescuees, mostly of Afghan origin, were transferred onto the Australian troopship *Manoora* to be taken away from Australian waters (Vogl 2015, 123).

The Afghani asylum seekers were soon joined on the *Manoora* (on September 7, 2001) by over 200 asylum seekers of Iraqi origins for the most part, whose vessel, the *Aceng*, had also been intercepted by the Australian military (HRW 2002, 13). Meanwhile, the Australian authorities, adamant that the claimants would not set foot on Australian territory, attempted to conclude deals with governments of other countries. The States of East Timor, Fiji, Kiribati, Palau, Tuvalu and even France (in relation to French Polynesia) were approached but deals did not go through (Mares August 2011 and Phillips 2012). New Zealand agreed to process 150 asylum seekers and to welcome those deemed to be refugees amongst them (Mathew 2002, 662). As for Nauru, it accepted to process asylum seekers on its soil in exchange of an additional aid package of $26.5 million (Australian Senate October 23, 2002, 6). However, the country refused to settle recognized refugees

(Mathew 2002, 662). The Australian government announced agreements with both countries on September 1, 2001. *MV Tampa* and *Aceng* asylum seekers were taken to Papua New Guinea on the Australian military ship. From there, they were then flown to New Zealand and Nauru (Mathew 2002, 662).

2 Political Context of the Tampa Incident

Why did the Australian government suddenly change its policy regarding spontaneous boat arrivals from Indonesia? The people of the *Palapa 1* (and then of the *Aceng*) had the misfortune of being caught in electoral manoeuvres. At the time of the *Tampa*, the Liberal and National coalition government (hereafter "the Coalition") led by Prime Minister John Howard was not doing well in the polls. The Coalition's key reform, the *Workplace Relations Act* (1996), had deprived workers of many rights (Stratton 2009). By showing a strong stance against unplanned boat arrivals, Liberal Prime Minister Howard hoped to boost his chances of reelection. At the previous Federal election, in 1996, the Coalition had already played on the Autralian people's "anxieties and fears around race and immigration" (Stratton 2009). The strategy had been successful.

Furthermore, the success of Pauline Hanson's political party "One Nation" in the 1998 Federal elections for the Senate had, again, demonstrated the receptivity of a part of the Australian electorate to anti-immigration rhetoric. Pauline Hanson, a "former Queensland shopkeeper", had raised the spectre of an Asian invasion and had insisted that "I should have the right to have a say in who comes into my country" (Hanson quoted in Jupp 2002, 130). Her party obtained 1 million votes in 1998, thereby becoming the most successful party after the Liberals and the Australian Labor Party (Jupp 2002, 135). Howard's electoral strategy was ultimately successful, as the Coalition retained power in the November 2001 Federal election. His promise that "We will decide who comes to this country and the circumstances in which they come" (this speech was reprinted in thousands of election pamphlets, cf. *The Guardian*, November 10, 2001) resonated well with the majority of voters. Now that the rationale for *Palapa 1* boat people's differential treatment has been explained, it is time to turn to the legislative measures that were taken in the wake of the *Tampa* incident.

3 The 2001 Acts or the Legal Foundation of the Excision Policy

Surfing on the crisis that it had itself contributed to create, the Australian government introduced amendments to the *Migration Act 1958* after the *Tampa* incident (Edwards 2003, 193). These amendments were presented to Parliament shortly after the 9/11 terrorist attacks in the United States. On September 26, 2001, the Australian Parliament passed three main pieces of legislation. The Act excising certain parts of Australian territory from the migration zone was one of them.

The *Border Protection (Validation and Enforcement Powers) Act of 2001*[2] validated the actions taken in relation to the Tampa. The Act declared that any action taken "by the Commonwealth, or by a Commonwealth officer, or any other person acting on behalf of the Commonwealth in relation to the *MV Tampa* or the *Aceng*" was lawful (*Border Protection Act 2001*, §5). This legislative piece shielded all the aforementioned actors from civil or criminal court proceedings (§7). It also enacted new border protection powers, including the power of interdiction (Mathew 2002, 663). The Act vested Australian officers with the power to detain a ship or aircraft as well as the individuals onboard. It also conferred officers the capacity to bring the latter to the migration zone, or to "a place outside of Australia" (*Border Protection Act 2001*, 3A). The Act legalized the interception of boats in and outside of Australian waters as well as their pushback.

As for the *Migration Amendment (Excision from Migration Zone) Act of 2001* (hereafter the "*Excision Act*"), it carved out certain territories from the Australian migration zone. These territories became labelled "offshore excised places". When the Act was first passed in 2001, the following territories were removed from the migration zone: Christmas Island, Ashmore and Cartier Islands and Cocos (Keeling) Islands. Importantly, the Act allowed the government to expand excision to other areas of Australian territory in the future, through gazetted regulations (Vogl 2015, 125). This piece of legislation created a new category of unplanned non-citizens arriving in an "offshore excised place": the "offshore entry person". The Act precluded offshore entry persons from applying for *any* visa. Onshore visas -including protection visa subclass 785 aforementioned- became inaccessible to foreign nationals setting foot in excised areas. This legislative piece, therefore, placed the national refugee determination system out of offshore entry persons' reach. The *Excision Act* made Australian sovereign territory -and the rights attached to it- vanish for a certain category of non-citizens. Ironically, in spite of asylum seekers being labelled "offshore entry person" upon arriving on excised territory, the Act also

2 The full name of the Act is "An Act to validate the actions of the Commonwealth and others in relation to the *MV Tampa* and other vessels, and to provide increased powers to protect Australia's borders, and for related purposes".

prevented them from applying for offshore humanitarian visas (such as the "refugee", the "global special humanitarian" and the "woman-at-risk visas").

While the French government presented the waiting zone legislation as progressive and human rights abiding (cf. chapter 2), the Australian government made the goal of excision in Australia very clear: prevent asylum claimants arriving by boat from filing a claim, and therefore, from benefiting from the country's refugee determination procedures. The explanatory memorandum that accompanied the *Migration Amendment (Excision from Migration Zone) Bill 2001*, stated that the purpose of excision and border protection was to "prevent [unplanned arrivals] from making a valid visa application simply on the basis of entering Australia at such place or installation". The *Excision Act* has to be examined in conjunction with the third amendment to the *Migration Act*.

The *Migration Amendment (Excision from Migration Zone) (Consequential Provisions) Act of 2001* (hereafter "*Consequential Provisions Act*"), enabled Australian officials to either detain offshore entry persons in Australia or send them to a "declared country", i.e. a country that had been declared by the government to meet certain minimum safeguards (Mathew 2002, 667). The Act allowed for the diversion of asylum seekers to third countries for processing, leaving it to the Immigration minister to determine what country to declare fit for asylum seekers intake:

> (3) The Minister may:
> (a) declare in writing that a specified country
> (i) provides access, for persons seeking asylum, to effective procedures for assessing their need for protection; and
> (ii) provides protection for persons seeking asylum, pending determination of their refugee status; and
> (iii) provides protection to persons who are given refugee status, pending their voluntary repatriation to their country of origin or resettlement in another country; and;
> (iv) meets relevant human rights standards in providing that protection; and
> (b) in writing, revoke a declaration made under paragraph (a).

Nauru and Papua New Guinea became declared countries as Australia negotiated agreements with both in September and October 2001 (DIMIA, 2005).

The *Consequential Provisions Act* created two new categories of visas for non-citizens sent to declared countries: visa subclass 447 (secondary movement offshore entry (temporary)) and visa subclass 451 (secondary movement relocation (temporary)). Both visas were in force until 2008 (Australian government February 2019). They were meant for asylum seekers receiving refugee status (or another protection status)[3] in declared countries. They were designed to allow persons deemed in need of international protection to *resettle* to Australia on a temporary basis. Visa subclass 447 was created for persons who had landed on excised territory ("offshore entry persons") before being sent to declared countries. By contrast, visa subclass 451 was crafted for people intercepted on boats *en route* to Australia, i.e. who had not reached Australian soil at an excised place before being taken to declared countries. Some of the recognised refugees from the *MV Tampa* and the *Aceng* were granted visa subclass 451 (others were resettled to other countries than Australia). Both visas carried stringent conditions: they only allowed their holders one entry into the country and precluded family reunion (Mathew 2002).

The Act made it more advantageous to receive a 451 visa than a 447 visa: holders of visa 451 could reside in Australia for up to five years compared to three years for visa 447 holders. Furthermore, visa 451 allowed refugees to gain access to a permanent protection visa after four years and a half if protection was still needed (Australian Senate October 23, 2002, 326). What was the rationale for treating offshore entry persons in a less advantageous manner than persons intercepted at sea? The Act seems to have sought to penalize non-citizens for having the audacity of landing in the country without prior administrative authorization; the closer foreign nationals got to Australian territory, the steeper the price they had to pay. People who never made contact with Australian land were, somehow, rewarded for staying away. The Australian Senate (October 23, 2002, 326-327) reflected on this differential treatment:

> The Committee finds it curious that those who have been intercepted or rescued at sea have a more favourable outcome, including the possibility of permanent protection, than those who reach Australian soil simply by virtue of not having completed the journey.

Importantly, the Act also precluded offshore entry persons from initiating legal proceedings relating to their status or to the lawfulness of their detention. As for passengers of boats intercepted in the high seas or in Australian territorial waters (i.e. non-offshore entry persons), they have been either taken to detention facilities in excised places, third countries or escorted back to the high seas or Indonesian waters. Excision has been part of a larger package of

---

3 Both visas were created for people who, at the time of application, are subject to persecution or substantial discrimination amounting to gross violation of human rights in their home country or for women registered as "persons of concern" to the UNHCR.

measures aimed at keeping unwanted non-citizens at bay. This legislative arsenal was dubbed the "Pacific Solution".

4 Why Australia's Excision Policy Was Built on Wrong Assumptions

The two new categories of visas aforementioned were created for claimants who sought asylum in Australia by engaging in "secondary movements", i.e. who attempted to or who actually reached Australian shores after transiting through one or more countries in which they could have sought asylum. The Australian Human Rights Commission (2005) explained that visas 447 and 451 "were introduced to encourage asylum seekers to remain in their country of first asylum, that is, the first safe country where they could have sought and obtained protection". The Australian government expressed its position towards individuals who arrive in Australia to seek asylum:

> [S]econdary flows disadvantage those in refugee camps who are often in greater relative need of assistance. Australia recognizes the greater need of such refugees by granting them permanent residence and providing a range of settlement services to enable them to fully participate in the Australian community.
>
> DIMIA 2001 quoted in HRW 2002, 89

In the eyes of Australian leaders, people in need of international protection had to seek permanent shelter in the first safe country in which they arrived (called "country of first asylum") after fleeing theirs. Those who did not (by engaging in "secondary movements") were not considered as deserving as those who stayed in refugee camps. In this statement, the Australian government implied that asylum seekers reaching the country shores were engaging in actions that were detrimental to refugees remaining in their region of origin. The UNHCR uses the term "resettlement" to describe "the transfer of refugees from the country in which they have sought refuge to another State that has agreed to admit them" (UNHCR June 2006). The Australian government depicted refugees waiting in refugee camps to be resettled as more worthy of protection than those who embarked on the journey to Australia.

According to HRW (2002, 11), secondary movement "is any migration by a refugee beyond the country in which she was first a refugee, irrespective of her legal status, and irrespective of the time she spent in the first country to which she fled". As the NGO explains, governments have equated "secondary movement" with "irregular movement". The UNHCR (Executive Committee

1989) uses the latter term to describe refugees who left a country of first asylum where they had obtained "effective protection" for economic reasons. Australia's excision policy was premised on two assertions: countries of first asylum are safe and, in the event that they were not, refugees could be resettled in an orderly manner.

Human Rights Watch, which interviewed fifty refugees located in Australia, Indonesia, New Zealand and Nauru in 2002, debunked these two affirmations central to the Australian government's reasoning. The NGO demonstrated that countries of first asylum (like Iran or Pakistan) offered neither effective nor lasting protection to refugees. As the NGO pointed out, protection against *refoulement* may not remain constant over time: while a person arriving in a bordering country may be protected on the first day of his or her arrival, protection may cease to exist as time passes. Life was particularly difficult for refugees in Iran and Pakistan, for they feared harassment by the police and other authorities and were not granted legal status (HRW 2002, 12). Refugees often had difficulties subsisting in the two-aformentioned countries where they faced obstacles finding work and accommodation, as well as accessing health care and education (HRW 2002, 3). As the NGO puts it (HRW 2002, 11), "The onward movement of refugees from the country where they first fled often reflects a serious failure of international protection there". As for the road to resettlement, it appeared to be paved with numerous obstacles: refugees may have difficulties applying for resettlement, UNHCR processing is not satisfactory and the number of places available for resettlement every year is insignificant compared to the number of people in need of protection worldwide.

To be resettled, refugees must first be able to apply for resettlement. Indeed, accessing UNHCR offices in the country of first asylum may be a challenging task in itself. For instance, several Iraqis interviewed by HRW recounted that the Iraqi security forces were watching the UNHCR offices in Jordan (HRW 2002, 26). An Afghan refugee told the human rights organisation that he was arrested by the Iranian police for lacking a residence permit on its way to UNHCR offices in Tehran. He was then placed in detention and finally forcibly returned to Afghanistan. Furthermore, those who managed to file a request with the UNHCR were not guaranteed a successful outcome. As Taylor (2006) remarks, UNHCR processing cannot meet the accepted standards of procedural fairness. Asylum seekers receiving a negative decision at the primary stage may have their cases reviewed by a second decision-maker. However, the review process is not independent, for the reviewer is also a UNHCR agent. Taylor (2006, 298) notes: "such a second chance is only of use if the reviewer is independent of the primary decision-maker and is free also of the biases and/or pressures that may have affected the primary decision-maker". This procedural flaw is inherent to the nature of the UNHCR, the latter being an organization rather than a State (Taylor 2006, 298). Statistics persistently indicate that only a handful of world refugees can be resettled annually. In 2001, when the excision policy was initiated, less than 0.3 percent of the world's refugees were resettled: 33,100 refugees were resettled under the UNHCR umbrella out of the 12 millions of refugees of concern to the UN agency worldwide (UNHCR, July 2002 and Del Mundo, June 18, 2002). Australia had 12,000 places available for resettlement, which, therefore, represented 0.1 percent of the refugees placed under the protection of the UNHCR (Edwards 2003, 202). Australia's excision policy, which aimed to punish and deter claimants from reaching the country soil, was built on wrong assumptions. Offshore entry persons simply could *not* have come to Australia through resettlement.

The Australian public reacted favorably to discourses delegitimizing boat arrivals. What was Australian people's reaction to the reality of excision? Their perspective on excised territory will now be presented.

5 "Why Are We Getting Kicked Out from the Rest of Australia?" Australian Citizens' Perspective on Excision

In France, individuals working in and on the waiting zone have displayed much confusion about the status of both the international and the waiting zone. Many have held the belief that, somehow, these areas were not French territory as far as non-citizens (and sometimes also French citizens) were concerned. The status of these zones has been a vexed issue. When asked: "Is the waiting zone French territory?" several stakeholders have expressed annoyance. Some have also attempted to take advantage of the ambiguous status of the waiting zone to escape French laws. The Australian people's perception of excised space was altogether different. The term "excision" did not resonate well with Australian citizens; it was very much a cause for anxiety, especially for the inhabitants of the large chunks of Australian territory that were carved out from the migration zone. Parliamentarians and indigenous communities alike expressed strong concerns about excision, which the government had to address. A senator asked the government for clarifications: "Does any other migration legislation apply within the zone? I note that we are only removing the application of selected legislation, but what other legislation does apply within the zone?" (Australian Senate August 22, 2002). In its response, the government tried to reassure the Senate, explicitly stating that excised places remained part and parcel of Australia: "An excised offshore place remains part of the migration zone and is part of the territory of Australia. All laws, including the provisions of the Migration Act, apply in an excised offshore place" (Australian Senate August 22, 2002).

The government, in the explanatory memorandum to the *Further Border Protection Measures Bill 2002,* explained that excised islands were still completely part of Australia (Coombs 2005):

> Australian citizens and other persons with lawful authority under the Migration Act to be in Australia will continue to be able to move about freely in these areas and make any applications permitted by the Migration Act. These amendments do not affect Australia's sovereignty over these islands. The islands remain integral parts of Australia.
>
> AUSTRALIAN SENATE October 21, 2002, 70

The Senate Legal Committee (Australian Senate October 21, 2002, 74) remarked that the government did not engage in adequate consultation with the communities whose land was affected by excision. Thus, Mr James Marrawal, speaking on behalf of the Warrawi community, expressed the community's concern; inhabitants of the islands of the Northern Territory feared that excision meant they were no longer part of Australia:

> In the back of our minds we were thinking: why are we getting kicked out from the rest of Australia? After all, we are enrolled for federal Commonwealth elections.
>
> AUSTRALIAN SENATE October 21, 2002, 74

The Minister for Immigration and Multicultural and Indigenous Affairs, Philip Ruddock, phoned and wrote to some community leaders and State Government Premiers on June 6, 2002, to inform them that regulations to excise additional islands were about to be made. DIMIA (August 6, 2002) explained that:

> In these letters the Minister advised these people of the extension of the definition of 'excised offshore place'. The Minister pointed out that this would not affect Australian citizens and other persons with lawful authority under the *Migration Act 1958* (the Migration Act) to be in Australia, and would only affect those who did not have this authority. Mr Ruddock reiterated that it had no other effect on the status of the islands concerned.

This extract shows that the Australian people were quite disoriented by the policy of excision of territory from the migration zone: it generated much insecurity at home, which the government had to soothe. It is now time to examine what excision meant for foreign nationals. What were the consequences of excision in terms of refugee and procedural rights?

6 Entering an Excised Space Equals Entering a Legal Space of Lesser Rights

The consequences of entering an excised space (or, as we shall see, a piece of Australia that was retroactively declared "excised offshore place") have varied significantly over the years. Between 2001 and 2008, excision was coupled with "exile": most asylum seekers landing in excised territory were taken to detention in third countries for processing (Foster and Pobjoy 2011). A total of 1,637 people were detained in the Nauru and Papua New Guinea facilities between 2001 and 2008, including 786 Afghans, 684 Iraqis and 88 Sri Lankans (Phillips 2012).

When Labor returned to power, offshore entry persons momentarily ceased to be taken to Nauru and Papua New Guinea. The Rudd government announced on February 8, 2008 that the centres on Manus and Nauru would no longer be used (Phillips 2017). Instead, offshore entry persons were placed in detention in excised Australian territory, on Christmas Islands, pending their refugee status determination. Rudd's Labor government stopped asylum seekers' transfers to third countries not because it was legally or morally wrong, but to save taxpayers' money (Phillips 2017). The time period between 2008 and 2012, which can be named "excision without exile", was short-lived: the excision and exile tandem was reunited in 2012 (Foster and Pobjoy 2011). The first asylum seekers arrived in Nauru on September 15, 2012 and in Papua New Guinea on November 21, 2012. Between 2012 and 2016, the number of people in offshore detention reached 2,450 (1,273 in PNG and 1,177 in Nauru in April 2014) (Karlsen 2016).

Gillard's Labor government opted for the reintroduction of the exile component on Nauru and Papua New Guinea following the recommendations of the Expert Panel on Asylum Seekers. The former had tasked the latter with producing a report on "how best to prevent asylum seekers risking their lives by travelling to Australia by boat" (Australian government 2012). The Panel insisted on the necessity to deter people smugglers from sending people to Australia by boat. For deterrence to work, the Panel recommended that offshore processing facilities in Nauru and Papua New Guinea be re-established and that boat arrivals *never* be resettled in Australia.

The Gillard's government had previously attempted to send claimants to Malaysia. The Prime Minister announced in May 2011 that bilateral negotiations were under way with Malaysia; the plan was to send 800 spontaneous boat arrivals to Malaysia for processing. In exchange, Australia would take 4,000 recognized refugees over four years. Gillard resorted to the "queue jumper" trope to explain her decision: "if someone seeks to come to Australia, then they are at risk of going to Malaysia and going to the back of the queue" (Sydney Morning Herald May 7, 2011). The message was clear: claimants entering Australia by boat would be sent to Malaysia where they would have to wait for their turn to be processed. The High Court of Australia struck down the "Malaysia Solution" in 2011, on the basis that Malaysia did not fulfill the criteria listed in the *Migration Act* to be a declared country (Roam 2018).

What has not changed over the years, however, is the excision policy's imprevisible character. For non-Australians, landing in excised space has constantly meant stepping into a legal space characterized by arbitrariness, legal uncertainty and diminished or inexistent legal protection. For offshore entry persons, the first uncertainty has revolved around the entry into the excision regime itself. The Australian government has indeed reserved itself the right to decide whether an offshore entry person could benefit from the regular onshore visa procedures. According to the *Excision Act* (section 46 A (2)), the Minister of Immigration may decide, "if (he) thinks that it is in the public interest to do so", to make the excision policy go away for an individual landing in an excised place. The latitude conferred to the Minister is consequential.

Secondly, asylum seekers landing in excised offshore place have had no guarantee of their claims being examined in so-called declared countries or in an excised place. In other terms, they have had no guarantee of having their claims examined at all. The aforementioned three amendments to the *Migration Act* have indeed to be read in conjunction. The *Consequential Provisions Act 2001* (198 A) states that an "offshore entry person *may* be taken to a declared country" (emphasis added): being brought to Nauru and Papua New Guinea is only an option. Under the *Border Protection Act 2001*, officers can also bring any person found on a detained ship or aircraft to a "place outside Australia". For example, 14 Turkish Kurds who landed on Melville Island were forcibly returned to Indonesian waters without having had the possibility of applying for protection in 2003 (Taylor 2005).

As for asylum claimants taken to "declared countries" (i.e. Nauru and Papua New Guinea) for processing between 2001 and 2008, they did not benefit from Australia's legislated refugee system (Taylor 2005). Instead, they were subjected to a changing and watered-down protection regime. The Australian government's goal was precisely to deny claimants access to the country's determination procedures. At a press conference on September 10, 2001, the Minister for Immigration and Multicultural and Indigenous Affairs, Mr Philip Ruddock, issued the following statement:

> What it means is there will be no basis upon which (people) will be able to land on Christmas Island and see it as a taxi rank to be brought automatically to Australia, engage our protection obligations, have the opportunity to have their claims considered first by the department, second by the refugee review tribunal and then enter into the judicial review process they are doing right now.
>
> AUSTRALIAN SENATE October 23, 2002, 316

Mr Ruddock refused that the claimants be processed according to onshore procedures.

When the first asylum seekers arrived to Nauru in 2001, the country was neither a Party to the 1951 Refugee Convention nor to its 1967 Protocol -it acceded to both international instruments on June 28, 2011 (UNHCR 2015). Having no refugee treaty obligations, Nauru had no refugee determination procedures in place. At the request of Nauru, the UNHCR processed the asylum seekers from the *Tampa* and the *Aceng*, i.e. the group that had been delivered to the country by the Australian troopship *Manoora*. While Australia paid for the expenses sustained by the international organization in Nauru, the UNHCR refused to process the claims of the asylum seekers coming from further boats, to protest Australia's policy (HRW 2002, 65).

Papua New Guinea also requested assistance from the UNHCR, but the latter declined. Papua New Guinea is a Party to the 1951 Convention but has entered significant reservations in respect to paid employment, housing, public education, freedom of movement, non-discrimination against refugees who enter "illegally", expulsion and naturalisation. In spite of being a Party to the Refugee Convention, Papua New Guinea did not have any refugee status determination procedures or framework to protect or settle refugees (HRW 2002, 63). This is why officials from the Australian Department of Immigration were sent to assess asylum seekers' claims on Nauru and Papua New Guinea (Australian Senate October 23, 2002, 316).

Although Australian immigration officials adopted UNHCR procedures and standards, evidence shows that claimants processed by Australian officials were disadvantaged compared to those assessed by UNHCR agents (Australian Senate 2002, 317). As of July 31, 2002, the UNHCR had recognized 84 percent of Iraqi asylum seekers in Nauru as refugees. By contrast, as of May 20, 2002, DIMIA had granted refugee status to, respectively, 53 percent and 76 percent of Iraqi asylum seekers in Nauru and Papua New Guinea (Taylor 2005, 61).

The status of Australian immigration officials carrying out refugee status determination in third countries was another issue. As Edwards (2003, 207) noted, Australian agents did not have to apply the Australian statute and case law that they would have been bound to apply on mainland Australia. Furthermore, appeals procedures for claimants in declared countries were unsatisfactory and much less protective than those applying to claimants subjected to Australia's onshore determination regime. At the time, those processed under Australia's onshore procedures were entitled to have their claims reviewed by the Refugee Review Tribunal (RRT) and/or the Administrative Appeals Tribunal, when unsuccessful in the first instance. They could also benefit from judicial review "on grounds of bad faith of jurisdictional error" (Taylor 2005, 58). By contrast, asylum seekers whose claims were rejected in third countries could only request a new assessment. DIMIA explained that the appeal was "essentially a fresh assessment" by a more senior departmental officer (HRW 2002, 71). As Taylor (2005, 60–61) pointed out, this procedure did not meet international procedural standards. The condition for appellate mechanisms to be fair is "that the review authority be an impartial tribunal independent of the initial decision-maker" (Taylor 2005, 61). Taylor (2005, 61) deplored the fact that the refugee determination regime was a purely administrative one. She remarked: "DIMIA officers have a decision-making discretion which is almost unbounded".

Furthermore, asylum claimants in the "declared countries" were left *without legal assistance,* as Australian lawyers, human rights and faith-based organizations could not access them. Visa applications from the association of legal professionals "Australian lawyers for Human Rights" were rejected by Nauru on two occasions. The lawyers had offered free advice to non-citizens detained on Nauru (HRW 2002, 72). Asylum claimants were therefore strongly disadvantaged compared to claimants onshore who were eligible for free legal advice under the Immigration Advice and Application Assistance Scheme (IAAAS) (HRW 2002, 73).

Last but not least, those granted refugee status in third countries had no guarantee of being accepted by Australia to rebuild their lives. Australian officials viewed the transfer of recognized refugees to Australian soil as an act of charity, akin to the act of resettling refugees from camps. A spokesperson for the Australian Immigration Minister stated that recognized refugees on Nauru and Papua New Guinea had "no greater claim on refugee resettlement than those waiting in camps in Africa and the Middle East in appalling conditions" (HRW 2002, 74). Australian officials clearly expressed the desire that refugees rebuilt their lives in countries other than Australia. DIMIA affirmed that Australia and the UNHCR strived to find a home for recognized refugees "as quickly as possible and consistent with the government's strategy of ensuring that a preferred migration outcome for people who are secondary movers essentially does not end up being Australia" (HRW 2002, 73).

In other words, Australian leaders behaved as if asylum seekers who arrived in Australian territorial waters or shores or who were taken to Australian warships had not triggered the country's protection obligations under the Refugee Convention. DIMIA officers did not consider the cases they dealt with on Nauru and Papua New Guinea as asylum applications. It is important to note that under international law, refugee resettlement is a voluntary scheme that cannot replace refugee status determination onshore.

The UNHCR (2012) insists: "Resettlement must be a complement to—and not a substitute for- the provision of protection where needed to persons who apply for asylum". The obligations stemming from the Refugee Convention are towards asylum seekers who arrive spontaneously to the country. In other words, people in need of international protection have the right to seek asylum but not to be resettled. The UNHCR (2012) explains: "resettlement is not a right, and there is no obligation on States to accept refugees for resettlement".

Hence, the UN refugee agency vigorously protested the Australian government's use of the term "resettlement" to describe the transfer of offshore entry persons to non-excised territory. Mr Michel Gabaudan, UNHCR's regional representative, observed:

> For those who are taken in from excised territory, we think the word "resettlement" is wrong and would create a precedent worldwide. That would not be proper, because resettlement is a discretionary authority of the country, while the granting of asylum is a convention ground.
>
> AUSTRALIAN SENATE October 21, 2002

Of the 1,637 non-citizens who were processed in Nauru and Manus between 2001 and 2008, 1,153 were found to be refugees (Australian Senate 2014, 4). 70 percent of the individuals transferred to declared countries were resettled to Australia or other countries such as New Zealand, Sweden, Canada and the USA. More precisely, 705 individuals (or 43 percent of the total number of non-citizens processed in Nauru and Manus) were resettled in Australia (Phillips 2012). It is my argument that Australian governments have used excision between 2001 and 2012 (since 2013, those receiving refugee status in declared countries can no longer rebuild their lives in Australia) as a device akin to a magic wand to turn the country's asylum obligations into resettlement generosity. Next section will put this argument in context.

7 Excision or the Pinnacle of Australia's Long-Standing Policy of Preference for Resettlement over Asylum

I argue that excision (and accompanying border control measures) should be considered as the ultimate manifestation of Australia's long-standing policy of preference for refugees and dislike for asylum seekers. Australian governments have used excision like a magic wand, to turn asylum into resettlement and thereby regain control over the country's borders. Indeed, Australia's humanitarian policy has not been so much about denying a safe haven as about standing up against unplanned, unauthorised arrivals. Historically, Australian government have consistently resettled recognised refugees and designed policies to discourage spontaneous asylum seekers. As Johnson (2014, 68) writes:

> (…) the underlying issue for the Australian State is not a distaste for refugee hosting or a dismissal of humanitarian objectives; rather, it is a firm position that asserts the ultimate power of the State to control and manage every aspect of migrant mobility and agency.

The excision policy should be considered as the continuity of Australian's humanitarian policy since the design of the Refugee Convention. Australia has been a humanitarian actor to reckon with on the world stage: the country's leaders actively contributed to drafting the Refugee Convention in the years 1950–1951 (HRW 2002, 91). Australia was one of the first countries to sign the treaty: it acceded to the Convention on January 22, 1954 and to the Optional Protocol on December 13, 1973. Over this time span, not a single asylum seeker claimed refugee status at the border: all refugees received authorization prior to travelling to the country. In other words, when Australia became a party to the Refugee Convention, asylum seeking at its borders was inexistent.

Australia accepted over 350,000 refugees and displaced persons between 1945 and 1975 (Price quoted in Gibney 2004, 177). During this period, there were no spontaneous arrivals. As Gibney (2004, 177) explains, "geographical isolation made the prospect of applications for asylum at the border nugatory, and virtually all the refugees accepted by officials entered pre-screened, as part of broader resettlement schemes that the government was free under international law to operate at its discretion".

Before 1975, refugees contributed to the Australian State's demographic, economic and foreign policy goals. Australian leaders had long felt isolated in the Asian region, "a lonely outpost of Western civilization in a profoundly alien sea. Too far from Britain for easy succour … perilously near the … storm centres of the world" (Harris 1938, 125 quoted in Gibney 2004, 170). Australians had felt particularly vulnerable during Word World Two, as Japanese forces had dropped bombs on Darwin and mini-submarines had invaded Sydney Harbour (Gibney 2004, 171). In the post-war period, Australian officials were therefore adamant that the country needed to increase the size of its citizenry to thwart an enemy invasion. New entrants made Australia stronger on the world stage. The country also needed a large workforce to build a strong manufacturing base and maximize economic growth (Gibney 2004, 172). Welcoming refugees from the Soviet Union was also a way for Australia to make a stance in the Cold War struggle. Prior to 1975, refugees came from Europe.

In 1976, for the first time, an uninvited, small boat of Vietnamese refugees arrived on Australian shores. By the middle of 1978, fifty-one boats carrying over 2,000 refugees had followed suit (Robinson 1998, 152 quoted in Gibney 2004, 178). The forced migrants were not welcome by the Australian public and by some sections of the Labor Party. In an attempt to regain control of migration to Australia by stopping the spontaneous arrivals, the Australian government led discussions with the UNHCR and the United States to resettle refugees from Thailand and later Malaysia (Gibney 2004, 179). A scheme ensued to enable refugees to come to Australia and the US through official routes. By 1981, Australia had accepted 50,000 Indo-Chinese (Gibney 2004, 179). The arrival of boat people coincided with an economic downturn, with Australia experiencing high rates of inflation and unemployment as the result of the oil shocks (Gibney 2004, 181). The rationale for taking in immigrants and refugees changed. In the 1980s and 1990s, "(...) public justification for accepting refugees began to be more closely tied to the virtues of humanitarianism" (Gibney 2004, 183). Australia secured agreements with Thailand and Malaysia (the Orderly Departure Programme in 1979) and Vietnam in 1987 (the Comprehensive Plan of Action), for these countries to stop spontaneous departures from their territories. In exchange, Australian government officials committed to resettle large numbers of refugees. Yet, in spite of Australia's best efforts to reduce the number of asylum seekers reaching its soil, the number of on shore asylum claims rose to 27,117 between 1989 and 1991 (Gibney 2004, 184).

In 1992, the *Migration Amendment Act* was passed. It provided for the detention of any person arriving by boat to Australia. In parallel to its endeavors to deter and penalize asylum seekers, Australia continued to resettle recognized refugees; between the mid 1980s and the mid 1990s, Australia welcomed between 10,000 and 12,000 refugees each year (Gibney 2004, 183). Excision is not an accident in but rather the pinnacle of Australia's humanitarian history, which has unwaveringly consisted in deterring and penalizing asylum claimants and in welcoming recognized refugees through resettlement.

Excision has enabled the Australian government to subvert the Refugee Convention while appearing to remain engaged with this international instrument. Successive Australian governments have not made statements that were *overtly* against the Refugee Convention. On the contrary, they have multiplied assurances that Australia abided by its convention obligations. At the occasion of the 50th anniversary of the 1951 Refugee Convention, ministers of States parties met in Geneva on December 12–13, 2001, at the invitation of the government of Switzerland and of the UNHCR. They issued a statement in which they reaffirmed their commitment to implement their obligations under the Convention and its Protocol. Australia signed onto this reassuring statement in December 2001, just a few months after putting in place the excision regime. Australian officials explicitly stated that *non-refoulement* was unacceptable, and that the excision machinery complied with this requirement central to the Refugee Convention. The Department of Immigration and Multicultural and Indigenous Affairs defended the excision policy to the Senate Legal and Constitutional References Committee in the following terms:

> The Australian government recognises that where asylum-seekers have entered Australian territory (which includes the territorial sea), Australia's obligations under the Refugees Convention are engaged. A key obligation under the Refugees Convention is not to *refoule* a person, directly or indirectly, to a place where his life or freedom would be threatened for a Convention reason. This obligation on a party to the Convention does not create a right for a person to decide where he or she may receive protection from persecution. Australia ensures that persons who enter Australia's territory are able to access a refugee determination process. This process may be undertaken either in an excised offshore place or in a declared country and is in line with United Nations High Commissioner for Refugees (UNHCR) processes.
>
> DIMIA August 21, 2002

In spite of the government's assurances, Australia has, in fact, undermined the Refugee Convention. It is not enough to make sure that persons entering Australian territory have access to *a* refugee determination process: the Refugee Convention provides that such persons shall have access to *Australia*'s refugee determination process. Australian leaders' disregard for and desire to circumvent the Refugee Convention became manifest in December 2014, when the *Migration and Maritime Powers Legislation Amendment (Resolving the Asylum Legacy Caseload) Act 2014* was passed by Parliament. The Act had most references to the Refugee Convention and to the country's *non-refoulement* obligations removed (Human Rights Law Center April 17, 2015-cf. section IX).

8 Contamination of the Regular Refugee Protection Regime by the Excision Regime

My argument is that the excision regime contaminated insidiously the regular immigration and refugee protection regime: the former slowly but surely penetrated the latter, until it completely disappeared. Contamination started when authorities denied access to the country's legislated refugee determination procedures to people who had landed in non-excised places. As previously explained, Kurdish asylum seekers were denied the right to have their claims reviewed in 2003, when they landed in Melville Island. The government hastily made regulations to excise Melville Island from the migration zone, and argued that the regulations applied retroactively. Dastyari (2007, 6 quoted in Johnson 2014, 77) observes: "Between the introduction of the Pacific Solution in 2001 and 2007, only 57 asylum seekers on two boats were able to land in an area that had not been excised. In some cases, this is because the land was retroactively excised after an arrival". Australian land was retroactively excised on more than one occasion.

Furthermore, for non-citizens landing within the migration zone on ground that was not retroactively excised, there was no guarantee of being processed in the mainland locations earmarked for people entering the regular onshore regime. In July 2003, 53 Vietnamese asylum seekers arrived to the Western Australian coast aboard the "Hao Kiet" boat. The government conceded that they had landed on non-excised grounds but refused to process them on Australian mainland. Instead of being taken to Port Hedland, the nearby and functioning detention center on mainland Australia, they were carried 1,800 kilometers away on a military ship to Christmas Island. There, the detention facility was not operational and had to be quickly re-opened (Taylor 2005, 67). The price of taking the claimants to Christmas Island was estimated at $10 million (The Sydney Morning Herald July 8, 2003). On a radio interview, the Prime Minister declared:

> We decide they should go to Christmas Island because we believe that if they were processed in Port Hedland that would run the risk of sending a message to the rest of the world that it was still possible to get to the Australian mainland and that in some way our policy on that had been changed. I think there is a big difference in the eyes of the world in being

> processed in Christmas Island, which is a long way from continental Australia, and being processed on the Australian mainland. I think psychologically there is a big difference.
>
> The Sydney Morning Herald, July 8, 2003

This statement shows that in 2003, the Australian government was already concerned with the fact that non-citizens landing on non-excised land would be treated more favorably than those landing on excised territory. Individuals who did not fit the "offshore entry person category" were somehow placed into it. To forcibly make the non-citizens fit into the category, the government either manipulated time (by declaring that the piece of land upon which the non-citizens arrived had already been excised prior to arrival) or space (by denying access to the regular physical locations dedicated to onshore processing).

9 Extension of the Space of Exclusion

> Refugees, the human waste of the global frontier-land, are "the outsiders incarnate", the absolute outsiders, outsiders everywhere and out of place everywhere except in places that are themselves out of place -the "no-where places" that appear on no maps used by ordinary humans on their travels. Once outside, indefinitely outside, a secure fence with watching towers is the only contraption needed to make the "indefiniteness" of the out-of-place hold forever.
>
> BAUMAN 2004, 80

Initially, when the 2001 *Excision From Migration Zone Act* was passed, the space of exclusion encompassed the Islands of Christmas, Ashmore, Cartier and Cocos. Since then, the exclusionary space has expanded significantly, until including the non-citizen's self and mainland Australia. Once again, the French and the Australian case present troubling similarities. In Australia, like in France, the expansion of the alternate legal regime's scope was triggered by perceived immigration crises. Expansion has been both personal and geographic in nature.

9.1 *Extension of the Space of Exclusion to the Non-Citizen's Self and Descendants*

As previously explained, in France the waiting zone status has been accompanying the individual wherever he or she goes since November 2003. Practitioners explain that non-citizens carry the waiting zone status like a "backpack" or are in a waiting zone "bubble". Christian, a lawyer, uses both terms (Interview, December 2013). In Australia, non-citizens were forced to *be* the border (Khosravi 2010) earlier, in March 2002. The excision status has followed the offshore entry person (and, from 2013, the person categorized as "unauthorised maritime arrival") when he or she entered mainland Australia at a later date. The *Migration Legislation Amendment (Transitional Movement) Act 2002* has precluded non-citizens from accessing the regular rights regime when entering mainland Australia from declared countries. In February 2002, DIMIA explained that the government favored deportations taking place directly from declared countries (HRW 2002, 76). Should this not be possible, the law has made sure that deportees would not take advantage of their physical location on the country's mainland to access legal rights. Those transferred to the mainland from Nauru or Papua New Guinea for medical treatment or deportation have been barred from applying for protection in Australia. They have been prevented from challenging their deportation before Australia's Refugee Review Tribunal or courts for a period of time of at least six months after arrival on mainland's soil (HRW 2002, 76). The Australian excision regime is, just like the French waiting zone regime, a particular legal space of lesser rights that follows the individual, no matter his or her physical location. Furthermore, this less protective legal regime premised on extra-territoriality has been transmitted from parents to their offspring.

The *Migration Amendment (Unauthorised Maritime Arrivals and Other Measures) Act 2013* had children inherit their parents' status of "unauthorised maritime arrivals", regardless of the location of the parent at the time of birth. The Act barred a child born in Australia's migration zone to unauthorised maritime arrival parents from applying for a visa. It also imposed that the child be taken "as soon as reasonably practical" to a regional processing country. The 2013 Act did not straightforwardly state that unauthorised maritime arrivals status was passed down from parents to children. Rather, the Act stated that a child born in Australia's migration zone who was *not* an Australian citizen (or an excluded maritime arrival),[4] who did not have a current visa at the time of birth and who entered Australia by sea was an unauthorised maritime arrival. A few steps of legal reasoning had, therefore, to be taken to reach this conclusion. As unauthorised maritime arrival parents gave birth to children fulfilling

4 Section 5AA (3) of the *Migration Amendment (Unauthorised Maritime Arrivals and Other Measures) Act 2013* states: "A person is an excluded maritime arrival if the person is a New Zealand citizen who holds and produces a New Zealand passport that is in force; or is a non-citizen who holds and produces a passport that is in force and is endorsed with an authority to reside indefinitely on Norfolk Island".

the aforementioned criteria, the Act provided *de facto* for the transmission of exclusionary status. Before the 2013 amendment, a child born to "offshore entry person" parents in a part of Australia that had not been excised was not an offshore entry person himself or herself.

Senator Sarah Hanson-Young introduced a Bill into the Senate on June 18, 2014: *the Migration Amendment (Protecting Babies Born in Australia) Bill 2014*. The Senate referred the Bill to the Legal and Constitutional Affairs Legislation Committee. The latter was due to report on the Bill on February 10, 2015. Senator Hanson-Young's Bill proposed to amend the *Migration Act* in such a way that children born in the migration zone to unauthorised maritime arrivals parents would no longer have been deemed unauthorised maritime arrivals themselves (Australian Senate February 10, 2015). However, before the Senate could submit its report, a new Act had been passed by Parliament. This time, the *Migration and Maritime Powers Legislation Amendment (Resolving the Asylum Legacy Caseload) Act 2014 overtly* stated that children inherited their parents' exclusionary legal status. This legislative piece *explicitly* provided for the transmission of unlawful non-citizen's status: children of "transitory persons" and "unauthorised maritime arrivals" became likewise classified. Let us now examine the geographic expansion of the space of exclusion.

9.2 *Extension of the Space of Exclusion to the Entire Mainland*

Before the House of Representatives on June 17, 2002, the Government, led by John Howard, affirmed: "There is no intention, and there never has been, to excise any part of the Australian mainland. That is an absolutely ludicrous proposition" (Australian Senate October 21, 2002). Yet, in 2013, Australian MPs passed a piece of legislation whose content was tantamount to excising the entire mainland from itself. Since this date, non-citizens have been denied the possibility of entering Australia spontaneously at any place.

In Australia, like in France, successive governments have significantly extended the scope of the extra-territorial zones of exclusion to thwart unwanted arrivals. In both countries, the perimeter of exclusion grew exponentially after unplanned boat arrivals. The excision policy began in 2001 when the islands of Christmas, Ashmore, Cartier and Cocos were carved out from Australia's zone of migration. These islands were the first to be excluded from Australia's regular legal regime as their proximity to Indonesia made them destinations of choice for people smugglers. The *Excision from Migration Zone Act* 2001 conferred to the government the power to make regulations to excise further places. In Australia, the space of exclusion was extended both through regulations (i.e. executive tools) and the law.

On June, 7 2002, the government excised about 4,000 islands in the Northern waters of Australia by regulations. Officials were concerned that smugglers might be considering new routes to reach Australia and possibly New Zealand. The government proceeded to excise all Australian islands located along such routes (Taylor 2005, 65). Opposition parties in the Senate disallowed the excision regulations on June 19, 2002 (Coombs 2005).

The government then introduced a Bill into Parliament on June 20, 2002: *Migration Legislation Amendment (Further Border Protection Measures) Bill 2002.* The Bill had the very same purpose and content as the previously disallowed regulations, and was, therefore, also rejected by the Senate on December 9, 2002. The government refused to be defeated, and introduced the Bill (*Migration Legislation Amendment (Further Border Protection Measures) Bill 2002 (No. 2)*) again into Parliament on March 26, 2003. But the Senate rejected the Bill again on June 16, 2003 (Taylor 2005, 66).

A few months after designating 4,000 Northern water islands excised offshore places, the government, alarmed by intelligence sources reporting a smuggling attempt, hastily passed regulations to excise four islands located next to the Western Australian mainland in December 2002 (Taylor 2005, 66): Bernier Island, Dorre Island, Dirk Hartog Island and Faure Island (Coombs 2005). When it appeared that intelligence sources had been mistaken (the boat was a Sri Lankan fishing boat), the government withdrew the regulations (Coombs 2005).

Then, on November 4, 2003, the Minister for Immigration issued *Migration Amendment Regulations 2003 (No 8)*, declaring about 4,000 islands (including Melville Island) in the Northern waters of Australia to be excised (Taylor 2005, 66) in emergency. This time, the regulations purported to prevent 14 Turkish Kurds from making valid visa applications. The asylum seekers had travelled from Indonesia aboard the Indonesian fishing boat the *Minasa Bone*, and had entered Australia's Melville Island without authorization (Taylor 2005, 66). Importantly, the 14 non-citizens landed in a part of Australia that had not been excised from the migration zone. Their boat, SIEV 14,[5] entered Australia before the *Migration Amendment Regulations 2003* were gazetted. The government violated the well-established legal principle of non-retroactivity, arguing that the regulations were effective retroactively, from midnight on the day of gazettal (Taylor 2005). The boat people were not sent to third countries for processing. Immigration, customs, defense and quarantine authorities interviewed them on a navy ship north of Melville Island. After the interview, the Australian Navy

5 SIEV stands for "Suspected Illegal Entry Vessel".

escorted the boat people back to Indonesian waters and left them there. The Senate subsequently disallowed the regulations on November 24, 2003, but it was too late for the asylum claimants (Coombs 2005). The Turkish Kurds were denied the possibility of applying for asylum. While the Australian government insisted that the Kurds had not asked for protection, the Kurds themselves, interviewed by the Australian media in Indonesia, said that they had asked for protection from the beginning (Taylor 2005, 75). The Minister for Immigration admitted that the 2003 regulations were similar to the regulations previously disallowed by the Senate and to the two Bills previously turned down by the Senate. She expected the 2003 regulations to be disallowed as well, but explained that they would serve their purpose until disallowed: ban the Turkish Kurds from applying for protection visas (Taylor 2005, 74).

The next round of excision was triggered by the arrival of 42 West Papuan asylum seekers by boat in May 2006 (Taylor 2005). They were all (except for one), granted temporary protection visas, which provoked a diplomatic backlash from Indonesia (Weber 2007, 87). The claimants originated from Indonesia-controlled West Papua, and the Indonesian government felt that Australia, by granting them asylum, was sympathetic to their claims to independence (Palmer and Matthews 2006, 28). The government introduced a Bill into the House of Representatives in May 2006: the *Migration Amendment (Designated Unauthorised Arrivals) Bill 2006*, which proposed to substitute the term "offshore entry person" for that of "designated unauthorised arrivals". The government wanted "designated unauthorised arrivals" arriving anywhere on the Australian mainland to be processed as if they had entered an excised space (Vogl 2015, 126). The government (2006) presented the Bill's purpose in the following terms:

> The amendments contained in the Bill propose to amend the *Migration Act 1958* (the Act) to expand the offshore processing regime currently applying to offshore entry persons and transitory persons to include, in addition, all persons arriving at mainland Australia (meaning other than at an excised offshore place) unlawfully by sea on or after 13 April 2006.

The Bill's proposal was therefore tantamount to extending the scope of excision to the entirety of Australian territory for boat arrivals. Non-citizens entering any part of Australia by boat without authorization were to be treated according to the excision regime. In the explanatory memorandum to the Bill, the Australian government (2006) justified the Bill by the need to not advantage asylum seekers who reach the mainland compared to those who land on excised territories: "This is designed to operate as a disincentive to people who arrived on the mainland unauthorised by boat to defeat the existing excision provisions".

Interestingly, the Bill also proposed to extend the offshore processing regime to certain categories of air arrivals: non-citizens who have undertaken most of their journeys to Australia by sea, and who use the plane for the last leg of their journeys. By a sovereign twist, the non-citizens' journey by plane would be transformed into a sea journey. The Australian government (2006) explained:

> The Bill will also deem certain air arrivals to be entry by sea so the persons will be subject to the new regime. Persons who travel most of the way to Australia by sea but travel the last leg by air, before entering (on or after 13 April 2006) and who become unlawful on entry, will be taken to have entered Australia by sea. These are basically situations where persons are airlifted into Australia at the end of their sea journey.

The House of Representatives approved the Bill. However, the Senate Standing Committee on Legal and Constitutional Affairs recommended that the Bill did not proceed (Australian Senate June 13, 2006). Faced with considerable public and political opposition within and outside of his ranks, Prime Minister John Howard decided to withdraw the Bill in August 2006 from the Senate (Palmer and Matthews 2006, 26).

The project to excise the entirety of the Australian territory failed in 2006, but succeeded in 2013. Up to May 2013, 4,891 Australian islands and territories were carved out from the migration zone (Vogl 2015, 114). After this date the entire Australian mainland was, *de facto,* excised from itself. More precisely, the excision regime was extended to the entirety of the Australian mainland upon the recommendations of the 2012 Expert Panel on Asylum Seekers. The latter recommended that all boat arrivals be treated under the same legal regime, regardless of the location where they arrive: "The Panel recommends that the Migration Act 1958 be amended, so that arrival anywhere on Australia by irregular maritime means will not provide individuals with a different lawful status than those who arrived in an excised offshore place" (Australian Government 2012). The rationale was to stop non-citizens from undertaking hazardous journeys by rendering arrival on mainland as unattractive as arrival in excised offshore places. Landing on the mainland was to trigger the same legal regime as landing on excised places: offshore processing in declared countries.

Yet, the *Migration Amendment (Unauthorised Maritime Arrivals and Other Measures) Bill 2012* did not use the language of excision; the government did not present this piece of legislation as excising mainland Australia. Vogl (2015, 143–144) explains:

> Significantly, the amending Act of 2012, which rendered those arriving by boat to the mainland subject to the same regime facing 'offshore entry persons', did not include the term excision in the title or the Act itself. Even more significantly, the amending Act did not add the mainland to the list of excised offshore places, which is how the policy was expanded on previous occasions. In this sense, in a somewhat knotty piece of legislative reform, the mainland was not excised, but those arriving on the mainland would be treated in the same way as those arriving at excised offshore places.

The government probably exercised great caution, as Australian nationals had not been comfortable with the terminology of excision.

Since 2013, all non-citizens arriving by boat to any part of Australia have been barred from applying for protection visas (or for *any* other visa) under the law, except at the discretion of the Minister for Immigration. On paper, the migration zone still exists. However, since 2013, those arriving by boat to a non-excised part of Australian territory have been subjected to the same legal regime as those landing to an excised part of Australia. The land from which it is possible to launch an asylum claim (i.e. the migration zone) has simply disappeared. From August 2012 until 2015, the government stopped carrying out refugee status determination for claimants who arrived by boat after August 13, 2012. The government began to allow some claimants to apply for protection in 2015. While the Department of Immigration and Border Protection allowed all claimants to apply for a protection visa in 2016, it also removed most access to government-funded legal advice, thereby creating long waiting list to access legal advice.

Boat people who arrived between August 13, 2012 and January 1, 2014 -and that were not taken to Nauru or Papua New Guinea- have been submitted to a fast track refugee status determination process. This process deprives them of the possibility of having their claims reviewed by an independent merits review tribunal.

On its website, the Refugee Council of Australia (February 26, 2019) regrets the lack of reliable and updated statistics when it comes to asylum claimants in Nauru and Papua New Guinea:

> The Australian Government does not provide many statistics regularly on offshore processing. Most of the information in this page comes through

> information provided through Senate estimates. Usually, the information provided in this way is already outdated by the time it is provided. As well, it should be noted that there are limitations and gaps in the data as the information depends on the way the question was asked and the frequency with which it is asked.

According to available data, 3,127 non-citizens have been processed on Nauru or Papua New Guinea since July 19, 2013 (on this date the Prime Minister announced that people taken to declared countries would no longer be resettled in Australia). Offshore processing resumed in September 2012, but statistics are unavailable for this period of time. On February 3, 2019, the Minister for Immigration, David Coleman, announced at a press conference that around 420 people remained in Nauru and 600 in Papua New Guinea. 456 refugees had been resettled to the United States and four children with their families were about to be resettled to the United States. The Minister refused to give the precise number of people who had applied for resettlement in the United States.

Part 1 Findings: Extra-Territorial Exclusion Comes in Two Forms that May Be Combined – the Case of Canada

The former chapters shed light on the two forms of extra-territorial exclusion that have sustained the creation and operation of nowhere countries. The Canadian case is interesting in that it combines traits of the first and second configurations of extra-territoriality previously outlined. Canadian authorities intercepted 599 individuals from China off the coast of British Columbia in July 1999. The non-citizens, who had been smuggled, arrived in four different boats over the course of six weeks (Mountz 2010). At the time, tens of thousands of smuggled non-citizens were arriving at Canadian airports every year, making this figure of 599 individuals rather unremarkable. Yet, the non-citizens from the Fujian Province were treated differently compared to those arriving by land or air. Their boats were towed and they were taken by ship or by bus to the Esquimalt naval base on Vancouver Island, which was declared a "port of entry".

Mountz (2010) pursued research with the Department of Citizenship and Immigration Canada (CIC) in the wake of the interceptions. The data presented here comes from her work, the sole ethnographic-based research studying the Canadian government's response to these events. She documented how the Canadian authorities developed the "long tunnel thesis" to claim that the Chinese people at the Esquimalt naval base had not reached Canadian soil yet, in spite of them being physically located on Canadian territory. At the naval base, the non-citizens were considered inside the tunnels of an international airport, not yet landed in Canada. The construction of the Esquimalt naval base as "Not-Canada" carried deep implications for the boat people's access to rights. Firstly, like in French airports in the 1980s, the non-citizens were denied access to rights. During processing at the base they were refused access to lawyers. Indeed, CIC, the federal agency in charge of managing immigration, refugee claims and border enforcement, wanted to gather as much information as possible about the boat people's journeys and their smugglers before allowing lawyer access. CIC was wary of lawyers, as they might have advised their clients to claim refugee status and to present their stories accordingly. In order to delay access to lawyers, the Canadian government temporarily designated the Esquimalt base as a port of entry. This designation carried important consequences, since migrants in detention do have the right to legal counsel under Canadian law, whereas migrants being processed at a port of entry do

 | DOI:10.1163/9789004383500_008

not. Lawyers protested this sovereign trick, observing that the Chinese people were undeniably detained, as evidenced by the presence of barbed wire, guard dogs and guards on the military base. Some individuals spent up to 14 days at the Work Point Barracks at Esquimalt, in "processing". During this time, immigration officials conducted preliminary interviews with the non-citizens with no legal counsel being present.

Secondly, the non-citizens' location in a space *declared* extra-territorial triggered a less protective legal regime. Unlike the legal regimes of the waiting zone and of excised land, the *de facto* alternate legal regime to which they were subjected was not enshrined in Canadian law. On paper, the Chinese non-citizens were accorded the regular protection of the law. However, *in practice*, they experienced less protection. After processing, 500 of the 599 non-citizens asked for refugee status. The asylum seekers were granted due process under the Canadian Charter of Rights and Freedoms: their cases were heard and they could exhaust all appeals procedures. However, their access to rights was mediated and subverted by geography. While claimants from the first boat were released after processing on Vancouver Island, those from the second, third and fourth boats were detained. At the time, detention of non-citizens in Canada for immigration purposes was quite rare. Many claimants from the first boat did not attend their refugee hearings; they were considered to have left Canada to work in Chinatown in New York City. Yet, as Mountz (2010, 77) notes, the fact that many boat people absconded did not justify the massive use of detention. After all, many non-citizens entering Canada by air or land also vanished after their release: "The reasons this group was treated differently through detention en masse went largely unexplained. Officials cited the involvement of organized crime, the failure of claimants to provide identity documents and the fact that they were likely to flee. The same could be said, however, of many arriving at airports and land borders who were released during the same time period".

Claimants from the second, third and fourth boats were detained in a provincial prison in the small city of Prince George, in the interior of the British Columbia Province. In this remote location, that stood ten hours away by car from Vancouver, the claimants experienced isolation from refugee lawyers, interpreters, human rights monitors and the Chinese community. Their cases were heard inside the prison, in provisional tribunals, and adjudicated by Immigration and Refugee Board officers who were especially brought to the prison. The claimants attended their hearings wearing prison outfit and handcuffs. Refugee lawyers and advocates argued that the claimants had not benefited from the regular rights regime on several accounts. The information that was collected by the government during preliminary interviews at the military base constituted the first point of contention. Indeed, the government used the data that was obtained in the absence of legal counsels to point to contradictions in the claimants' stories. Lawyers also deplored the fact that claimants were not identified and treated as individuals but as a homogeneous group. Mountz (2010, 104–105) explains: "At routine detention review hearings, federal lawyers used the same document to provide background information on each claimant and to argue for continued detention, which lawyers and advocates suggested was a form or racial profiling". Furthermore, refugee advocates argued that Immigration and Refugee Board members, who were temporarily accommodated in Prince George, were in a hurry to decide on the cases, as they were keen on returning home. While the Immigration and Refugee Board argued that the cases were prioritized because the claimants were detained, lawyers lamented the expedited character of the hearings, pointing that they did not have enough time to collect evidence. Last but not least, the four lawyers who were selected by the Legal Services Society to represent the asylum seekers held in Prince Georges were not recognized as experienced refugee lawyers by their counterparts: they did not regularly attend the immigration subcommittee meetings of the Canadian Bar Association and were not well-known in Vancouver. The fact that they could represent diligently such an important number of claimants was also questioned.

Importantly, almost all of the claims that were heard in Prince George were ultimately rejected. Only 24 asylum seekers had their claims accepted out of the 577 claimants.[1] At the time, asylum seekers from China had a 58 percent approval rate. By contrast, the approval rate dropped to less than 5 percent for the claimants who arrived by boat in 1999. The majority of those who were conferred refugee status had not been detained in the regular criminal system in Prince George but had been hosted or detained in the surroundings of Vancouver in youth facilities or prisons. There, they enjoyed access to experienced refugee lawyers, and their claims were heard in a more individualized manner at the regional headquarters of Citizenship and Immigration Canada. Claimants that were detained in Prince George simply did not enjoy the same quality of access to the refugee determination process. One lawyer argued that they experienced "skeletal justice", by opposition to the "thick justice" taking place in Vancouver. Many of the claimants who had been detained were deported back to China in 2000, after they exhausted all legal recourses. The media, public opinion and the government depicted the asylum claimants as illegal

1 Mountz (2010, 178) notes that the number of refugee claimants was contested and changed over time, as people's legal status evolved. She explains: "Some migrants misrepresented their ages, and minors were identified distinctly by the federal and provincial governments".

migrants trying to abuse Canada's generous refugee system. The inscription of the "bogus refugee" identity to the Chinese claimants triggered their detention in "Not-Canada" and in the remote location of Prince Georges as well as the subsequent subversion of the access to the regular rights' regime. As Mountz (2010, 113) puts it: "the narrative of *who* these migrants were explains *where* they were located and vice versa". "Those designated outside the definition (of the Convention refugee) are detained where their access to sovereign territory and claim and processes is inhibited, illustrating the relationships between discourse, representation and identity".

PART 2

Inside Nowhere Countries: Enforcement Practices and Mental Landscapes

Previous chapters established the conceptual framework, exploring the ways in which exclusion of non-citizens through extra-territoriality took place in France, Morocco, Australia and Canada. I would now like to change the level of analysis to concretely describe daily practices and discourses occurring in one nowhere country. The study will focus on CDG's waiting zone. Is it a homogeneous space? What happens to non-citizens confined there? What organizations or actors are working in CDG's waiting zone and how do they relate to non-citizens and each other? In the two following chapters, I will share ethnographic findings, unveiling practices and mental landscapes in spaces inaccessible to the public.

 | DOI:10.1163/9789004383500_009

CHAPTER 6

Airport Terminals: the Border Police's Realms. The Less Visible Part of CDG's Waiting Zone

This chapter will focus on airport terminals while the next one will turn to the detention center, "ZAPI 3". Airport terminals are truly the border police's realms: there, asymmetrical power relations prevail and both detainees and researchers experience arbitrariness. Airport terminals constitute the less visible part of CDG's waiting zone. I begin with a description of the geographical and legal path followed by passengers prior to and upon conferment of the waiting zone status. Some passengers may have difficulties reaching the waiting zone status, deprived of the "right to have rights" (Arendt 1968) in the international zone.

1 Path Followed by Passengers Prior to and upon Placement under the Waiting Zone Regime

Passengers arriving at the airport may meet the border police as soon as they get off the plane at gangway checks (also called "on-board inspections") or at built-in border checkpoints. In both cases, passengers may be returned immediately, without conferment of the waiting zone status. For these individuals, the international zones of Paris' airports remain, as Basaran calls it, a "zone of non-rights" (2011, 63). They are the only space where individuals may experience a legal vacuum. Indeed, those who have not been registered yet as non-admitted travelers or as asylum claimants at a border checkpoint do not benefit from the rights attached to the waiting zone framework (among them the right not to be returned before 24 hours or the right to communicate with any person of their choosing). Because they are not registered as having been denied entry, they are not accounted for under the law. As their existence is not acknowledged in the border police's records, it is possible for border agents to intercept them as soon as they get off the plane and to return them immediately.

Christian, a lawyer representing foreign nationals in the waiting zone and in *rétention*, flew from Kinshasa to Belgium a few years ago. He explains that authorities boarded the plane where they identified travellers who did not meet the criteria to enter Belgian territory. These passengers were forbidden from exiting the plane, which was returning to Kinshasa (Interview, December 2013).

 | DOI:10.1163/9789004383500_010

Christian wondered how people could claim asylum in such circumstances. At CDG, on-board inspections have been common practice since 2005 (Iserte 2008). According to Iserte (2008, 16), 40 onboard inspections are carried out daily at CDG. The practices witnessed by Christian in Belgium also take place at CDG and have been denounced by several European reports. In 2007, the European Parliament recommended that France "prohibit the almost immediate removal of illegal immigrants during 'on-board inspections', which is contrary to asylum law" (European Parliament 2007). The Commissioner for Human Rights also noted in 2004:

> A final matter to address is that of foreigners who are not allowed to enter the waiting zone. Representatives of specialist NGOs passed on several reports to me which show that gangway checks are on the increase and lead on occasion to immediate expulsion or removal to international areas of the airport terminal, preventing the persons concerned from being registered or reaching the waiting zone.
>
> GIL-ROBLES 2006, §193

Therefore, people are sometimes returned without even leaving the runway, as in the 1980s and early 1990s. Jean, an Air France employee at CDG in the 1980s, describes the practices at the time: "When the border police caught someone, this person would not even cross the gangway, the person was left on the plane, the airline company had to deal with the person" (Interview, February 6, 2014). Issues pertaining to the absence of legality in the international zone have endured after 1992, in spite of the Law on the Waiting Zone.

Luc, a lawyer who occasionally represents non-citizens at airport borders, had a client who never reached the legal guarantees attached to the status of the waiting zone (Interview, October 2013). He recounts that the family of a pregnant Moroccan woman contacted him in 2008 or 2009. Living in France with her husband, Leïla had requested administrative permission to reside lawfully in the country. She was given a receipt acknowledging that her request was under examination. Mistaking the receipt for proof she had been entitled to stay in France, Leïla travelled to Morocco. When she returned and presented herself at Orly airport's border, the police denied her entry and kept her at the terminal, in their offices. When Luc arrived at Orly, two hours after his client had landed, he found no trace of her. The border police had not issued the usual administrative paperwork: there were no documents certifying she had been denied entry or placed in the waiting zone. Leïla was completely unknown, her name absent from police electronic records: it was as if she had never come. Luc understood how events had unfolded later, when Leïla contacted her family from Casablanca, Morocco. Already six or seven months pregnant, the police had attempted to beat her back on the plane and she had not resisted her return. There are frequent flights to major Moroccan cities, perhaps making it easier for authorities to return travellers without registering them. When denied registration under the waiting zone regime, those turned away at the borders at French airports are rendered nonexistent, as in the 1980s and early 1990s. While the rights conferred to those placed under the waiting zone regime are no panacea, they are nonetheless better than being denied legal existence. In particular, the waiting zone framework grants the right not to be returned before 24 hours.

The international zone remains an "abject space" (Isin and Rygiel 2007) only for those left outside of the waiting zone regime. To illustrate this point, imagine two individuals detained in the same holding room in one of CDG airport's terminals. One of them possesses paperwork indicating he has been turned away, while the other will be left unregistered and thus never receive such documents. Both are geographically located in the international zone. However, from a legal standpoint they do not share the same space: the former is detained in the waiting zone, while the latter is located in the international zone. The illegal practice of non-registration under the waiting zone status may have dramatic consequences on people's lives. As in the era preceding the birth of the Law on the Waiting Zone, asylum seekers may experience *refoulement* in Paris' airports' international zones.

Travelers may also spend lengthy amounts of time in the international zone, in a legal vacuum, before reaching the waiting zone status. The CDG airport is not a homogeneous place: terminals were built at different points in time and do not have the same shape or length (cf. map 1).

In some terminals, passengers have no choice but to reach the border checkpoint immediately. However, in other terminals, passengers have to walk for a while and/or take a shuttle to reach the border checkpoint: the international zone covers a vast amount of space. Extended stays in the international zone may be voluntary or involuntary. According to the Ministry of the Interior (Interview with Clotilde, December 2013), some travelers avoid reaching the checkpoints immediately so that it becomes impossible to track their point of departure and therefore to return them. But others are confronted with the police's refusal to register their asylum claims (Anafé February 2016).

I will now explain the path followed by those who are granted the waiting zone status. When authorities suspect the traveler of lacking the appropriate documents to cross the border, the individual is put aside and taken to meet another authority called an *officier de quart*. This border officer proceeds to conduct further checks, interrogating the individual. The *officier de*

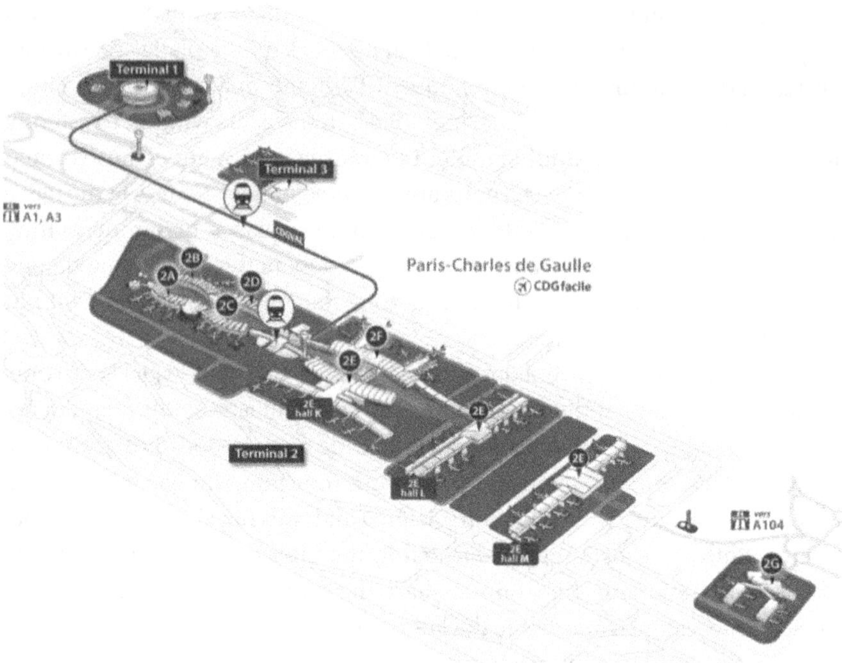

MAP 1 Map of terminals at Roissy-Charles de Gaulle airport
SOURCE: AIRPORT WEBSITE AUGUST 2016

quart ultimately decides whether or not the individual should be admitted to the country. Upon placement in the waiting zone, this authority issues the following administrative documents: a form certifying that entry was denied (or requested on asylum grounds), a form certifying the placement under the waiting zone regime, the transcription of the hearing and documents detailing the types of control that were carried out by the *officier de quart*.

After—but also sometimes prior to—conferment of the waiting zone status, rejected travelers and asylum seekers are detained in small cells located in or outside of police stations at airport terminals (in terminals 1 and 2A, 2C, 2D, 2E and 2F).[1] Individuals await their transfer to the detention center (ZAPI 3) in these small cells, which are also the last stop before boarding of those who are to be returned. Men, women and children of all ages (accompanied or unaccompanied) are all detained together, sitting on rough benches that are attached to the walls. Conditions of detention in these transitional places of confinement are anything but homogeneous. These rooms present different

1 At the time of visits, terminal 2B was closed for renovation.

degrees of cleanliness and are of varied surface area (from five square meters to 28 square meters). Some walls are covered with sentences such as "Put your trust in God", "Jesus is Lord", "No one is a stranger in this world" or *Dieu est grand* (God is great). Some of the cells' doors are opened, being guarded by one or several police officers at the entrance. However, others are locked without a door handle on the inside, creating a very claustrophobic atmosphere to the space. Most rooms are windowless except for a small window that cannot be opened—about the size of an A4 paper—on the door itself. None of the rooms I visited had windows allowing natural light into the room. Although my visits took place during the winter, some of the rooms were very hot. They were more or less crowded, depending on the level of activity and the destinations covered by the terminal in question.

Some terminals receive significantly more passengers than others. According to one authority, 70 percent of the flights land in terminals 2E (including Air France flights) and 2F combined. Many flights from Africa land in these two terminals. The border police consider African citizens as presenting a "high migratory risk". Not surprisingly, during each of my two morning visits to terminal 2E, the detention room (about 18 square meters) was quite full, with detainees occupying most of the benches' space. I met Arnaud, a border agent, in terminal 1. Having previously worked in terminal 2E, he explained that, although holding cells in the two terminals were of the same surface area, terminal 2E hosted twice as many individuals. Arnaud remarked: "Terminal 2E's holding room really looks like a prison. And from the point of view of hygiene it is not great. There is a ventilation system but no air conditioning, while terminal 1 has both" (observations). A picnic is served to detainees during meal hours, but according to an agent in terminal 2F, there are no meals for babies. During a February 2014 visit to terminal 2D, I met a family with two small children (aged thirteen months and three years). The toddler was eating the solid food provided: potato crisps and a tuna salad, in spite of the choking hazard.

2 Hassan's Understanding of His Location

How do individuals subjected to the waiting zone framework comprehend their situation? Evidence suggests that the notion of legal space can be difficult to grasp for those detained in Charles de Gaulle's waiting zone. The aforementioned family had fled Syria. Hassan, the father, explained that he was a descendant of Palestine refugees, born in Kuwait. He confided that he wanted to go back to Israel but that "the country did not want him". Hassan and his family had refugee cards from the UNHCR and wanted to know whether they could seek refugee status again in a European country. Hassan explained that they had undertaken a long journey travelling from Syria to Lebanon, Turkey and then Cyprus before finally arriving at CDG two days before my visit. The family's final destination was Sweden, where his wife's family was living. They had not asked for asylum at French borders and the police had attempted to return them to Cyprus that very morning. The father enquired: Was this France? My explanation: Yes, this was France but they were detained in this small room for they had been refused entry as they lacked valid travel documents, was met with a puzzled look. The detainees' confusion surrounding their physical location may be compounded by the official posters located in some police stations at terminals, which remind border policemen of the rules by which they must abide. I saw one such poster in terminal 1, reminding policemen to be courteous, say "hello" and "welcome to France". Not without irony, they are located in rooms where people are taken to be further interrogated about their travel motives, i.e. after the agent at the checkpoint determined they could not be admitted, at least not before more thorough checks. It is in these rooms that travelers, when applicable, are informed of their placement under the status of the waiting zone.

3 Isolation

The presence of third parties is very rare in airport terminals. These spaces are the realm of the police; most of the time non-citizens are alone with border agents. Detainees are therefore highly isolated there. Many actors equate Charles de Gaulle's waiting zone with ZAPI3: in common language, the term "waiting zone" refers to the detention center. Usually, when I presented myself at police stations' entry desks in terminals, border agents were surprised and tried to divert me, claiming that the waiting zone was not located in airport terminals, but at the detention center. This attitude may denote that policemen are not used to receiving visitors in terminals. The law entitles legal counsels to visit their clients anytime and anywhere within the waiting zone. But in practice, lawyers are generally turned down when they present themselves in airport terminals (Anafé January 2013, 40–41). I met four lawyers who, at the time of interview, represented or used to regularly represent non-citizens detained in CDG's waiting zone. None of them visited their clients in terminals.

As for *ad hoc* administrators, they do not visit unaccompanied minors in airport terminals either. Unaccompanied minors are alone when placed under the legal regime of the waiting zone: they sign the administrative paperwork without their *ad hoc* administrator being present.[2] *Ad hoc* administrators are normally designated upon placement of the child in the waiting zone (CESEDA 2016, art. L.221–5). However, in violation of the law, some time may elapse before the public prosecutor office designating an *ad hoc* administrator. Anafé (January 2013, 29–30) explains that border officers may question the person's age even if he or she carries official documents establishing minority. When border officers question minority, they contact the public prosecutor's office. The latter may then order a medicalized procedure: a bone test. Yet, this way of assessing a person's minority is controversial; the medical community contests its accuracy, pointing out that such method only offers a rough estimation of a person's age (Anafé 2013, 31). When individuals are finally recognized as minors, they usually have already been transferred to ZAPI 3. Even when the *ad hoc* administrator is swiftly designated, he or she does not meet the child in the terminals' holding cells (interview with Anafé employees Anne and Lise, January 2014 and conversations with border officers).

Family members and friends are also banned from terminals. As far as NGOs are concerned, some of them carry out sporadic visits. Anafé and the Red Cross secured access to the international zone (including airport terminals) but face multiple barriers to the fulfillment of their mission. Both organizations signed a Memorandum of Understanding with the Ministry of the Interior, detailing conditions of access.

As Anafé employees Lise and Anne explain, the agreement prevents the organization from carrying out unannounced visits: the former has to inform the border police one day in advance of their intention to visit (Interview of Lise and Anne, January 2014). The memorandum also precludes Anafé members from speaking to foreign nationals when they are the "object of an ongoing procedure"[3] (Anafé 2007, 1). Raoul, an Anafé volunteer, observes:

> An ongoing procedure can mean anything and we say it very often. Depending on the agent that we have in front of us, an ongoing procedure can mean that the person has just arrived and has not signed yet his or her administrative forms, that the person will be boarding in two hours

2 Cf. chapter 4 for a discussion of the role played by *ad hoc* administrators.

3 The Memorandum of Understanding reads: "habilitated individuals (…) can talk to non-citizens, except for those who are the object of an ongoing procedure, and access places where these people are waiting" (*les personnes habilitées (…) peuvent avoir des échanges avec les étrangers, à l'exception de ceux pour lesquels une procédure est en cours, et accéder aux locaux où ces personnes sont en attente*).

> or refused to board two hours ago, it can be anything and everything (Interview, October 2013).

The Red Cross faces the very same limitation as Anafé. The organization's 2013 report (18) reads: "The argument of an ongoing procedure is often used, mediators are invited to come back later". Furthermore, agents often assert to Red Cross employees (mediators) that confinement cells are empty in an attempt to thwart them.[4] In general, officers do not seem to understand the rationale for mediators' visits:

> (…) policemen present in terminals' police stations do not seem well aware of the precise role of our mediators and of what motivates their visits to terminals. Some civil servants are surprised by their presence, even though this is a contractual task which is an integral part of the mission that has been assigned to us.
>
> RED CROSS 2013, 18

Both Anafé and the Red Cross lack the necessary resources to frequently visit the terminals. As per the memorandum, Anafé is entitled to visit the airport terminals four times per week (Anafé January 2013, 2)[5] but cannot allocate members to meet detainees in terminals that often. According to Noémie, who had volunteered for Anafé for nine months at the time of interview, the NGO only visits terminals once a month (Interview, September 2013). As for the Red Cross, it had to reduce the number of visits due to its shortage of personnel. While the organization's report (2013, 9) does not specify any visit number, it suggests that they are infrequent: visits can only take place when there is little activity at ZAPI 3 and when teams are complete.

Other NGOs are authorized to access the waiting zones, including CDG airport terminals. Determined to break detainees' isolation in terminals, NGOs struggled to obtain access to these sensitive spaces, extracting from the government one NGO access after another. NGO clearance has fluctuated tremendously over the years. The Prime Minister first issued a decree (*décret*, i.e. an administrative act) on May 2, 1995, allowing a UNHCR delegate as well as eight

4 Mediators understand that the confinement cells were not empty when they witness non-citizens arrive in ZAPI 3 shortly afterwards from these very same cells (Red Cross 2013,14).

5 Anafé first signed a Memorandum of Understanding with the Ministry of the Interior on March 5, 2004. The Convention was subsequently renewed. At first, the organization only had the authorization to visit twice a week. This number was then extended to three visits per week in 2005.

NGOs (of which six were Anafé members)[6] to access the waiting zones. Conditions of access were stringent: each NGO was allocated ten visitor's cards but could not carry out more than eight visits per year and per waiting zone. Visitors had to request the Ministry of the Interior's permission prior to visiting. Visits had to take place between 8:00 am and 8:00 pm, and only two visitors were allowed each time. Then, other NGOs requested a visiting pass. In reaction to ongoing court proceedings, the Minister of the Interior authorized thirteen NGO s to access the waiting zone on May 30, 2006[7] (of which ten were Anafé members). In 2009, two additional NGOs gained authorization to visit waiting zones (French Minister of Immigration, May 27, 2009). In 2015, fifteen organizations, including Human Rights Watch (HRW), had fought their way to waiting zones. These organizations' visits to terminals depend on each NGO's mission and priorities.

HRW sought accreditation in the Fall 2013 when I offered to work collaboratively to update the 2009 report on unaccompanied minors.[8] HRW dedicates itself to the production of reports documenting human rights violations, reports upon which an advocacy strategy is then devised and implemented. For such an organization, fieldwork takes place to collect enough data in order to write thorough reports. Dedicated to fact-finding, fieldwork is limited in time. I carried out a few visits alongside with HRW researchers (two of CDG's and one of Orly's waiting zones) and pressed on by myself after they had collected enough data. Conditions of accreditation to waiting zones are listed in the CESEDA (art R223-8 to R223-14). NGOs willing to apply need to have had legal existence for at least five years and must aim to provide social or medical assistance, defend human rights or assist non-citizens. Accreditation is granted for three years and one NGO can request up to ten visitor's cards. The law specifies that representatives from different NGOs cannot visit the same waiting zone

6 The following Anafé members were granted access to waiting zones: The French section of Amnesty International, Anafé, Cimade, Forum réfugiés, France Terre d'asile and MRAP. The other two non-Anafé members to be granted access were the French Red Cross and Doctors Without Borders.

7 Cf. French Minister of the Interior, May 30, 2006. In addition to the eight NGOs that were granted access in 1995, the following organizations obtained the right to visit waiting zones in 2006: Association d'accueil aux médecins et personnels de santé réfugiés en France, Groupe d'accueil et solidarité, Groupe d'information et de soutien des immigrés, Ligue des Droits de l'Homme, Médecins du Monde.

8 For the 2009 report (*Lost in Transit, Insufficient Protection for Unaccompanied Migrant Children at Roissy Charles de Gaulle*) the HRW researcher did not access terminals. The interviews that took place in the waiting zone were conducted at the detention center, in the visitors' room (accessible to the public). Cf. p. 6 of the report.

on the same day. However, this was never an issue: over the course of my visits to terminals, I never ran into any other NGO visitor from these 14 organizations. NGO presence in terminals is limited in time and irregular: most of the time detainees are alone with the police.

For all of these aforementioned reasons, airport terminals are not places where detainees can exercise their rights satisfactorily. Both Dominique, high-ranking border officer, and Luc, legal counsel who represents non-citizens in waiting zones, agree on this point. Dominique admits:

> It is [ZAPI 3] a more appropriate structure to exercise rights than the terminal. At the terminal, where the person's rights are notified, she has access to a phone and can make international calls. There are no difficulties but it is not a place that is suitable to host the person over a long period of time. It is not suitable at all to ensure confidentiality for interviews with lawyers or others so she is transferred to this structure [ZAPI 3] (Interview, September 2013).

Yet the law considers the waiting zone as a homogeneous space; it does not distinguish between airport terminals and the detention center. Lawyers representing the border police in proceedings before the custody and liberty judge often state that "the waiting zone is one and indivisible", in response to the other party's counsel who claims that his or her client's access to rights was impeded by extended stay in terminals (observations).

Several officers that I met during the course of my visits insisted that detainees spent as little time as possible in airport terminals. For example, Philippe asserted: "Detainees are normally kept four to five hours before their transfer" (observations). However, the testimonies of the detainees I spoke with, did not match the policemen's affirmation. Time spent in confinement can be lengthy. Rosalita, a young Nicaraguan woman whose trip to Madrid was interrupted at CDG, contended that she had spent 12 hours in terminal 2E's holding cell upon her arrival from Nicaragua. As for Alfredo, a Cuban national who had departed from Bamako with the intent of reaching Sweden, he claimed having spent 12 to 13 hours per day in terminal 2E for the past week. Inspectors of places of liberty also noted that time spent in confinement in terminals was extremely variable: from five minutes to 14 hours (CGLPL 2013, 47–48) in terminal 2F. They arrived at this conclusion after studying terminal 2F's police registries from December 1 to December 10, 2013. About one third of individuals had spent more than four hours at the station. Makaremi (2007) observed that officers at CDG had a strategy to curtail detainees' willingness to resist return; non-citizens were sleep and food-deprived in order to make them more compliant.

Those that I met in terminal cells had not been subjected to such measures. However, confinement in a restricted space with other individuals without easy access to water (distributed only during meal times) or sanitary facilities is in itself trying. Detaining those who are to be returned in the airport's terminals for lengthy periods of time may be a strategy to discourage them from staying. Luc, a legal counsel, deplores the lack of transparency that surrounds the time of transfer from terminals to ZAPI 3. He points out that exercising rights in terminals is much more challenging:

> You are told that the person in question or the non-citizen is in a position to exercise his or her rights from the first minutes. The issue that we run into today and that I lament is there is no transparency regarding the transfer of people from the terminal to the accommodation zone [*zone d'hébergement*]. Why? Because the person who stays in the terminal from 7:00 am to 5:00 pm is not in the same conditions to exercise his or her rights than in the accommodation zone where he or she can have access to family, talk, receive family members and send a fax through the Red Cross which is on site, or ask to meet a doctor anytime if he or she wishes. There is a minimum of infrastructure. But in terminals these individuals are put in a room and access is closed (Interview, October 2013).

Detention at ZAPI 3 is not devoid of challenges when it comes to exercising rights (cf. chapter 7). But, at least, detainees can receive the visit of family members, lawyers, consulate employees and friends as well as communicate more easily with Anafé and the Red Cross. In addition to experiencing isolation, detainees are also subjected to arbitrariness in airport terminals.

4 Arbitrariness and Asymmetrical Power Relations

Generally, those confined and their visitors are subjected to arbitrary and diverse rules, varying greatly from one authority to the next. The treatment an individual receives, therefore, varies significantly from one terminal to the next, and even within one terminal under the supervision of the very same authority. Not unlike Melville's characters of Turkey and Nippers, whose energy levels and behaviors fluctuate according to the time of day (in the short story *Bartleby, the Scrivener*, 1853),[9] the very same official might display distinct attitudes

9 In this story, the characters Nippers and Turkey are law-copyists, working for a Wall Street lawyer. Turkey is a great employee in the morning but becomes too energetic in the afternoon,

as time unfolds. For example, during the first visit to a terminal at Charles de Gaulle airport I witnessed a border officer's transformation: within the range of an hour Philippe went from being very welcoming and eager to please to quiet and aggressive, reaching a point where he stopped answering questions. At the end of the visit he explained the reason for his anger: his colleagues had not come to relieve him of his duties. Having started his shift at 5:00 am, by the time of the lunchtime visit Philippe was starving. In a place where people must rely on authorities for everything, every change in mood or well-being affects both detainees and researcher's access to information.

Belcher and Martin (2013, 408) explain that policies of access to detention centers in the United States "changed randomly and without notice, or were interpreted differently by detention center staff members". In airport terminals, similarly, there is no guarantee that NGO visitors will be able to effectively communicate with detainees. On a Saturday in February 2014, I experienced first-hand at Charles de Gaulle what Martin had observed in the United States. The police officer accompanying me attempted to silence both detainees and myself by affirming that I could not discuss any "procedures" with the individuals confined in terminal 2E, claiming that my mandate was limited to verifying detention conditions. This precluded any conversation about rights or administrative or judicial procedures pertaining to the detainees' status. When challenged with the observation that these requirements were nowhere to be found in the law, Jérémie replied that they were specified in an internal policy note, which I could not see as I was not a civil servant. The visit posed a significant ethical dilemma: the officer, standing less than one meter apart from myself and detainees, listened closely to the conversations. I attempted to bypass the police officer's illegitimate conditions by first engaging with English and Spanish-speaking detainees in their language. When it became apparent that the police understood neither English nor Spanish, I could still gather some valuable information: I heard about an allegation of mistreatment at the hands of the police of a woman named Maria for the second time. This incident probably explained why the authority did not want me to speak openly with detainees.

However, this strategy was limited by the common word origins of French, Spanish, and English. Jérémie put an abrupt end to the conversation after hearing the word "court", which is the same in French and Spanish (*tribunal*). It was particularly heart-breaking not to be able to explain asylum procedures to an exhausted and obviously traumatized Syrian asylum seeker (who kept

making mistakes at work. As for Nippers, his attitude is inversely proportional to that of Turkey: he is irritable and nervous in the morning and calmer in the afternoon.

saying: "please, don't attack me"). The officer told me it was forbidden to discuss "political asylum". When it was time to speak to Francophone detainees, I asked the only question I could think of that would not endanger them: Had they eaten? The answer to this question was evident as garbage and picnic leftovers were scattered all over the room. Fearing that detainees could be the targets of retaliation if they complained, I chose to ask the minimum amount of information possible.

Ironically, this uncomfortable situation repeated itself shortly afterwards. After exiting terminal 2E, I took a small break before heading towards terminal 2A. During the previous visits, I had learned that different police officers were in charge of the different terminal clusters (terminals 2E, 2F and 2G constitute one such cluster: every morning the 300 policemen assigned to this cluster are distributed across the three terminals). According to what I had observed, the police officer in charge of terminal 2E was different from the policeman in charge of terminal 2A. However, when I presented myself at the entrance of terminal 2A, asking to visit the detention cell there, the same policeman greeted me. Apparently, on Saturdays, the same officer covered multiple terminals. Unfortunately, the two individuals held in terminal 2A were both Francophone. I quickly left. Ultimately, it is the researcher's ethical duty to decide when to stop asking questions and leave, however frustrating the situation.

Officers also referred to detainees' possible dangerousness to oppose private conversations. Arnaud, border officer in terminal 1, contended that he could not leave me alone with the detainees, as "we do not know who these people are". This measure, justified by reference to my own safety, prevented me from talking privately to the detainees. As Agier (2008) points out, by isolating migrants, States convey the message that there is something wrong with them: they must be isolated for a reason. Arnaud displayed a friendly attitude and probably meant well, frequently interrupting my conversation with detainees to provide extra information ("I am helping you a little"). Arnaud used the third person to refer to the non-citizens sitting next to us, explaining the procedures applicable to detainees in general. Not only was this situation ethically problematic, it also confused my position in the eyes of detainees, who associated me with the authorities and felt I was not to be trusted. Establishing rapport with both policemen and detainees at the same time constituted an impossible task. Although NGO workers possess more power and freedom than detainees, they too are subjected to the arbitrary power of authorities. Noémie notes the fundamental power gap between officers and NGO affiliates:

> I know that we try to be diplomatic with the border police. We know very well that otherwise they can shut all doors; they make the decisions.

> When we visit terminals, we chat with officers as if we were friends and afterwards we are astonished [by their answers]. But we should never forget that it is them who have the power to open the waiting zone for us, it is a constant negotiation and we have to play along (Interview, September 2013).

Power differential, isolation and barriers to accessing rights combine to create an environment conducive to psychological and physical mistreatment.

5 Psychological and Physical Violence

Terminals are the waiting zone's spaces where detainees are more likely to experience the highest levels of psychological and physical violence. Mistreatment is particularly prevalent prior to or upon placement in the waiting zone, when officers try to assess the individual's travel motives over interviews of varying duration. It is also very likely to happen during attempts to return the individual, especially against his or her will. Different detainees confided having been subject to instances of abuse. Rosalita, a young Nicaraguan national who landed in terminal 2E in February 2014, told me that her final destination was initially Madrid, a city that she wished to visit as a tourist. The border police thought otherwise, and tried to force her to admit that her intent was to work in Madrid. Officers told her that if she did not tell the truth, they would make her clean the airport. She was certain she had understood correctly, as her interpreter had conveyed the officers' words. Several detainees complained that officers made fun of them and applied pressure. For example, Carmen, another Central-American national, explained to the police that she was a masseuse; but she was ridiculed and called a prostitute.

During the challenging visit aforementioned (February 22) when I was forbidden to discuss any "procedures" with detainees, I heard about an allegation of mistreatment for the second time. Alfredo, a Cuban national, recounted that policemen had beaten Maria, a Central American woman on the morning of the previous day (February 21). Maria had been seated just outside of the holding cell when he himself was brought to detention. Although Alfredo had not personally witnessed the event, when he arrived she was crying and had many bruises on her stomach. His testimony concurred with that of a group of Central American women I had met in the afternoon of the 21st at the detention center. In the morning, they had been held at the terminal in a room close to that of Maria and had heard the incident. They had heard officers telling Maria that she was going to be put "in a dark room alone".

Because the group of Central American citizens in ZAPI 3 had told me that Maria was now confined in terminal 2F, I decided to visit this terminal's holding room. After waiting for a fairly long time, I was finally invited to observe the end of the interview of a non-admitted Nicaraguan national. Philippe, the officer, insisted that this constituted a favor: usually it was forbidden for visitors to witness interviews, but he was making an exception for me. Was this an attempt to distract me from the case of Maria? It is impossible to know, but when I finally got to see the holding cell, there was no trace of her. Philippe was very tense and inquired when I left: "Could you see everything that you wanted to see?" I shared Maria's case with Anafé employee Lise, who explained that Anafé had never managed to get the border police convicted for violence on detainees. Usually, such cases are riddled with issues: eyewitnesses are lacking, and the alleged victim has left the country and cannot testify. The case of Maria was no different: she had been returned and nobody had witnessed directly her abuse. Nothing could be done.

Lise explained that she had attended a meeting with the Ministry of the Interior during which she had mentioned instances of violence. The Ministry refused to take the allegations of mistreatment into account, challenging her instead to present proofs and to state what criminal procedure had been launched (Interview, December 2013). Yet, France is a party to regional and international conventions prohibiting torture and other cruel, inhuman or degrading treatment or punishment.[10] As such, France has an obligation to prevent and repress torture and other acts of ill treatment. But the Ministry of the Interior is not pro-active in terms of safeguarding human rights when it comes to the waiting zone. This case is representative of the government's approach to the waiting zone in general: the Ministry of the Interior will not take steps to address alleged rights violations unless forced to do so by legal proceedings. To unveil the mechanisms behind abuse, it is important to study how authorities perceive detainees.

10 Amongst other Conventions, France ratified the UN Convention against Torture and Other Cruel, Inhuman or Degrading Treatment or Punishment in 1986 and the Council of Europe's European Convention for the Prevention of Torture and Inhuman or Degrading Treatment or Punishment in 1994. Furthermore, the prohibition of torture and other forms of ill-treatment is an established *jus cogens* norm. Cf. Weissbrodt and Heilman, 2011.

6 Authorities' Perception of Detainees

In order to determine who should come in or not, border agents screen passengers and their stories, on the lookout for suspicious elements. Some traveling rationales trigger red flags. Salter (2007, 59) observes:

> Border guards build up a common stock of acceptable travel narratives and traveler characteristics ... In addition to being from a refugee-prone country or region, guards are attendant to other risk factors: buying a plane ticket in cash, having another person purchase the ticket, purchasing a ticket close to departure time, traveling a long distance for a short time ... Travelers are reduced from citizens, foreigners, and refugees, with complex identities and claims to home into objects of danger or benefit, which perhaps afford entry or exit into the national population.

At CDG, after this screening, those denied entry or seeking asylum are placed in waiting zones,[11] carrying the category that has been assigned to them at the border. They are either to be returned or to be heard by the refugee agency. In either case, those placed in waiting zones are suspect and not to be trusted. In fact, some agents are so convinced that detainees are liars, resorting to any possible method to deceive them, that they dismiss everything they say as unreliable. During one March visit to terminal 2A, I met Laurent from Senegal, whose journey to Portugal had stopped at CDG. Laurent recounted that he had previously been refused entry into Schengen territory at Lille (a city in the North of France). As I was not aware of Lille having an airport, I asked Laurent to confirm that I had understood him correctly. Laurent explained that he had flown from Senegal to Algeria and then to Lille, where he was turned away. After this visit, Henri, the agent accompanying me, was concerned that I might be too gullible. He asserted: "There is no airport in Lille. I hope you do not believe everything that they tell you! " He went on: "These people do not have money for tourism; it is impossible to come from the other end of the world for just three days". When I left Henri, he reiterated his point: "Whatever you do, do not go to the airport in Lille!" Yet, Lille does have an airport, serving flights to and from Algeria as well as Portugal.[12] In the eyes of some authorities, people lose their individuality once in the waiting zone: they join the ranks of faceless "*Inads*" whose word is necessarily untrustworthy. The term "*Inad*"

11 Unless immediately returned, in which case they will never reach the waiting zone status.

12 According to the brochure edited by Lille Airport for the Fall and Winter 2013. The brochure was no longer available from the Internet at the time of writing.

comes from the International Air Transport Association (IATA) and is used by French border agents. It designates an "inadmissible person", defined as "a person who is or will be refused admission to a State by its authorities" (IATA October 15, 2014, 4). As anthropologist Agier (2008) observes, what makes a foreigner (*étranger*) is not an identity but a place (from a material and symbolic standpoint) and a context. The waiting zone is one of several places creating the foreigner. To some authorities, the waiting zone embodies an outside as well as a supposedly natural inequality and difference (Agier, 2008). Detainees are lumped together based on their administrative status; they have not been admitted to the country.

Henri envisioned his border-enforcement job as necessary to protect his own welfare as well as that of the country. Sociologist Bauman (2004, 5) contends that modernity produces "wasted humans", i.e. "redundant" or "excessive" beings. As new ways of making a living emerge, previous ways are degraded and devalued, thereby stripping individuals of their livelihood. Present times are also characterized by the fullness of our planet: there are no territories left to colonize, "no man's lands" have disappeared. Bauman (2004) demonstrates how, in the past, such territories were used as "dumping grounds" for the wasted humans who had been rendered undesirable by the processes of modernization. The conjunction of these two phenomena (i.e. the production of human waste and the fullness of our planet) results in "an acute crisis of the human waste disposal industry" (Bauman 2004, 6). Bauman equips us with conceptual tools to understand the perspective of some border agents towards both their jobs and individuals placed in the waiting zone. Henri insisted that we (French people) should help ourselves first, our family and our neighbors, otherwise we would be committing suicide (*hara kiri* were his precise words). He noted that from a humanistic perspective, everyone should be able to come in. However it was not possible, due to current (unfavorable) economic conditions. Henri therefore conceived his job as a shield against social redundancy: "excessive beings" had to be kept outside of the country for it to thrive. Bauman (2004, 56) writes:

> Immigrants, let us note, fit better into such a purpose than any other category of genuine or putative villains. There is a sort of "elective affinity" between immigrants (that human waste of distant parts of the globe unloaded into "our own backyard") and the least bearable of our own, home-grown fears. When all places and positions feel shaky and are deemed no longer reliable, the sight of immigrants rubs salt into the wound. Immigrants, and particularly the fresh arrivals among them, exude the faint odour of the waste disposal tip which in its many disguises haunts the

> nights of the prospective casualties of rising vulnerability. For their detractors and haters, immigrants embody-visibly, tangibly, in the flesh- the inarticulate yet hurtful and painful presentiment of their own disposability. One is tempted to say that were there no immigrants knocking at the doors, they would have to be invented.

Financial matters occupied a central place in my conversation with Henri, who was disgruntled by a recent talk he had had with an inspector of places of deprivation of liberty. According to Henri, the inspector used to work for an NGO "whose role was to annoy the government". Now retired, the inspector worked in such a position five days a month and allegedly complained to Henri that his salary was low. Henri remarked that "the inspector did not realize that some people did not make as much", especially since this money was supplementing his retirement pension. As for asylum seekers, Henri told me they were receiving many State subsidies. I remarked that French law prohibited asylum seekers from working during the assessment of their claim. To my observation, Henri replied: "I do not say that they live well, but my wife works in the department in charge of allocating subsidies, and they do receive some!" He continued: "People who live in poverty at home will always be better off in France, because here there are NGOs distributing meals and helping out". Henri also admitted that he was not in favor of people receiving benefits from the State, but preferred when people made their own money through entrepreneurship.

Henri was not the only agent to resent non-citizens. Valentin, whom I met at a terminal's reception desk, confided that he was about to leave the force, as he was terribly disappointed with the way he and his colleagues were treated by their superiors. He explained that work conditions were disastrous, with superiors refusing to permit breaks to be taken or to take into account doctor's notes. According to this young policeman, four colleagues had committed suicide over the course of a year and a half and their superiors could not care less. He expressed resentment, deploring the fact that, according to him, foreign nationals received more attention and care than themselves. No NGO was interested in checking how police officers were treated.

Authorities are not a monolith and should not be essentialized: agents do have different stances on both their work and non-citizens placed in the waiting zone. On a different day, Simon, a policeman at one of the terminal's reception desks looked at my access card. When he saw the name Human Rights Watch, his interest was piqued. He asked: "It [the NGO] is well-known, right"? He said he regretted his career choice and confided the torments that his job entailed. He lamented that some of his colleagues were racists and that detainees were just "Inads" to them. He explained that some colleagues did their job without asking themselves any questions: "They come here, do their job and go home. They are happy with themselves at the end of the day". Simon recalled: "One of my superiors told me, 'you are like me, you would prefer borders to be closed'. But it is not my wish at all, I have never asked for anything like that". He reminded me that, historically speaking, we all came from Africa and confessed that there were things he was pressured into doing. Simon was visibly tense and scared. He told me he had a lot more to say and wanted to meet again but outside of his workplace. He explained that he would call from a public phone and use a pseudonym to set a meeting. Unfortunately, Simon was never interviewed, as he did not call. I do not claim to have depicted comprehensively the viewpoints of representative of all of the border agents at CDG. Instead, I have merely attempted here to present some of the perspectives of some of the agents I met during my terminal visits.

To conclude, while the law treats the waiting zone as a homogeneous space, exercising rights in airport terminals is particularly challenging. Individuals may spend lengthy periods of time in holding cells where they experience a high level of isolation. Despite the existence of formal agreements between NGOs and the Ministry of the Interior, access to detainees is subject to the border officers' goodwill. Conditions of access are highly variable, reminding the researcher and NGO worker of the pronounced power differential at play in this part of the waiting zone. When HRW retrieved visitor's cards, the civil servant working for the Ministry of the Interior explained that we could visit whenever and as much as we wanted. However, HRW's office soon received a call (after two visits) from the Ministry of the Interior explaining that it would be appreciated if we could inform authorities of visiting plans in advance. I had planned to carry out more visits of CDG's terminals but stopped after eight visits,[13] as I was starting to feel really unwelcome. Officers ridiculed me with remarks such as "you must really like it here to come back so often" or "she has taken a subscription: 10 entries with one free!" Some were rather threatening, telling me that I was very well known on the airport platform (*connue comme le loup blanc*) or that I should stop coming.

Some authorities' mindsets towards non-citizens and their border enforcement jobs may be conducive to ill treatment. Those placed in waiting zones are seen as being impoverished and as undifferentiated masses to be kept at bay for the economic sake of the country. Once categorized as "non-admitted" or "asylum seekers", individuals disappear. As Bauman (2004, 78) argues: "All

13 I carried out one visit in January, five visits in February and two visits in March 2014. Terminal 1, 2A, 2C, 2D and 2E were all visited three times. Terminal 2F was visited twice.

waste, including wasted humans, tends to be piled up indiscriminately on the same refuse tip. The act of assigning to waste puts an end to differences, individualities, idiosyncrasies". The very structure of the waiting zone is also conducive to abuse: individuals who are wronged are usually returned and do not testify. This chapter has unveiled practices and discourses that occur in airport terminals, spaces where third parties rarely venture. The following chapter explores the second part of CDG's waiting zone: the detention center.

CHAPTER 7

ZAPI 3: a Place of Deprivation of Liberty Where Access to Rights Remains Challenging

The detention center is called ZAPI 3 (*zone d'attente pour personnes en instance*- waiting zone for persons whose case is pending). It constitutes the most accessible part of CDG's waiting zone. Anne, an employee from Anafé explains: "(…) It (CDG) is the most visible of waiting zones, taking into account the fact that waiting zones are not very visible" (Interview, December 2013). Since 2004, Anafé noticed that the situation of non-citizens significantly improved inside the detention facility, which became a "showcase" (*vitrine*). Police officers are used to showing ZAPI 3 to visitors. The officer accompanying HRW researchers and myself during a visit in January 2014 told us that ZAPI 3 was a "very sensitive" place (*c'est très sensible*) as they received the visits of MPs, UNHCR, NGOs, embassies and lawyers. Previously, in September 2013, Dominique, the high-ranking officer who gave me a tour of the detention center, had insisted that I had seen ZAPI 3 as it always was. Nothing had been modified for me: "It has been said that it is a place where people are tortured, but you can see, they were not told about our visit, it is always like that. We do not embellish anything for visitors". NGO presence in ZAPI 3 is unique: Anafé volunteers are at the detention center two (or three) days a week. As for the Red Cross, its employees work in ZAPI 3 seven days a week, twenty-four hours a day. I observed that liberty and custody judges at Bobigny often told non-citizens that they could find Anafé and the Red Cross at ZAPI 3, as if NGO presence made confinement acceptable and guaranteed the respect of rights.

Yet, the presence of visitors or third parties does not guarantee satisfactory access to rights in ZAPI 3. In this space, the issues are not so much the material conditions of detention but rather the issue of confinement as well as access to rights. ZAPI 3 very much remains a place of deprivation of liberty characterized by limited visibility and police omnipresence. ZAPI 3 is a place where abuse and tension transpire, in contradiction with euphemistic discourses presenting it as a hotel or a place of recreation. NGOs and their individual members face multiple challenges in the daily exercise of their mission, forcing them to reflect on and negotiate their positioning.

 | DOI:10.1163/9789004383500_011

1 Background Information on ZAPI 3

ZAPI 3 was built specifically to confine individuals spending the night in CDG's waiting zone. In 2010 and 2011, detainees spent an average of 3.10 days and 3.5 days at CDG respectively (Anafé January 2013, 67). ZAPI 3 is unique in terms of its capacity: 163 detainees in the adult area and six in the minor zone. On the ground level the following spaces can be found: the offices of the border police unit in charge of analysis and follow up of immigration affairs (*GASAI*), the refugee agency office and three rooms for visitors (such as family, friends, lawyers, embassy or consulate representatives and others). CDG is the only waiting zone where OFPRA, the refugee agency, has an office. Detainees are kept away from these spaces by a set of closed doors. However, they can circulate in the rest of the ground level and access phones, two TV rooms, the dining room and the medical facility as well as a small outside yard. The "minor zone" (*zone mineurs*), specifically dedicated to unaccompanied minors, is also located on the ground level but only opens from inside. The detainees' bedrooms and showers are located on the first floor, as well as Anafé's and the Red Cross' offices and a small children playroom. What are these two NGOs' missions?

The Red Cross' mandate in the waiting zone is fourfold. The organization has been offering psychological support and provision of "any useful information" to those detained in the waiting zone since 2003. It also commits to providing detainees with material support through the distribution of phone cards, childcare products, hot drinks, and clothes. Last but not least, the Red Cross acts as a mediator between foreign nationals and civil servants fulfilling their duties in the waiting zone. The term "mediator" (*médiateur*), which designates a Red Cross employee working in the waiting zone, seems to derive from this mission statement. The organization's internal report states that: "The Red Cross facilitates in general the relations between the police and the persons who are held (*personnes maintenues*), as well as with all the other stakeholders in the waiting zone" (Red Cross 2013, 11). The Red Cross intervenes on behalf of non-citizens, requesting information from the border police regarding their individual cases. Employees also forward to the police any specific request a non-citizen may have, such as being returned to a country other than that of his or her departure. Mediators may help the asylum seeker "to structure his or her asylum story and encourage him or her to be specific by asking questions". This assistance has to take place "while respecting the Red Cross' neutrality principle" (Red Cross 2013, 11). As of 2012, twenty-three plurilingual mediators worked in small teams in rotating shifts, enabling the Red Cross to be present in ZAPI 3 twenty-four hours a day, seven days a week.

Anafé's mission differs from that of the Red Cross. On March 5, 2004, Anafé signed a Memorandum of Understanding with the Ministry of the Interior whereby the organization secured the permission to access ZAPI 3 permanently, which is at any point in time and without any time limits. Anafé employees explained that the NGO decided to use this privileged access to offer legal aid to those placed in waiting zones to compensate for the lack thereof. In practice, Anafé is present at the center two or three days a week (Interview, December 2013). Employees Lise and Anne described the organization's mission: Anafé strives to ensure the respect of existing laws applicable to individuals arriving at the border, but also tries to modify laws and practices by either legal action or negotiation, although the latter is more complicated. In addition, Anafé also aims to inform the public about practices and proceedings at the border and to assist those placed in waiting zones (Interview, December 2013).

During the course of my research, I visited ZAPI 3 five times. Dominique, a high-ranking border police officer, accompanied me for the first visit, which occurred after I interviewed him in my capacity as doctoral researcher. I carried out the four other visits as a Human Rights Watch volunteer; half of these visits took place with HRW researchers, and half were conducted alone. Formally interviewing Red Cross employees working in the waiting zone proved impossible. The Red Cross mediator I had secured an interview with (outside of ZAPI 3), cancelled the meeting at the last minute. She explained that her supervisor, the director of the Red Cross in the waiting zone, had forbidden her to answer any questions until I specifically obtained permission from the headquarters' Department of Communication. After numerous emails and phone calls, the contact person at the communication's department announced that I would receive permission, provided I signed a confidentiality agreement. However, I never received the said agreement and was always told to continue waiting. Hence, the data comes from conversations with mediators during participant-observation in the waiting zone or from interviews with former Red Cross mediators. In general, the Red Cross' mission in the waiting zone appears to be shrouded in secrecy. Previous researchers also failed to obtain detailed material on the Red Cross' activities. Bacon (2013), who explored the relationships between ZAPI 3 actors in her masters' thesis, explained that she could not interview any mediators. The Red Cross director for the waiting zone told her that he had forwarded her request to the communication's department but had never received any answer (Bacon, 2013). Some mediators are aware of this culture of secrecy. During one visit of the minor zone, one of them told me: "The less we talk, the better it is at the Red Cross". The detention center is a place either marked by secrecy or euphemistic discourses.

2 Euphemistic Discourses: ZAPI 3 as a "Hotel"

In the early 1990s, some discourses minimized the issue of confinement, obscuring what was at stake for those detained in the international zone or in what was construed as its extension. Some actors expressed the idea that those confined in the waiting zone were hosted in desirable hotel-like conditions. Before parliamentarians, Marchand, the Minister of the Interior who introduced the 1991 amendment that later became the waiting zone legislation, insisted that non-citizens in transit zones were not detained: they were not on French territory (cf. chapter 2). Contrary to non-citizens detained on French territory, those in waiting zones were free to move and therefore did not need as many legal safeguards. Marchand introduced a new legal term to distinguish the two categories of non-citizens: *retenus* (detained) are to be removed after staying illegally in the country whereas *maintenus* (held) are placed in waiting zones. This different vocabulary conveys the idea that people in waiting zones experience a greater degree of freedom, the term *maintenu* not expressing as strong a constraint as *retenu.* This semantic distinction having no legitimate basis (chapter 2), I use the English term "detention" to refer to the deprivation of liberty to which people are subject when placed under the legal regime of the waiting zone.

In turn, parliamentarians embraced the government's discourse and legal language. In June 1992, just before the National Assembly adopted the law that established the waiting zone, MP Pezet told parliamentarians of his recent visit to the hotel Arcade at CDG airport, where non-admitted citizens were confined. Pezet was both a lawyer and the National Assembly's law commission rapporteur: his discourse carried a certain weight. He was addressing the MPs as a person who had examined the proposed bill scrupulously and therefore had a better understanding of it.[1] This is how he describes his visit:

> I had the opportunity of going to Roissy very early in the morning, accompanied by an administrator from the National Assembly. We could

1 According to the website of the National Assembly, permanent commissions have a double function: preparing the legislative debate as well as informing MPs and controlling the government. The law commission (*commission des lois constitutionnelles, de la législation et de l'administration générale de la République*) is a permanent commission. Cf. Summary sheet n°24: permanent commissions (*Fiches de synthèse n°24: les commissions permanentes*), available at: http://www2.assemblee-nationale.fr/decouvrir-l-assemblee/role-et-pouvoirs-de-l-assemblee-nationale/les-organes-de-l-assemblee-nationale/les-commissions-permanentes. Accessed January 22, 2016. See also the Regulation manual of the National Assembly (*Règlement de l'Assemblée Nationale*), Chapter IX.

> observe what was going on. We saw the Arcade hotel of which so much has been said. A hotel just like any other! We go to the first floor: the doors are just like all the others. Of course, the police are there, there is a register with the name of the people staying on this floor and their room number. We visited these rooms. They brought back old memories. They look like youth hostels-three beds per room-but they are quite decent [*correct*] and each one has a shower. There are no bars to the windows.
>
> French National Assembly debates June 24 1992, 2696

Chapters 1 and 2 traced how, in the 1980s and early 1990s, non-citizen populations were detained in a legal vacuum. Asylum seekers were particularly at risk of *refoulement*. Pezet compared the situation of those detained indefinitely after fleeing their countries to that of young travellers staying willingly in a youth hostel. This comparison ignored the plight of the former.

The government's willingness to understate the deprivation of liberty also transpires in the legal terminology still in use to refer to the waiting zones' physical spaces of confinement. The Law on the Waiting Zone reads that the waiting zone may comprise "one or several hotel-like accommodations" located in or nearby the train station, port or airport (CESEDA December 2015, article L221-2).[2] Charles de Gaulle's waiting zone is equipped with the biggest of such "hotel-like accommodation": ZAPI 3. It is the only structure that was built specifically to detain non-admitted travelers. The number "three" is attached to the place's name as other structures previously served to detain those subjected to the waiting zone framework at CDG. ZAPI 3 opened in January 2001. Before this date, rejected foreign nationals were confined in nearby hotels (such as Arcade and Ibis, called "ZAPI 1") and then in a part of the Mesnil-Amelot *rétention* center (ZAPI 2) (Médecins du Monde March 2003).

Fieldwork revealed that some people currently working in Charles de Gaulle's waiting zone also adopted the legal language. During a terminal visit in February 2014, I saw a young and dynamic interpreter explain to Isabela, a distressed Nicaraguan national whose final destination was Madrid, that she would be taken to the "police hotel" (*hotel de la policía*). Inspectors of places of deprivation of liberty (cf. chapter 3) also witnessed an officer explain to a

---

2 *Elle peut inclure, sur l'emprise, ou à proximité, de la gare, du port ou de l'aéroport ou à proximité du lieu de débarquement, un ou plusieurs lieux d'hébergement assurant aux étrangers concernés des prestations de type hôtelier* (CESEDA December 2015, L221-2).

rejected traveller that "ZAPI is a hotel managed by the police" (CGLPL 2013, 64). Interestingly, several detainees I met referred to ZAPI 3 as a "hotel".

Some actors still consider CDG's detention center as a place of recreation, particularly for young people. Pierre, one of the doctors working at ZAPI 3, depicts the detention center as a sort of summer camp: "When you are 25, it is nice here; they make noise, they prevent the others from sleeping" (observations). With regard to unaccompanied minors in the minor zone, he remarks that they have access to toys. The Red Cross manages the minor zone in ZAPI 3. The organization's internal report (2013) presents the typical daily schedule for children in the minor zone. This schedule curiously resembles one that could be found in a summer camp or in day care:

7:45 am:	waking up, shower
8:30 am:	breakfast
9:00 am:	minors do their laundry if necessary
9:30 am:	writing down the date, seasons, holidays: in order to be able to situate themselves in time alphabetization is offered to those willing to learn French language[3]
10:30 am:	several activities are offered to minors in the morning: dancing, singing, soccer, etc ...
12:30 pm:	lunch at the cafeteria
1:00 pm:	free time: reading, watching TV, napping
3:00pm:	collective activities: artistic activities, board games, etc ...
4:00 pm:	snack preparation with the minors' participation
4:30 pm:	snack at the cafeteria
5:00 pm:	return in minor zone
5:30 pm:	collective activities: dancing, music, wii, etc ...
6:30 pm:	dinner
7:00 pm:	return in minor zone
Activities:	reading, stories, board games, TV ...
10:30:	bedtime

In spite of these discourses idealizing ZAPI 3 by portraying it as a hotel or place of recreation, it remains a detention center where individuals are deprived of liberty and face forced return.

3 The term "alphabetization" implies that all non-Francophone minors are illiterate, which is not true.

3 A Place of Deprivation of Liberty Where Tension Transpires

Even google maps, google's mapping application, designates ZAPI 3 as a "hotel" (but places the expression "holding area" in brackets next to it). Yet, when exploring Charles de Gaulle airport's compounds with google maps, it is impossible to get too close to ZAPI 3, no doubt for security reasons. Surrounded by a high fence topped up with barbed wire, ZAPI 3 hardly resembles a hotel (cf. figure 2).

According to an internal report from the Red Cross (2013), about 15 video surveillance cameras are posted both within and outside the building. Windows cannot open and the furniture is attached to the floor for security reasons. Border officers frequently police the corridors, 24 hours a day. They call detainees through speakers between 7:00 am and 9:00 pm (Red Cross, 2013 and observations). Raoul, an Anafé volunteer with three years of experience, describes ZAPI 3 as a place "where the level of stress is unbelievable" (Interview, October 2013). Furthermore, detainees routinely experience psychological mistreatment and humiliation at ZAPI 3. Raoul witnessed countless racist jokes on the part of the border police. For example, he heard the police call a Chinese national through speakers with a strong fake Chinese accent: "M. Chang is called downstairs with his luggage". He narrates another incident that

FIGURE 2 ZAPI 3 (June 2019). Copyright Rafael Moreno.

took place during a summer. In response to a detainee's request to lower the blinds to block out the sunlight, an agent replied, "Kirikou, you are not used to sunshine over there?" (Interview, October 2013). Kirikou is the name of a small African boy in the eponym-animated film.

Red Cross and Anafé employees and volunteers explain that working at ZAPI 3 takes a toll. Being in ZAPI 3, as a detainee or as a worker, is physically and emotionally draining. Laura, a former Red Cross mediator, explains that she had to leave her job after two years because it was a "very tough and tiring job" (Interview, August 2013). As for Raoul, the Anafé volunteer, he explains that he regularly needs breaks from the waiting zone, as assisting individuals there is too trying:

> Humanly it is not always easy. I went a lot to the waiting zone, and it is true that since three years I am there a lot, but there are times where I stop going to the waiting zone. Because I go there a lot and after going there three times a week for three months I stop, I cannot do it anymore, I have a knot in the stomach before going (Interview, October 2013).

In the past, tension used to reach even higher levels in ZAPI 3. Paul, former Red Cross mediator, explains that over the course of the eight years he spent in ZAPI 3, the Red Cross managed to secure some progress:

> It was very difficult at first for everybody. When we arrived, the waiting zone [ZAPI 3] was packed with a capacity of 164, anyway I do not recall. Tension was tangible, officers were waking up people at 4:00 am in order to present them to the Court of First Instance at 10:00 am, they make them go downstairs, with calls through speakers at any time of the day and night, with a [very loud] volume. Persons and their sleep were not respected, which meant that tension was more tangible.
>
> Interview with PAUL, August 2013

The Red Cross managed to reduce tension, by waking up people individually by knocking gently on their bedroom doors, instead of the police calling individuals through speakers or knocking on their door violently with their guns. Paul also credits the Red Cross for stopping overnight calls through speakers. When ZAPI 3 first opened, there were barely enough beds and detainees had to be returned promptly to make room for the next wave of arrivals. Paul recalls: "Policemen were under pressure, some people had to leave to be replaced, otherwise, if you do not have 60 individuals leave and today there are 60 individuals, there will be no more space and as the result ZAPI will be full, overloaded (Interview, August 2013)". Tension diminished over the years as fewer individuals were placed in the waiting zone.

ZAPI 3 is a place of confinement where detainees are subject to rules and constraints and have limited agency. People who are strangers to one another are assigned to the same bedroom, provided they are of the same sex. Women, men and families are all detained in the same facility. Women and men are detained together but do not share rooms, unless they are family members. Individuals are infantilized in ZAPI 3 and lose control over the simplest actions, like choice of TV channel. Detainees do not have direct access to the remote controlling of the television and need to ask the Red Cross to change channels (observations). Frequently, those confined in ZAPI 3 do not have access to their checked luggage, and have no choice but to spend the entire duration of their stay in the same set of clothes. There are no washing machines on site (observations and 2013 Red Cross report). A Bulgarian national I met in terminal 2C's holding room asked me to speak to the police on his behalf, explaining that he had spent 15 days without access to his luggage.

Anafé volunteer Raoul, believes that confinement in the waiting zone constitutes a form of violence in itself: "So violence is already here. It is inherent to the waiting zone. It is detention, presence of cameras, presence of police officers, lack of information, lack of interpreters, disgusting food that does not respect your religious convictions. Violence is inherent to the waiting zone" (Interview, October 2013). Some detainees find comfort in the presence of compatriots at ZAPI 3, while others experience their confinement as trauma. Amine, a young Algerian man I met in a terminal's holding cell in March 2014 confided: "At the hotel you are panicked in your room. At the hotel you do not understand anything". Lea, a liberty and custody judge at Bobigny, laments that some individuals are locked up in spite of them fulfilling all the criteria to enter France. The border police could release them but prefer them to be taken to court after four days in the waiting zone. Léa worries about the consequences:

> The administration forwards to us [liberty and custody judges] all the documents that we need to support our decision but does not release them before. It waits for us to take this decision. And it is a bit unfortunate because we have individuals who are shattered, who miss their connection, who miss their stay, who are traumatized. And it is unfortunate. Let us say that there are mistakes that are very unfortunate. And it happens quite often (Interview, November 2013).

FIGURE 3 Detainees in ZAPI 3's courtyard (June 2019). Copyright Rafael Moreno.

Detainees who explain that the conditions of detention are good in ZAPI 3 confide the difficulties of detention *per se*. Cherif, an Algerian national I talked to in February in terminal 2A's holding room, explained: "In ZAPI the accommodation conditions are acceptable, but we can feel that we are locked. There is a fence, you are not free" (cf. figure 3).

Detainees usually compared the entry policies at home and in the Schengen area. During a March visit, a woman from Burkina Faso told me it was the first time she was locked up, which was "humiliating":

> When you are locked up at home it is because you committed a very serious offence. At the airport in Burkina Faso if you do not have a visa it is possible to buy one on site at the airport. It costs the double: you pay 100 euros instead of 50. In Burkina Faso you can enter the territory without passport and visa. They give you the slip and you come back two days afterwards.

Many detainees do not understand why they are deprived of liberty and feel that they are being treated like criminals. This feeling may be compounded by police omnipresence in ZAPI 3.

4 Limited Visibility and Police Omnipresence

ZAPI 3 is more open to NGOs than other waiting zones. Nevertheless, it remains a structure with very limited visibility. ZAPI 3 is located in the freight area of the airport, close to the runway: detainees can watch planes take off and land from the small, enclosed yard where they are allowed to smoke. It is possible to reach ZAPI 3 using public transportation: a bus serving the airport compounds can be taken from the train station "Charles de Gaulle 1". However, ZAPI 3 visitors may well get lost on the way for lack of directions. At the time of research, the detention center was not featured on the bus map at the train station "Charles de Gaulle 1". Similarly, the bus stop's name (*Rue des Vignes*, Vineyard street, cf. figure 4) did not give any hint regarding the location of ZAPI 3 and there were no indications between the bus stop and ZAPI 3. Drivers faced the same issues, as no road signs indicated the center. No sign advertised ZAPI 3.

The public knows nothing or very little of ZAPI 3. For example, documentaries about CDG airport simply omit the presence of ZAPI 3. Public TV channel "France 3" (December 12, 2013) produced an extensive report (duration: 1h50) on the airport in December 2013, called "Roissy Charles de Gaulle, immediate boarding" (*Roissy Charles de Gaulle, embarquement immediat*). Explaining that

FIGURE 4 Bus stop *Rue des Vignes* (June 2019). Copyright Rafael Moreno.

Roissy was "a possible entry point for illegal immigrants", the report did talk about the work of the border police and showed a gangway control of passengers arriving from Istanbul. The voice over explained that several passengers were brought to the airport police station and returned to their countries of origin. However, the report failed to mention the confinement of these young women, eluding the existence of both terminals' holding cells and of ZAPI 3 entirely. In November 2018, I registered for a visit of the airport entitled "Exploration of Charles de Gaulle airport with access to the secure zone". As a researcher, I wanted to understand how ZAPI 3 was currently presented to the public. The visit was organized by "Explore Paris", an entity created by several stakeholders interested in the promotion of tourism in the greater Paris area. The visit started by a power point presentation on and by *Aéroports De Paris*, which manages CDG airport. The projected map of the airport grounds omitted the detention center and its attenant Court of First Instance. After undergoing thorough security checks at the entry point reserved for airport staff, participants were invited onto a bus and taken to the roads that surround the runways. As the bus drove by different buildings or installations, a speaker offered comments on their function. Although the visit bragged about taking the visitor "behind the scenes" of the airport plateform, the existence of the detention center and of the annex to the Bobigny Court of First Instance was not mentioned.

In general, ZAPI 3 is a place where detainees are highly reliant on the police. Phones with cameras are confiscated, as it is forbidden to take pictures on airport compounds. As a result, detainees have to request permission from the police in order to access their phone book (observations at the Bobigny Court). Furthermore, as Dominique explains, the police are in charge of the entire "administrative proceedings" in ZAPI 3 (Interview, September 2013). This means that asylum seekers first have to see the police in order to lodge a request to enter France on asylum grounds. The police then issue and forward a document (*procès-verbal de demande d'asile*) to the refugee agency (OFPRA) in ZAPI 3. This document "mentions the identity of the individual, the date of his or her entry to France, the documents he or she possesses, and policemen also explain to the individual the proceedings as well as his or her rights in the waiting zone. And we cannot hear anybody without this document" (Interview with Miriam, OFPRA agent in ZAPI 3, November 2013).

Likewise, the police notify claimants of the Ministry of the Interior's decision. Miriam explains: "We (OFPRA agents) send our opinion to the Ministry which forwards its decision to the border police which inform non-citizens". (Interview, November 2013). During the hearing, OFPRA agents write down the claimants' declarations. Asylum seekers have the right to receive a copy of this document (in French), which is of particular use should they decide to appeal the Ministry of the Interior's decision. Again, individuals receive their declarations from authorities in ZAPI 3. While officers swear that they do not read them, Anafé finds these practices problematic, and insists that it is not a practical matter but a question of principle: the police should not have access to these documents (Interview with Raoul, October 2013).[4]

Georges, an *ad hoc* administrator, observes that the detention center is a continuous space, making it a complicated structure to navigate, especially for asylum seekers. ZAPI 3 is not legible to detainees, as establishing the distinction between the police unit and the rest of the center is challenging:

> The waiting zone is not necessarily the best place to make an asylum-claim, this is certain. What I reproach is that it is always the same premises. In the same place we have the dormitory, the cafeteria, the TV, we go through a door and we are at OFPRA, we go through another door and we are at the GASAI [i.e. police unit in charge of following the administrative cases of those placed in the waiting zone], the lawyers, the visits it is almost the same rooms, we are at the same place, it is the same spatial unity. It is really unpleasant because I am convinced that one is not at ease over there. Even for myself, with my years of experience I do not go to the GASAI light-heartedly. To me it is a place of deprivation of liberty and at the GASAI I am not in my element, I am not home because it is a place … I know it is not a prison, but we are in a place that is not neutral (Interview, October 2013).

As George's observation shows, ZAPI 3 is a place where asymmetrical power relations prevail, and manifest spatially. NGO members have to be constantly aware of the power relations at play in ZAPI 3. Otherwise, they may put at further risk the individuals whom they are trying to assist. One day at ZAPI 3, I was confronted with instances of mistreatment. While I was conversing with Anafé's volunteers in the small room allocated to the organization, a group of six women from Central America burst into the office showing signs of great distress. Veronica, Joyce, Amanda, Jazmin, Gabriela and Lola recounted mistreatment by police during the attempt to force them on the plane. They

4 Anafé and OFPRA gave me inconsistent information. According to OFPRA, agents print off the declarations and forward them to the police in a sealed envelope (Interview with Stéphanie, Miriam and Charline, November 2013). However, according to Raoul, OFPRA faxes the declaration to border officers, who then put the document in a sealed envelope (Interview, October 2013).

showed the multiple contusions that covered their bodies. Jazmin had a certificate from the facility's doctor documenting the wounds.

Anafé's employees (contacted at the headquarters over the phone) told the volunteers that the women could file a complaint if they so wished. The Central American nationals agreed. As none of the volunteers spoke Spanish, I was the only one who could collect their testimonies. Anafé's employees warned us that we had to be careful and act with the highest discretion when preparing the complaints for the public prosecutor. The mistreated detainees could be returned overnight should the officers in ZAPI 3 realize they were launching complaints against their colleagues. We did manage to send the complaints to the State prosecutor without attracting the immediate attention of the police in ZAPI 3. However, the State prosecutor did not investigate the allegations of abuse. Gabriela and Amanda were returned shortly afterwards while Veronica, Joyce, Jazmin and Lola were sentenced to a few months in prison by a criminal court for remaining illegally on French territory (cf. section VI). In general, detainees experience multiple barriers to accessing remedies in case of mistreatment.

5 Barriers to Accessing Remedies in Case of Mistreatment

As the case of the Central American women shows, ZAPI 3 is the place where abuse that occurred in other spaces of the waiting zone becomes visible. Red Cross and Anafé workers usually do not witness first-hand the alleged facts (especially when it comes to physical violence) but hear of them upon the individual's return to the detention center. The presence of Anafé and of the Red Cross in ZAPI 3 does not guarantee that individuals who experience mistreatment will be able to obtain remedy. Red Cross workers have been constrained by their organization's mandate and positioning. The organization has been reluctant to engage in any action that could damage its relation with border authorities. Anafé workers have not faced the same issues, as their organization chose to be vocal in the denunciation of abuse. However, launching a complaint for allegations of mistreatment is a challenging process. Furthermore, State prosecutors rarely investigate such allegations in the waiting zone. This leaves those who experienced abuse with very limited (or no) recourses.

Police violence in this space was documented by regional human rights monitoring bodies such as the European Committee for the Prevention of Torture and Inhuman or Degrading Treatment or Punishment (2003, paragraphs 10–15 and 2007, paragraphs 54–56). Detainees have long complained of mistreatment taking place outside of ZAPI 3. Noémie, who worked in ZAPI 3 as an Anafé volunteer for ten months, attempts to analyze the causes of police violence:

> There is a police violence that is legal. The boundary is not very clear; a return with escort is a return where officers have the right to tie you and there is an entire set of movements that are authorized, techniques, and therefore when you possess legitimate violence, the point where it becomes illegitimate it not really clear in your head. For me it is rather clear! And also there are orders from above, superiors that tell you "this person has to be returned" for example. It also has to do with the fact that in waiting zone non-citizens are considered a migratory risk, often liars, they are completely humiliated, they are nobody, their word is not worth anything if they do not have official documents they are nobody, and therefore it is part of the same process of infantilization, humiliation, the fact of being violent even verbally, there is a lot of verbal abuse, more than physical abuse ... .
>
> Interview with NOÉMIE, September 2013

As Noémie mentions, instances of mistreatment have been particularly prevalent during attempts to force detainees on planes or during transfer from planes to ZAPI 3 after the attempts have failed. Those placed in waiting zones can be sent back with or without escort. The decision to escort is made by the border police on a case-by-case basis, and depends on the individual's willingness to comply. Makaremi (2009 b) has analyzed violence during return attempts with escort. As she explains, the French government created a police unit specifically dedicated to forced returns and deportations in January 1999: UNESI or National escort, support and intervention unit (*Unité nationale d'escorte, de soutien et d'intervention*). UNESI was created following the death of a Sri-Lankan asylum seeker. UNESI officers receive specific training; they learn technical professional gestures (*gestes techniques professionnels*) developed with the assistance of doctors. Escorting techniques are rationalized and the use of force is reduced to managing life and bodies: violence is denied. Makaremi (2009 b) remarks that during the flight, the use of force is extremely codified. Moreover, flight crew and passengers watch officers. However, before or after the codified procedure (i.e. before boarding or after disembarking the plane), brutal mistreatment occurs, in places far away from the public gaze: airport corridors, the van bringing the individual back to ZAPI, or police stations in terminals.

Red Cross workers wishing to address the issue of violence have been constrained by their organization's mandate and positioning. When ZAPI 3 first opened, allegations of mistreatment were particularly numerous. Several Red Cross mediators tried to address the issue but their efforts were to no avail. Former Red Cross mediator Paul, describes the procedure that had to be followed by mediators in such instances. Mediators were instructed to collect the person's testimony and to forward it to their superior who would then raise the issue with the border police director at a weekly meeting (Interview, August 2013).

Journalist De Loisy spent six months in ZAPI 3 from October 2003 to April 2004. She conducted an undercover investigation, taking on the role of a mediator. She was a colleague of Paul. She wrote that, at some point, mediators received testimonies of abuse every day (De Loisy 2005, 143–159). Strongly resembling one another, the stories were often backed by medical certificates issued by the medical service in ZAPI 3. De Loisy and her colleagues felt powerless when confronting police violence. Different teams of mediators raised the issue to their superior, who routinely answered: "The issue will be addressed at the next meeting with the border police. Meanwhile, remain NEUTRAL". Their superior insisted: "We do not judge the work carried out by the border police, in any circumstance. We ask you, in the respect of the Red Cross neutrality principle, to stop writing sarcastic comments in the correspondence notebook" (used for communication between Red Cross mediators and their superiors) (De Loisy, 157–158).

While allegations of violence greatly diminished over time, Paul regrets the police's attitude towards the issue: "It is true that the police ask us not to talk about it anymore. If the person arrives with traces of handcuffs, these are not mistreatments, it is procedure. If we say, this is how it happened, they say (the police): 'It is absolutely normal, it is the law that enables it when people are escorted'. For them it is not mistreatment". (Interview, August 2013). Paul no longer works in ZAPI 3, but follows events occurring in the waiting zone in his current capacity at the Red Cross. The Red Cross report (2013) also laments that the border police stopped the dialogue with the Red Cross regarding allegations of mistreatment.

Contrary to the Red Cross, Anafé chose to denunciate these issues, releasing reports documenting violence at the hands of the police (see for example Anafé April 2001; March 2003; November 2015) as well as supporting the alleged victims' claims to relevant bodies. However, more than ten years after De Loisy's experience, Anafé employee Lise is as disheartened and frustrated as De Loisy. Lise deplores the impunity of officers involved in mistreatment (Interview, December 2013). The aforementioned case (cf. section IV) of the six Central American nationals illustrates her statement: two women were returned shortly afterwards while four were sentenced to a few months in prison by a criminal court for remaining illegally on French territory. Their complaints never went through; the State prosecutor never contacted them, and thus the police were not held accountable for their actions. Anafé 2015's report documents the obstacles faced by those who experienced mistreatment at the hands of authorities. Lodging a complaint is itself a challenging process. As detainees cannot complain to the police, their only recourse is to file a claim with the State prosecutor, for which they need to be assisted. In many cases, individuals cannot be heard, as they are returned shortly after lodging the complaint. Moreover, State prosecutors seldom launch an inquiry for these types of events. As for liberty and custody judges, they usually consider such allegations outside of their mandate, therefore not allowing them to impact the decision to extend the duration of detention after four days (Anafé, November 2015). The presence of NGOs in ZAPI 3 does not guarantee that detainees will access (effective) remedies in case of mistreatment. Neither does it guarantee the implementation of the rights set out in the Law on the Waiting Zone.

6 Barriers to Accessing Legal Aid

In this section, I will show that detainees in ZAPI 3 experience barriers to accessing legal aid, in spite of the NGO Anafé providing such assistance a few days a week. Absence of accessible and sufficient legal aid leaves the door open to fraudulent practices: detainees may fall prey to unethical legal counsel. Although detainees are entitled to certain rights under the Law on the Waiting Zone, the implementation of these rights remains challenging. Accessing legal aid is more difficult for detainees in the waiting zones than for those deemed on the territory.

Legal assistance and the possibility to communicate in one's language are crucial to accessing rights. According to the law, any person placed under the waiting zone status must be informed of his or her right to contact a lawyer and seek the assistance of an interpreter (CESEDA 2016, article L221-4). But in practice, hiring a lawyer or an interpreter may prove an uneasy task. Indeed, the detainees themselves must incur these expenses. Non-citizens can benefit from free legal counsel and interpreter only when presented to judges (CESEDA 2016, articles L222-3 and L222-7). Apart from the actual hearing at the court, detainees are left without state-paid legal or interpretation assistance.[5]

5 Border officers must also notify the placement in the waiting zone as well as the attached rights to the individual in a language that he or she understands.

Barriers to legal assistance are many: detainees must know whom to contact and must be able to afford such assistance. Allophone detainees may also need an interpreter to communicate with their legal counsel, which entails an additional cost.

Anafé mitigates this situation by providing free legal aid in ZAPI 3 a few days a week (two to three days). But this assistance is insufficient and cannot guarantee access to rights for all detainees. Only a fraction of those detained in ZAPI 3 benefit from this service: about one tenth go through Anafé's office, an ordinary bedroom that was turned into a legal aid clinic (Interview, December 2013). Trained Anafé volunteers also rely on volunteers to provide interpretation services. The availability of these interpreters is limited and may affect the ability of Anafé volunteers to assist Allophone detainees. Their neutrality and skills may also be open to question.

In France, NGOs are paid by the State to provide legal aid to non-citizens who are detained for illegal residence in the country prior to their deportation (i.e. who are in *rétention*). NGOs compete to get this market in a public tender; the government then funds the activities of the tender winners. The government therefore allocates funds for legal assistance when detainees are considered on the territory, but not before. Those placed in waiting zones are disadvantaged compared to those in *rétention.*

Anafé employees insist that the organization cannot and does not aspire to legally assist all detainees in Charles de Gaulle's waiting zone. Anafé advocates for a legal aid clinic financed by the State and staffed with lawyers. Lise from Anafé explained:

> The law does not provide for lawyers in the waiting zone. There is nothing. So it is us who supply a part of this legal aid, knowing that it is out of the question for us to replace a service that should be financed and organized by the State. We do not, and we will never guarantee that noncitizens' rights are respected in the waiting zone. We are first of all an observer and we use the law to support our demands and observations (Interview, December 2013).

Anafé decided to use its privileged access to ZAPI 3 to provide legal aid to some detainees but, as previously explained, the organization's mission is much broader.

Anafé and its member organizations have long pondered the NGO's involvement at the detention center. As early as 2004, Amnesty International feared that Anafé's presence might be counterproductive and contribute to legitimization and reinforcement of the system rather than its denunciation (Amnesty

International, 2004).[6] I asked Raoul whether this debate was over. At the time of our interview (October 2013), Raoul was a member of the administrative council of the organization. He answered: "It is a question that we still ask ourselves nowadays". At my invitation to expand discussion of the legal aid issue, Raoul confessed: "There is a crisis at the moment at Anafé. I will not go into details but the legal aid clinic is currently called into question; each organization [composing Anafé] has its own vision of non-citizens' rights, of its realm of action, of its own mandate too" (Interview, October 2013).

Anafé functions mainly with private donations: it does not receive money from the State to offer legal aid. Anne and Lise lament that many people fail to understand Anafé's objective. Many stakeholders think that it is Anafé's duty to offer legal aid to all ZAPI 3 detainees. Lise said: "There are false assertions regarding the mission of Anafé. Sometimes in court the administration lawyer affirms 'Anafé is very well paid to do what it does'. No, we are not publicly funded to do what we do". (Interview, December 2013). On several instances, I indeed heard stakeholders complain about Anafé not fulfilling its mission well. For example, at the Appeal Court in October 2013 the administration's lawyer asserted: "Anafé is never here (in ZAPI 3), does not do its work in spite of receiving subsidies".

Fraudulent practices thrive in the absence of accessible and sufficient legal aid. In France, lawyers do not have the right to approach potential clients first. This is explicitly forbidden by article 10.2 of the lawyers' internal regulations manual (2007). However, there is evidence that lawyers contravene this rule regularly. At CDG's detention center I met José, a Nicaraguan national who introduced himself as a professor of literature in Nicaragua. His initial goal had been to visit a friend in Spain. He recounted that he had been standing on the first floor of the detention center, near the phone booths. All of the sudden the phones started to ring "like magic". He picked up and was surprised to hear the voice of a Spanish-speaking lawyer offering her services in his language. He hired her. Paul, a former Red Cross mediator, confirmed that these practices were indeed frequent in spite of the Red Cross tirelessly denouncing them. He explained that it was lawyers' practice to offer a discount to clients bringing other clients (Interview, August 2013).

---

6 At the early research stage, I had the opportunity to meet with scholar Makaremi who had researched Charles de Gaulle's waiting zone as an anthropologist, taking on the role of an Anafé volunteer. She gave me access to materials produced by either Anafé itself or its member organizations. The document to which I hereby refer was an internal document produced by Amnesty International.

When Anafé is not here, rejected asylum claimants are left to their own devices. Upon expiry of the time allocated to appeal, they move from the category of "asylum seeker" to that of "inadmissible person". Once assigned to the latter, they can be sent back at anytime.[7] As chapter 9 will show, barriers to accessing legal aid at CDG's detention center are a serious issue for asylum seekers. Due to unsatisfactory access to legal recourse, rejected claimants risk *refoulement* to countries where their lives or freedom are at risk. For some detainees, having access to legal assistance may literally be a matter of life or death.

To summarize, ZAPI 3 is not a spotless space; in the adult area the floor felt sticky below my feet, bathrooms were smelly and the family room I visited with Dominique was a bit run-down. However, overall detention conditions are quite good in ZAPI 3, especially compared to other administrative places of confinement or accommodation for non-citizens.[8] In ZAPI 3 the issues are not so much material conditions of detention but rather confinement in and of itself as well as access to rights. NGO workers try to remedy these issues but are constrained by their organizations' mandates and asymmetrical power relations.

7 According to Anafé, in some instances the border police may also attempt to send back claimants before the expiry of the legal time allocated to appeal to the administrative court. This constitutes a serious violation of domestic and international law. It was the case at Orly around 2011 (Interview with Lise and Anne, December 2013 and Anafé December 2013, 25).

8 For example, Agnès, Cimade employee, describes the administrative detention center of the Mesnil-Amelot, nearby Charles de Gaulle, where non-citizens are confined prior to their deportation after residing illegally in the country: "And after three years it is almost insalubrious in many areas because there are water infiltrations, the paint is completely flaked … There are no more locks on toilets' doors, there are no more tables, the bedrooms had small tables, there were water fountains, nothing is working anymore, there are water drainage issues so water flows back including in the toilets, so there are unsanitary water inundations, it stinks, it is disgusting … (Interview with Agnès, March 2014)". \ "Likewise, George, the *ad hoc* administrator, explains that some group homes for unaccompanied minors on what is construed as the territory are incredibly filthy (Interview, October 2013)".

Part 2 Findings: Nowhere Countries Are Vanishing Points Where Border Control Takes Precedence over Rights

Following Agamben's conceptualization of a "vanishing point" as "a hidden point of intersection between the juridical-political institutional and the bio-political models of power", Gregory (2007, 206) analyses the war prison (through a study of US Naval Station at Guantanamo Bay and Abu Ghraib prison in Iraq) as a "dispersed series of sites where sovereign power and bio-power coincide".

Drawing on Agamben (1998, 1999 and 2005) and Gregory's work (2007), Mountz (2013) argues that nation States create "vanishing points" through geography to prevent and diminish asylum seekers and migrants' enjoyment of the rights attached to presence on sovereign territory. Vanishing points are "sites where national security is prioritised over human security and where the protection of human rights and human life disappear". Mountz, researching asylum seeking in Australia, considers the islands of Christmas, Manus and Nauru to be such vanishing points. International NGOs, organizations and Australian parliamentary committees and experts have tirelessly denounced the severe human rights violations taking place in declared countries. Reports documenting the abuses abound. For example, a joint press release published by Amnesty International and Human Rights Watch in 2016 concluded that Australia and Nauru were violating asylum seekers and refugees' rights to be free from torture and other ill treatment and from arbitrary detention. The life and physical integrity of those confined in Nauru was endangered, as the latter suffered frequent attacks from local Nauruans. Appalling detention conditions (in tents where the temperature reached 45 to 55 degrees Celsius) and poor access to health care were found to have exacerbated the trauma that the detainees had suffered at home. Paediatricians observed that children who had spent several months in Nauru were amongst the most traumatized children that they had ever seen (Elliott and Gunasekera October 16–18, 2015). Importantly, the two human rights organizations concluded that the Australian government was both well aware of and condoning the abuses taking place on the island in the hope of deterring future seaborne asylum seekers.

Those confined on Manus Island have been similarly exposed to grave human rights abuses in the name of deterrence. Asylum seekers' and refugees' health and lives have literally been at risk on the equatorial island. Violence is endemic in Papua New Guinea, a country where poverty and police abuse are

 | DOI:10.1163/9789004383500_012

rampant (Amnesty International 2013). In 2017, the country's human development index was in the low category according to the indicator developed by the United Nations Development Programme (i.e. the UN agency tasked with helping people build a better life).[1] As for the Australian Department of Foreign Affairs and Trade (February 15, 2019), it has advised travelers to exercice a "high degree of caution" in Papua New Guinea due to "high levels of serious crime" in the country. One Iranian asylum seeker was killed and others were seriously harmed during a riot that took place over two days at the detention centre on Manus Island in February 2014. A parliamentary inquiry (Australian Senate December 2014) determined that the Australian government had failed to protect asylum seekers detained on Papua New Guinea. Local residents, service provider staff and the Papua New Guinea police were found to have engaged in criminal actions against detainees. The inquiry concluded that despair and uncertainty about the future had constituted the root cause of the violence that had taken over the detention center:

> Of the factors that contributed to the events of 16 to 18 February, the committee is of the view that delay and uncertainty about refugee status determination and resettlement arrangements was the main cause which, if it had been addressed, would have been most likely to prevent the escalation of protest activity at the centre to the point where violence ensued. The committee believes that the hopelessness of the situation transferees found themselves in, with no clear path forward and no certainty for the future, was the central factor in the incident of 16 to 18 February.
>
> Australian Senate December 2014, 146

Confronted with the report's findings, the immigration minister, Scott Morrison, denied Australia's responsibility and emphasized the necessity of border control: "We've stopped the boats, and we are getting on with the job of resettlement, once again cleaning up a Labor mess in partnership with the government of Papua New Guinea, who retains sovereign control and responsibility for the center" (Innis December 11, 2014). The Supreme Court of Papua New Guinea declared, in April 2016, that the asylum seekers' confinement on Manus Island ignored constitutional protections of personal liberty. The Court ruled that the detention was illegal and ordered the governments of Papua

---

1 The UNDP (2018) explains that the Human Development Index (or HDI) is "a summary measure for accessing long-term progress in three basic dimensions of human development: a long and healthy life, access to knowledge and a decent standard of living".

New Guinea and Australia to put an end to it (Ramzy April 26, 2016). The detention facility was shut down in 2017 but Australia refused to bring the remaining non-citizens to the mainland and to offer them protection, leaving them exposed to violence on Manus Island (Perrigo February 1, 2019).

Although Mountz' concept of vanishing points applied to offshore locations, she notes that the same mechanisms are at work on sovereign territory. It is my argument that Charles de Gaulle's waiting zone and the waiting zone legal framework in general are an example of such vanishing points on mainland territory. In the eyes of the State, the categorization of individuals in waiting zones as illegal migrants trumps their status of rights-holders. This translates into dramatic consequences for those entitled to specific protection under international human rights and refugee law on account of their vulnerability. Asylum seekers and unaccompanied minors (these categories not being mutually exclusive) are perceived and treated as economic migrants (and therefore as bogus applicants), undeserving of the guarantees applicable to their counterparts who have crossed the legal border.

Strikingly, even those entrusted with safeguarding the rights of individuals in CDG's waiting zone can embrace the State's perspective according to which border control should take precedence over rights. The general inspector of places of deprivation of liberty (*Contrôleur général des lieux de privation de liberté*) is an independent public body whose mission consists in controlling the conditions of management and transfer of people who are deprived of liberty in order to ensure their fundamental rights are upheld (Law of October 30, 2007).[2] This public body came into being following France's ratification of the Optional Protocol to the Convention against Torture and other Cruel, Inhuman or Degrading Treatment or Punishment. 21 inspectors assist the head of this monitoring body (called the "general inspector"). An interview with one such inspector, Jacques, reveals that even those tasked with safeguarding the rights of detainees can endorse the State's perspective.

When asked whether there were vulnerable groups in the waiting zone, Jacques explained that during his visit to the CDG waiting zone (on January

2 Law n° 2007-1545 of October 30, 2007. Article 1 reads: "*Le Contrôleur général des lieux de privation de liberté, autorité indépendante, est chargé, sans préjudice des prérogatives que la loi attribue aux autorités judiciaires ou juridictionnelles, de contrôler les conditions de prise en charge et de transfèrement des personnes privées de liberté, afin de s'assurer du respect de leurs droits fondamentaux. Il exerce, aux mêmes fins, le contrôle de l'exécution par l'administration des mesures d'éloignement prononcées à l'encontre d'étrangers jusqu'à leur remise aux autorités de l'Etat de destination. Dans la limite de ses attributions, il ne reçoit instruction d'aucune autorité*".

27 and 28, 2009) he met with Yin, a seventeen-year-old Chinese girl at the detention center. She told him (via an interpreter) that she had been smuggled to France after the death of her parents. The smuggler had taken the land she had inherited as payment for her passage.[3] Jacques acknowledged that this situation was absolutely terrible in the sense that it was very difficult to determine the best course of action. Should Yin be taken to a group home? In this case the smuggler would be happy, as she would have managed to cross the border: he would take it as a signal that more people should be sent and get rich as a result. Or should she be returned to China? But she had nothing left at home. Jacques' dilemma was not framed in terms of determining the best course of action for the young Chinese but rather in terms of what was best for the control of borders. Yet, the Convention on the Rights of the Child, to which France is a Party, explicitly states: "In all actions concerning children, whether undertaken by public or private social welfare institutions, courts of law, administrative authorities or legislative bodies, the best interests of the child shall be a primary consideration" (article 3). Furthermore, Article 20 of the same convention specifies that "A child temporarily or permanently deprived of his or her family environment, or in whose own best interests cannot be allowed to remain in that environment, shall be entitled to special protection and assistance provided by the State". Instead of envisaging people in the waiting zone as rightholders, Jacques embraces the State's perspective by being overly concerned with border control.

Even George, an experienced *ad hoc* administrator who explicitly presents himself as an activist ("I am an activist"), observes that it is impossible to end the detention of unaccompanied minors at the borders as this would clearly constitute a "suction effect" (*appel d'air*): it would incite more people to come (Interview, October 2013).

Stakeholders whose task it is to assist and comfort detainees in the waiting zone in a spiritual or medical way appeared overly concerned with security and lacked empathy with detainees. Several places of worship and prayer for Christians, Jews and Muslims can be found on Charles de Gaulle airport's compounds. Catholic priests, pastors, rabbis and imams are allowed to visit those placed in waiting zones should detainees expressly call for them. Such visits rarely take place, as detainees are often unaware of this possibility: the information is nowhere to be found in spaces of confinement. During data collection

3 The case of this young Chinese is briefly described in the 2009 report of the general inspector of places of deprivation of liberty (p. 58).

two Catholic priests were listed on the airport's website.[4] One of them, Cédric, refused to talk to me: he was very angry and told me that "he knew people like me, who just want to sell their products and are not even thankful afterwards". But the other one, Raphaël, agreed to a short phone interview.

Raphaël explained that he had been to Charles de Gaulle's detention center twice. He was first called by an Orthodox priest and then by a Catholic priest. Both were lacking one document to enter the country. He had the opportunity to talk with Red Cross agents and doctors working onsite and could visit the entire center. He was very suspicious of those in CDG's waiting zone, denouncing individuals who "abuse the system". For example, some detainees pretend to be sick. He noted that some priests might be frauds: sometimes there are "false priests" and "false nuns". The border police must be careful, as nothing proves their identity: "In detention centers there are people of all kinds. There are people who may be terrorists or wanted by Interpol". Raphaël remarked that CDG airport was a very sensitive zone: "Should the slightest problem arise, an entire plane crashes with many passengers onboard". Raphaël did not find the detention of children problematic, explaining that ZAPI 3 was well equipped to receive families: conditions are satisfactory (Interview, June 2014).

During one visit to the detention center, I met Pierre, one of the doctors working onsite. He described the medical unit comprised of three doctors and three nurses, working in shifts. I asked Pierre: "What is the impact of detention on children?" Pierre did not answer my question directly but observed that parents were to be blamed for putting their children through this: "They take their children all around the globe for 15 days, giving them hazardous food to eat [*n'importe quoi*], not to mention the presence of fleas". According to him, the parents were at fault for making the decision to carry their children to the other end of the world. As far as unaccompanied minors are concerned, he wondered whether it was better for them to be hosted in hotels with nannies (i.e. before the minor area opened) or at ZAPI 3, in an area with toys. Clearly, Pierre did not find the confinement of minors problematic. He admitted: "As a clinician, I really do not care about the age [of detainees]". I remarked that a different legal framework applied to children. Pierre insisted: "I do not care about the legal regime". Once again, the law is something that can be dispensed with. As a doctor, Pierre sees minors under 13 every day and those older than 13 once during their stay at ZAPI 3. Even though he "agrees to check on the little ones", he thinks that this policy has been established so as to please NGOs and

4 I also contacted a pastor who was willing to talk but could not provide me with information as he had not been called yet and therefore did not know waiting zone issues. Due to time constraints, I did not contact rabbis or imams.

the Ministry of the Interior. Generally, Pierre minimized detention, explaining that ZAPI 3 was "a hotel from which one cannot leave". Like Raphaël, Pierre thinks that many detainees are frauds. He explained: "Every time there is a conflict somewhere, people take advantage of it". For example, some claim they are Syrians but they are not. Pierre espouses the State's perspective; in waiting zones, people are first and foremost illegal migrants who seek to take advantage of the country. He added: "The majority of people come for economic reasons or to get cured here". CDG's waiting zone is a physical and legal space where border control takes precedence over rights.

PART 3

Nowhere Countries or One Non-Entrée *Mechanism amongst Many*

CHAPTER 8

The Symbiotic Relations between Carrier Sanctions and the Waiting Zone

The number of individuals seeking international protection at French borders has dwindled over the years. While in 2001 OFPRA's border division heard 7,018 claimants, this number had shrunk to 1,093 in 2014 (OFPRA April 10, 2015, 64). The refugee agency's border team was comprised of 14 agents in the early 2000s, but only three were needed at the time of interview (Interview with Stéphanie, Miriam and Charline, November 2013). This dramatic drop in claimants is to be explained by the numerous (literal and figurative) fences that have been erected between refugees and France, or desired destination countries in general (Anafé, January 2013; Rodier, 2012). Hathaway first referred to such fences as *non-entrée* practices in 1992. They take extremely varied forms and present various degrees of formality. They include extra-territorial airport international zones (cf. chapter 1) or excision of zones of arrival in general, airport transit visas, carrier sanctions, maritime interception on the high seas, immigration liaison officers at departure points, safe third country agreements such as the 2004 Canada-US agreement. Recent *non-entrée* mechanisms rely heavily on cooperation with States of departure or transit. For example, they encompass "reliance on diplomatic relations; the offering of financial incentives; the provision of equipment, machinery, or training; deployment of officials of the sponsoring State; joint or shared enforcement; assumption of a direct migration control role; and the establishment or assignment of international agencies to effect interception" (Hathaway and Gammeltoft 2015, 243). One of the latest of these mechanisms includes the EU-Turkish agreement signed on March 18, 2016. Under said agreement, individuals reaching the Greek islands irregularly were to be returned to Turkey. EU member States pledged to resettle one Syrian refugee for every Syrian refugee readmitted to Turkey.[1]

This chapter will study one of these tools that may come into play thousands of kilometers away from countries of destination: carrier sanctions. What are the relations between carrier sanctions and the institution of the waiting zone?

1 As many scholars and NGOs have observed, the agreement is in violation of international human rights and refugee law. Kenneth Roth, Human Rights Watch Executive Director, remarked: "resettlement can be a very helpful supplement to asylum but can never be a substitute for the right to seek asylum" (HRW March 15, 2016).

 | DOI:10.1163/9789004383500_013

A brief history of the emergence of carrier sanctions at the international and French level will first be provided, before demonstrating that they constitute a formidable mechanism to keep claimants at bay. The perspective of governmental actors on this device will be explored.

1 A Brief History of Carrier Sanctions at the International and National Level

Dauvergne (2016, 4) explains that "settler societies" are "nations built through extensive migration, and which as a consequence led the world in developing migration regulation". Settler countries like the United States and Australia started to impose financial and criminal sanctions on carriers bringing inadmissible passengers as early as the 1950s (Feller 1989). In Europe, these developments occurred over the 1980s, a key decade in the history of measures designed to keep undesirable migrants, and asylum seekers in their midst, at bay (Feller 1989). By 1989, the following countries had adopted laws providing for carriers sanctions: Australia, Belgium, Brazil, Canada, Denmark, the Federal Republic of Germany, New Zealand, Thailand, the UK and the US. Many European countries introduced repressive legislation against carriers specifically to curb the number of asylum seekers. For example, the German Parliamentary State Secretary for the Ministry of the Interior explained (in August 1987) the rationale for introducing legislation imposing penalties in Germany: the number of asylum seekers had risen from 35,000 in 1984 to 100,000 in 1986, and many of them were running from economic hardship, not political persecution (Feller 1989). Therefore, when the Schengen Convention was signed on June 19, 1990, many States worldwide had already equipped themselves with repressive legislation against carriers bringing undesirable travelers.

By contrast, the concept of carrier sanctions only made its way into French law in 1992, when the country integrated the requirements of the Schengen Convention into its domestic legislation (cf. chapter 2). In the early 1990s France, like any party to the Chicago Convention, was already bound by the standards developed by the International Civil Aviation Organization's (ICAO) executive council.[2] At first, the Facilitation division of the ICAO had considered that the carrier's obligation to transport back inadmissible travelers constituted

2 Pursuant to article 37 of the Chicago Convention of 1944, the executive council of the International Civil Aviation Organization (ICAO) is responsible for developing standards and recommended practices regarding customs and immigration matters. Such standards are listed in Annex 9 to the Chicago Convention.

sufficient punishment: in 1986, standard 3.36 specifically stated: "Operators shall not be fined". However this quickly changed: at the 1988 facilitation meeting, the possibility of fining carriers was introduced (Feller 1989). Prior to ratifying the Schengen Convention, France was therefore already compelled to *consider* administering fines to carriers bringing rejected passengers. Other Annex 9 standards were also in force: carriers had to return passengers lacking proper documents and to cover the cost of their stay prior to return. France waited until 1992 to incorporate these requirements into its national legislation, via the Law of February 26, 1992. This law imposed financial penalties on those carriers bringing an inappropriately documented "foreigner who is not a national of a member State of the European Economic Community" (article 3).[3] It also obligated companies to transport back non-admitted passengers and to pay for their living expenses before return (article 7).

Importantly, both the Schengen Convention and Annex 9 to the Chicago Convention mention the need for States parties to respect their obligations under the Refugee Convention. Article 26.1 of the Schengen Convention clearly states: "The Contracting Parties undertake, subject to the obligations resulting from their accession to the Geneva Convention relating to the Status of Refugees of 28 July 1951, as amended by the New York Protocol of 31 January 1967, to incorporate the following rules into their national law". But, are carriers sanctions and refugee protection compatible? Or were contracting parties merely paying lip service to their obligations under the Refugee Convention and its additional protocol?

The French Constitutional Council found that the Schengen Convention was compatible with the French Constitution on July 25, 1991. Nevertheless, several parliamentarians persisted in questioning the impact of the Schengen Convention on the right to seek asylum, a constitutionally protected right. For example, Allouche, a Socialist senator, observed that he preferred "a foreign national staying illegally, but alive, in the Schengen area, to a foreign national persecuted or killed in his country because he was turned away when he wanted to flee" (French Senate debates January 16, 1992, 206). Communist MP Gilbert Millet remarked that this bill proposed to turn airline companies' employees into police auxiliaries (French National assembly debates December 19, 1991, 8267). As for Lederman, another Communist senator, he pointed out that the experience of European countries that had undertaken to enforce sanctions against carriers revealed that such sanctions were both harmful and dangerous. Finally, he observed that paving the way of asylum seekers with obstacles

3 10,000 francs per inadmissible passenger.

could only result in clandestine arrivals, the only option left to those fearing for their lives (French Senate debates January 16, 1992, 215). Marchand, the Minister of the Interior, brushed aside parliamentarians' concern by explaining that the carrier would only be responsible when bringing an asylum seeker whose claim was "manifestly unfounded". He argued that no special knowledge was required to identify such a claim; for example, an asylum seeker declaring that his goal was to find work in France had a manifestly unfounded claim (French Senate debates January 16, 1992).

The law was adopted, notwithstanding these concerns. The Law of February 26, 1992 exempted companies from the fine of 10,000 francs when the asylum claimant was admitted to French territory or when the claim was not "manifestly unfounded" (article 3). These legislative provisions have not changed since then. Parliamentarians were rightly concerned: carriers sanctions and refugee protection are fundamentally at odds. This should not come as a surprise, as countries introduced sanctions against carriers precisely to curtail the number of claimants arriving at their gates. Let us now examine carriers' obligation to cover the costs of accommodation and return.

2 Carriers' Responsibility (Part 1): Accommodation and Return

CESEDA (2016) currently provides the domestic legislative basis for carrier sanctions. Transport companies bringing a non-EU national to France from a country outside the Schengen area pay a heavy price when the individual in question is found inadmissible at French borders. Companies are responsible for returning the rejected passenger to the point where he or she started his or her journey with the company. When it is impossible, carriers have to return the individual to the State that delivered the travel documents or to any other place where the person is admissible (CESEDA 2016, article L.213–4). Furthermore, carriers are financially responsible for the non-EU citizen from the moment he or she is declared inadmissible until his or her return (CESEDA 2016, article L.213–6).

The law does not specify whether the company's financial obligations are limited to accommodation costs or if they also encompass medical and other expenses.[4] It proved challenging to gather reliable data regarding the precise expenses incurred by companies under article L.213–6. But evidence suggests

4 The precise wording in French is *les frais de prise en charge de l'étranger*, which translates in English as "the expenses to support the foreigner".

that these costs may be non-negligible at both CDG and Orly airports. In ZAPI 3, I talked to Gilles several times, as he accompanied me during my visits to the adult zone. Gilles occupies an important function in the police hierarchy. According to him, "the stay of an individual in the waiting zone costs 200 Euros per day" at CDG. Gilles explained that this amount included the maintenance of the building as well as civil servants' salaries. I also asked Clotilde, from the Ministry of the Interior, about the cost of a non-citizen's confinement at CDG per day. She replied: "It is a matter on which my colleagues are currently working. They are trying to put in place a frame of reference, to set a price for a day so that it integrates both accommodation expenses and medical expenses if needed"[5] (Interview, December 2013).

Those placed in the waiting zone at Orly airport are confined in a rather spacious room (about 50 square meters)[6] at the airport's south terminal during the day and transferred to the nearby Ibis hotel at night.[7] I visited both parts of Orly's waiting zone and met with Guillaume, a high-ranking police officer at Orly, and Anna, who occupies an important managerial position at Ibis Orly airport. The State requisitions 12 rooms at Ibis hotel to detain those placed under the waiting zone regime. These rooms are on the fourth floor, all located in the same aisle. According to Anna, the allocated rooms are the same as regular ones, except for the fact that windows cannot open. Sometimes the hotel even rents the rooms in question to "ordinary customers" (*clients ordinaires*). I asked Guillaume how expensive it was to maintain a non-citizen in Orly's waiting zone. He answered that the cost varied: the price of a hotel room at Ibis Orly fluctuates from one day to the next, but averages 130 euros per night. Guillaume pointed out that there could also be additional costs, for example if the person needs an interpreter or a doctor. Guillaume concluded that it was impossible to provide a precise number.

From a financial standpoint, it is certainly in the State's interest to have undesirable individuals returned before they legally enter the country. According to the Senator Bernard-Reymond, in 2008 the State spent 20,970 Euros per individual removed from the French territory (i.e. deportating individuals

5 I asked Clotilde in July 2016 whether this frame of reference had been put into place. Clotilde replied that she was no longer working at the department in charge of administering fines, and encouraged me to contact the person that had replaced her. Her colleague said that the department was still working on the document establishing accommodation costs. As it had not yet been finalized, the information could not be shared with me.

6 According to Anafé's 2011 report on Orly's waiting zone.

7 According to Anafé's 2011 report (p.4) non-citizens may also be confined for a significant amount of time in police stations before being transferred to the holding room at the South terminal.

already deemed present in France, not in the waiting zone). This estimate included detention centers' running expenses, transport costs (boat, plane or train tickets), costs pertaining to legal and medical assistance in detention centers and costs of guarding and escorting detainees. Although high, this number did not reflect expenses actually incurred: for example, the costs of providing court-appointed lawyers and of financially compensating claimants winning their trials against detention and removal were left out of the estimate (Lipietz 2012). There is also a second component to the carriers' responsibility framework: financial penalties.

3 Carriers' Responsibility (Part 2): Fines

In addition to costs pertaining to confinement in the waiting zone and return, air and sea companies are legally compelled to pay fines to the French State when the non-EU traveler is turned away at the French (and therefore Schengen) border for reasons pertaining to travel documents; i.e. when the passport and/or visa are at issue (article L.625-1).[8] Companies are also responsible for ensuring that a non-EU citizen possesses the required documents to reach his or her final destination outside of the Schengen area, in cases where transit occurs through France. Likewise, failure to comply with this requirement will result in a fine payable to the French State (article L.625-1). The website of the Ministry of the Interior (December 2015) specifies the circumstances under which a company's responsibility is triggered: when the passport or visa are missing, when the passport is invalid or when either is falsified, usurped or forged.[9] Clotilde, a civil servant working for the Ministry of the Interior's department in charge of administering fines to carriers, gives examples of unacceptable passports:

> You also have a very interesting variety, which are fantasy passports. For example, if you show a "Groland"[10] passport, you will not be let in.

8 Appropriate travel documents are just one of the criteria (listed in article 5 of the Schengen border code) that third country nationals need to fulfill to enter the Schengen area. When entry is denied for non-documentary reasons such as lack of sufficient financial means, medical insurance or proof of accommodation, carriers are not fined. However, transport enterprises still have to pay for the non-national's stay and must provide for his or her return.

9 http://www.immigration.interieur.gouv.fr/Europe-et-International/La-circulation-transfrontiere/Les-conditions-d-entree-dans-l-espace-Schengen. Accessed April 4, 2016.

10 Groland is the name of an imaginary country in a notorious French TV show.

> It exists. There are also "citizen of the world" passports; it is pure fantasy. There are also other cases that are a bit different; it is the passports of the Sioux nation for example. You have nations, you have groups like the Sioux who consider that the border does not run through the United States and Canada so there is a Sioux nation passport, that is not recognized either. There are also passports that we do not recognize because we do not recognize the country. The fantasy passport is another notion (Interview, December 2013).

Since I interviewed Clotilde, in December 2013, the amount of fines actually doubled. Clotilde had explained that fines amounted to 5,000€ per traveler turned away at the border. This meant that an airline company paid 30,000€ when a family of six was turned away at the border for inappropriate travel documents. The CESEDA was modified by law n°2016–274 of March 7, 2016. Since then, companies face fines of 10,000€, not 5,000€ per inadmissible traveler. The fine's amount may be lesser in cases where companies co-operate with the French government. As Clotildes explains:

> The usual rate is 5,000€ [10,000€ at the time of writing] and we go below when the company helped the administration. It is often persons in transit. For example, the person comes from Ouagadougou, transits through Paris on her way to Canada. When she is about to embark for Canada -so she stayed in international zone, she did not present herself to the border police, she did not have to- Air France realizes that the person does not have a visa for Canada. The company has a responsibility problem because it should have noticed it from the start … They [company agents] notice it late but do a favor to the French State because, had nobody noticed, the person would have been returned from Canada, she would have come back to us and we would have had to deal with the file. So we consider that the company helped and we issue a fine at 3,000€ instead of 5,000€. Objectively it did not fulfill its obligation but it rectified the situation. We will issue a smaller fine (Interview, December 2013).

Both the amount of the fine and the procedure to be followed are different in the case of unaccompanied minors (article L.625-4). Carriers may pay up to 20,000€ when bringing a child with no legal guardian (previously this amount was capped at 10,000€). Immediately after a *procès-verbal* (i.e. the administrative document establishing the infraction) is issued, the company has to place 10,000€ on an escrow account. This sum could then be partially or totally reimbursed to the company at the end of the procedure, after it has had the opportunity to defend its practice. If the carrier refuses to disburse the money and its responsibility is indeed engaged, the fine will be 20,000€. This is how Clotilde justified this difference of treatment:

> Isolated minors are a particular public, no matter which topic we are dealing with. There are ICAO norms, Community norms, and there is an obligation of particular vigilance towards minors … personnel in charge of control have to be particularly vigilant regarding the situation of the child, to ensure that he or she is accompanied by persons having authority: parents, or, if it is not the case, to check the quality of the person accompanying the child (Interview, December 2013).

Clotilde explains these specific norms on account of children's vulnerability: there are international kidnappings within family settings but also human trafficking for sexual exploitation. Clotilde, espousing the perspective of the State, also notes that unaccompanied minors place a heavy burden on the State when brought in by an immigrant trafficking ring (*filière*)[11]: "So the kid voluntarily threw away his or her passport, he or she was told to throw off the passport. He or she will not utter a word and will be placed in group homes managed by regional councils (*conseils généraux*) until his or her majority. The arrival of a foreign minor within these frameworks is an enormous burden for the State" (Interview, December 2013). Fines do represent a significant amount of money for transport companies.

4 The Impact of Fines on Companies' Budgets

Fines certainly weigh heavily on carriers' budgets and can even force carrying companies to shut down. Dominique, the high-ranking authority who accompanied me during my first visit to ZAPI 3, told me:

> You know, I think in Africa in particular, there are less and less airline companies that endure. There are airline companies that appear that do not necessarily have the means to focus on control. For us the objective is, rather than to have to deal with difficult human cases upon arrival, not to uproot these people and to sort [people] it is easier to tell someone "you will not be able to enter France". So, some companies do not always

11 Cf. footnote in chapter 4 on the use of the term *filière* (network).

> have means [to control] and we will have populations coming because a company opens. Six months later, it shut down because initially it faces penalties or has difficulties functioning. So, if a route stops, a route that existed and was a heavy immigration provider, I am thinking for example about the African company [inaudible company name]: when the company closed it was over. Now there is "Camair-Co" that is a bit in the same situation and we tell ourselves: "If it closes it will be over, we will have less [unauthorized migration]". It is not necessarily only Cameroonians: sub-Saharan population transit through these airports because it is easier, there is a company serving France directly (Interview, September 2013).

Only companies that possess sufficient financial resources will be able to train their employees and withstand a few fines. Others, particularly those based in Southern countries, will perish.

Even companies that invest consequential resources in personnel training are not fine-proof. Clotilde explains that, at Air France, entire departments are dedicated to training. However, Air France is still, in absolute numbers, the company that pays the most fines to the French State. This high number of fines derives from volume of traffic: Air France gets fined less than other companies, proportionally to its activity (Interview, December 2013). According to Clotilde, each year the border police forward to the Ministry of the Interior approximately 2,000 decisions taken against carriers (*procès-verbaux*) that transported sea and air passengers unequipped with the required travel documents. Astonishly, the Ministry of the Interior seldom receives decisions to penalize sea carriers from the border police. Yet, Clotilde pointed out that many boats from North Africa arrived at the port of Marseille and that, surely, not all passengers were in possession of the required travel documents. Clotilde could not provide me with an explanation as to why sea carriers were fined less than air carriers, proportionally to their activity (Interview, December 2013). What is certain is that air carriers bear the brunt of the fines. As Charles de Gaulle is the first airport in France, it is safe to assume that most of the fines incurred by airline companies are taken to penalize irregular arrivals at this airport.

Upon receiving the *procès-verbal*, the Ministry of the Interior informs the company of its intention to fine it. The latter may then dispatch a representative to the Ministry of the Interior to access its file. The carrier has one month to provide a written rebuttal to the Ministry of the Interior (CESEDA 2016, L.625-2). This procedure allows the company to present its side of the story and may lead to a fine annulment. Indeed, the law provides for exemption from fines in two cases: when the individual is admitted to the territory after his or her asylum claim was declared not manifestly unfounded or when the carrier demonstrates that the inadmissible individual was in possession of the required documents upon boarding and that these documents were not "openly irregular" (CESEDA 2016, L.625-5).[12] Dialogue may benefit the company: for example, it may demonstrate that an impersonation case was impossible to detect to the naked eye and, thereby, be exempted from the fine. In cases where the passenger presents a valid passport (and a valid visa if applicable) upon boarding but then disposed of his or her travel document before reaching the border, the fine will be cancelled if the company can prove (with a photocopy for example) that the passenger was indeed in possession of a valid document upon commencing the journey (Interview with Clotilde, December 2013).

Financial issues may be one of the most important rationales behind gangway checks: by controlling passengers as they exit the plane, border agents can connect passport-less individuals to a specific flight and therefore collect the carrier's fine. They can also make sure that the individual is transported back by the company that brought him or her to France.

Ultimately, the company may contest the fine in court (CESEDA 2016, L. 625-2). Clotilde and her colleagues noticed that companies resorted to litigation more often when the price of airline fuel increased: the number of cases rose from 30 to 70 (at the time of interview, according to Clotilde) per year. According to her, the government wins in 98 percent of the cases. Once the final fine has been set, it is impossible for the company to waive it. While in some countries companies can negotiate with the government, there is no such practice in France. When companies do not pay, the government's budgetary services do not hesitate to take retaliatory measures against those having their headquarters in France. Clotilde gave the example of a company whose bank account had been recently frozen (Interview, December 2013).

For all the aforementioned reasons (price of fines, low odds of winning court cases, impossibility of negotiating the fine's amount) letting undocumented asylum claimants on board is not in carriers' economic interest. Feller's observation, although dated (Feller 1989, 57), is still relevant: "A high risk-taking and profit-oriented transport carrier cannot reasonably be expected to make humanitarian decisions based only on a possibility that sanctions will later be waived, particularly when the burden of proof is on the carrier". Refusing

---

12 Article L.625-5 of the CESEDA (April 2016) reads: "*Les amendes ne sont pas infligées: 1. Lorsque l'étranger a été admis sur le territoire français au titre d'une demande d'asile qui n'était pas manifestement infondée. 2. Lorsque l'entreprise de transport établit que les documents requis lui ont été présentés au moment de l'embarquement et qu'ils ne comportaient pas d'élément d'irrégularité manifeste*".

improperly documented refugees makes sense for carriers, especially since they face fines in many countries.

5 France within the Landscape of Carrier Sanctions: One Country among Many

France is one country among many in the carrier sanctions' landscape. A European Directive (2001/51/EC) on carriers' liability of June 28, 2001 compels EU countries to fine transport companies bringing inappropriately documented passengers. The said Directive gives leeway to countries to set the fines' amount but forces them to impose penalties no less than 3,000€ or the equivalent in the national currency (article 4). The Directive specifically refers to member States' obligations under the 1951 Refugee Convention and its 1967 Protocol, stating that these obligations remain unaffected by the Directive. In particular, article 4 reads that the States' duty to administer fines to carriers is "without prejudice to member States' obligations in cases where a third country national seeks international protection". However, such a provision is very vague and, unsurprisingly, has been interpreted differently by member States. They use different criteria. Some EU countries exonerate companies only when asylum claimants are subsequently recognized as refugees, while others also provide for exemptions when claimants receive some form of subsidiary protection (EC-EMN, December 2012).

For example, the UK belongs to the former group of countries: fines will be waived only after the asylum seeker is granted full refugee status (Scholten 2015). Austria is more generous, as stated by its legislation: "The fine will be void in case the foreigner in question receives asylum or subsidiary protection or cannot be sent back to his country of origin for reasons of *non-refoulement*" (EC-EMN December 2012). Other countries go one-step further, waiving penalties in cases where the inadmissible person seeks international protection, irrespective of the outcome. This seems to be the case of Lithuania, according to the information that the country itself provided: "A carrier shall not be imposed any fine where: 1) the alien being carried applies for asylum in the Republic of Lithuania in compliance with the Law of the Republic of Lithuania on the Legal Status of Aliens" (EC-EMN, December 2012).

France can be situated somewhere in the middle of this European spectrum: fines will be waived provided that the individual's request to enter the territory on asylum grounds was not found "manifestly unfounded" (Interview with Jeanne, November 2013). A claim is found to be not "manifestly unfounded" when considered worth examining on merits for both refugee status and subsidiary protection (Interview with Stéphanie and Miriam from OFPRA, November 2013). In any case, the European Council on Refugees and Exiles points out that legislation relieving carriers of their liability is not applied consistently.[13] Discrepancies and unpredictability in implementation may incite companies to outwardly reject inappropriately documented asylum claimants. What is the perspective of some governmental actors on this *non-entrée* tool?

6 Governmental Actors' Perspective on Fines and Asylum Seeking

To some actors working on Charles de Gaulle's waiting zone, measures blocking asylum seekers' access to sovereign territory do not constitute an issue. My conversations with Clotilde and Jeanne, civil servants working for the Ministry of the Interior, were particularly enlightening. I told Clotilde that, according to some NGOs, the carriers' responsibility framework was detrimental to asylum seekers. At first, Clotilde acknowledged that my remark was interesting, but quickly went back to her role, refusing to change her perspective and finally justifying measures keeping asylum seekers away from France's territory, explaining that it was not in the State's interest to handle too many claimants. Clotilde was very welcoming, eager to share her experience and knowledge with me. However, her tone changed when answering my question, betraying exasperation and anger. The issue of asylum was emotionally charged for her.

RESEARCHER: According to NGOs, carriers' responsibilities hurt asylum seekers.

CLOTILDE: In what way?

RESEARCHER: In the sense that asylum seekers are not able to reach French territory to make their claim.

CLOTILDE: They can make them at the embassy. And there are other ways of applying for asylum, I think. You need to ask, the department in charge of asylum would tell you better than myself.

RESEARCHER: I do not know if it is possible to do it at the embassy anymore.

CLOTILDE: It is, objectively, a remark that seems interesting. But my job is to prevent people from setting foot in France!

13 Cf. European Council on Refugees and Exiles' (ECRE) website. Available at: http://www.ecre.org/topics/areas-of-work/access-to-europe/7-carrier-sanctions.html Accessed April 6, 2016.

> But everyone has one's own position, like we were previously saying. Everyone is in one's role. But here there is a massive influx, as you know we are in the first ranks in terms of asylum claims in Europe and there is saturation. The colleagues from [the department of] asylum probably told you, the CADA [accommodation centers for asylum seekers] are fully packed, the system is ready to implode because the delays of instruction became too long; it is neither in the interest of the claimant nor in the interest of State services because people remain on the territory, in overloaded structures. People who, once rejected, do not want to leave. It is really, really heavy to handle and to find ways out afterwards (Interview, December 2013).

According to the report published by the Intergovernmental consultations on migration, asylum and refugees (ICG) in 2012, it is possible to apply for an asylum visa at French embassies.[14] However, according to the information submitted by the French government itself, "There is no provision in French law that governs this procedure, which means that asylum applications at diplomatic missions are dealt with on an exceptional basis" (IGC December 2012, 186). After the individual has described the merits of his or her case, the diplomatic mission will decide whether or not to transfer the request to the Ministry of the Interior or to the UNHCR. The Ministry of the Interior will then consider the visa request along with the interview report (IGC December 2012). It is important to note that the refugee agency may not have a say at this stage of the procedure. As the IGC notes, "The case is then examined by the Ministry of Interior, which *may* include a consultation with OFPRA" (December 2012, 186, emphasis added). Once granted an asylum visa, the claimant still has to go through the regular procedure on French territory.

Earlier in our conversation, Clotilde had told me that visas should not be granted lightly. She had pointed out that, in the past, some individuals had taken advantage of visas, in order to claim asylum once on French territory:

14 The IGC defines itself as "an informal, non-decision making forum for intergovernmental information exchange and policy debate on issues of relevance to the management of international migratory flows" (ICG 2012). The IGC 2012 report reads: "The IGC brings together 17 Participating States, the United Nations High Commissioner for Refugees (UNHCR), the International Organization for Migration (IOM), and the European Commission".

> The Commission initiated with member States a policy of liberalization of visas, which means that we explain to third countries currently subject to visas that, if they make efforts, especially with regard to the readmission of illegal individuals, we can liberalize visas. And we noticed that this liberalization could have very negative effects: for example when we liberalized for the Balkans we ended up with an exponential increase of asylum claims. Because until then, since a visa was needed to come to Europe, I mean to the Schengen area, people were blocked at consulates. Now, with a biometrical passport in general, they enter without a visa, so the first thing they do when they arrive is rush to the *préfecture* [i.e. where claims are registered]. They are considered mostly unwarranted claims, but they weigh on everything: on the system, on the system's slowness, financially. It leads to expenses in terms of administrative functioning and in terms of accommodation in the CADA [i.e. the centers accommodating claimants] (Interview, December 2013).

Clotilde's statement matched Macklin's observation that we are witnessing an "erosion of the idea that people who seek asylum may actually be refugees" (2005, 1). Clotilde did not think that some people may genuinely need international protection, and therefore advocated for a *non-entrée* mechanism: visas. Just like Clotilde, Jeanne refused to ponder the implications of carriers sanctions on asylum claimants. Clotilde and Jeanne both elected to confine themselves to the role that had been attributed to them, refusing to consider the issue in its entirety. Both used the sentence "everyone is in one's role" (*chacun dans son rôle*) that summarized their refusal to adopt a holistic perspective. In response to my question "have you noticed some changes since you have occupied this position"? Jeanne replied:

> Yes, a significant decrease in asylum claims at the border. When you will meet NGOs, you will hear them complain about this. The border police's services have correspondents in States.
>
> RESEARCHER: Liaison officers?
>
> JEANNE: Immigration [officers]. They already do really important checks in airport zones and prevent them from boarding. Every year we meet NGOs who deal with asylum at the border. They [NGOs] complain about this regularly, saying that we seriously impinge on the right to seek asylum. It is their version; we do not think that it is the case. You really have both perspectives (Interview, November 2013).

Governmental actors are not the only ones to consider asylum seekers' lack of access to the territory to be a non-issue. Louise used to be a lawyer representing individuals claiming asylum and was a senator at the time of interview (January 2014). To my question "do you not think that there are some genuine asylum seekers that can never reach the territory?" Louise answered:

> But of course, we know it very well. Some did not go through, but well ... And there are others that did not go through. But the worst is not this, the worst is those who entered and claimed asylum but were turned down in spite of being real political refugees. I met some (Interview, January 2014).

Louise accepts that some claimants will never be able to file a claim, blocked by measures taken kilometers away from the waiting zone. However, she truly laments the system's lack of fairness: some true political refugees -who managed to cross the border and entered regular procedures- are denied status. In her eyes, this is the most blatant injustice, not the extra hurdles created by *non-entrée* mechanisms.

The vocabulary used by Clotilde in the statement below both reveals and contributes to the dehumanization and trivialization of asylum claimants. She explained that the border police should refrain from forwarding decisions taken against carriers to the Ministry of the Interior when individuals have been admitted to the territory on asylum grounds in the meantime. However, mistakes may occur, forcing the Ministry of the Interior's departments in charge of asylum at the border (i.e. Jeanne's department) and in charge of administering fines (i.e. Clotilde's department) to exchange information. Clotilde explained:

> Normally the DCPAF [border police] should not send me the procedure [i.e. when the person was admitted on asylum grounds], they cancel it; it is the only case. It happens sometimes that they send it to me anyway because they have a problem with organization. When we see files of individuals who presented themselves without passports it happens that we check with Jeanne to see if she has these names. Because it happens that DCPAF sent us by mistake people ['s names] that have been considered as having a non-manifestly unfounded claim. In these cases the fine is cancelled [by the Court] right away. Normally the DCPAF should not send me the file. If they sent it and we did not check and we go to court it is an automatic cancellation with interests to be paid because we should not have pursued this case. So when we have a doubt with my colleague, we seize Jeanne's department. We ask: "We have this person arriving from this flight pretending to be x, do you have an asylum claim?"

> Sometimes there is one but the person was not admitted. So we can press on with the procedure. We call this *flushing out* [*purger,* a strong term in French, associated with dirt, disease and excrements] the asylum petition proceedings from the record, so we check. Normally we should not have to do it since the DCPAF should forbid themselves from sending us the document [*procès-verbal*] while the asylum procedure is not *flushed out* [*purger*] (Interview, December 2013).

Contrary to civil servants, trade unionists resisted the carrier responsibility framework.

7 "We Are Not Border Police Auxiliaries!" Trade Unionists' Resistance to the Carrier Responsibility Framework

Air France trade unionists campaigned against carriers sanctions. They protested about having to play the role of border agents. At the time of the interview (February 2014), Aurélien and Christophe were still affiliated with the airline section of the CFDT trade union, while Jean had just left. CFDT stands for *Confédération française démocratique du travail* (Democratic French Work Confederation). CFDT is a trade union of employees that belong to different professions and work in different companies, ranging from public to private. Aurélien, Christophe and Jean all worked or used to work for Air France in varied capacities. All three of them were instrumental in shaping the history of CDG's waiting zone and of French waiting zones in general. They participated in the creation of Anafé and were all very active in CFDT, some of them occupying key functions in the trade union's airline section. Christophe recounts:

> It was also an action that we launched around this time [i.e. from 1999–2005]. It was [about] the role that Air France employees had to play upstream, in source countries. We worked a lot on these questions. Furthermore, we had situations that were a little strange. I remember that I intervened because, in Turkey, Air France personnel were Turkish and obviously had a position, commonly shared amongst Turks ... they were not favorably inclined when it came to Kurds. In our personal capacity we told them "wait, you do not have to ...[discriminate against Kurds]". Since Air France paid a fine if the person did not have [the required documents)] there was some pressure on these people: "be careful if at the other end we realize that the person

does not have the required documents ... it is your job to check, you, company employees". So we also worked with the help of ITF

RESEARCHER: What is ITF?

JEAN: The International Transport Workers' Federation. It dates back to the eighteenth century.

CHRISTOPHE: It gathers all trade unions worldwide that work in transports- seafarers, bus drivers, as well as those working in road and urban transport, [with] the railways and civil aviation.

JEAN: 150 countries, the headquarters are in London, they organize conferences in several languages

CHRISTOPHE: They had worked at our request: the CFDT had asked [them] to work on the Chicago Convention and on the role that airline employees have to play; they are asked to check and recheck, to do the job of immigration officers. Companies put a lot of pressure because at the other end they had to pay so they said: "I am going to train my staff to avoid paying". So we worked on these issues.

RESEARCHER: Did it pan out?

CHRISTOPHE: No, it is still the case.

RESEARCHER: The same system is still in place. When did this action take place?

CHRISTOPHE: Between 1999 and 2005. Around this time. We worked a lot during these five or six years (Interview, February 2014).

Not surprisingly, the trade unionists' action was not successful. How could it have been? The notion of carriers' sanction was then well enshrined in international, regional and domestic laws. In order not to perish, airline companies had to align their practices with legal requirements and this directly entailed putting the burden of document control on their own personnel.

Today, airline companies' personnel have no other option but to receive training in document control. This training is achieved in close cooperation with government officials. Clotilde's department at the Ministry of the Interior receives the representatives of companies who wish to analyze their fines. Clotilde and her colleagues establish a typology of the fines administered and provide tips on how to avoid them. Border agents also deliver training in companies' headquarters (Interview, December 2013). As Guiraudon (2006 b) points out, companies' employees are forced to engage in practices that violate human rights. She writes:

> There are reasons to believe that carrier sanctions will result in discriminatory practices. The competition between airlines (and airport authorities) is ferocious and they are keen to save time on passenger processing and speed transfers. Airline security personnel have therefore spoken in favour of "profiling", i.e., selecting a few individuals for additional checks rather than delaying boarding time by submitting everybody to the same treatment.

Christophe, who had already alluded to Air France's discriminatory practices against Kurds in Turkey, specifically described passenger profiling in this country:

> I saw things in Africa and in Turkey, in these places at the confines of Europe where Air France personnel was asked many things; they were told to photocopy passports otherwise people afterwards ate them, destroyed them, put them down the toilet and then "look, you let this person through without a passport". "But how should we proceed? Do we make photocopies of everybody ['s documents]?" "Oh no, only those that you think … [we will have issues with]". I remember talking with Turks in Turkey, Air France employees, who said "I do not want to make photocopies, how do I do? This one sounds dodgy; I make a photocopy. This one will maybe attempt something so I make a photocopy" (Interview, February 2014).

Aside from advocating against carriers sanctions, trade unionists also resorted to artisanal methods to try to stall returns of individuals in danger in their countries of origin. Aurélien recalls:

> Monica from Anafé often called us at the last minute: "be careful on this flight". There were really tense situations when it came to returns. I would say that we were improvising a little, and we only had one possible interlocutor in such emergency, it was the captain. So regularly with Jean we burst into cockpits as they were preparing their flight. We were not always received well; I remember a strong anecdote. It was the case of Christian Iraqis during the war, Barbarin had forwarded the case to Anafé, he was probably the archbishop of Lyon.[15] He had indicated that

15 According to the official website of the Catholic Church in Lyon, Philippe Barbarin was transferred to the Parish of Lyon on July 16, 2002. On October 21, 2003 Pope Jean-Paul II ordained him Cardinal. http://lyon.catholique.fr/?Biographie,1 Accessed May 3, 2016.

> these persons would meet their death if sent back to Iraq. There was a family with children and a general who was a deserter. We climbed on the cockpit with you, I think [talks to Jean]. We had explained [the situation] to the captain who had said "but I really do not care". So the plane went to Amman, because they were not landing in Bagdad anymore and they stayed on the plane and came back. We made a lot of noise on this case. You see the extreme difficulty (Interview, February 2014).

The trade unionists explain that they are still very sympathetic to Anafé's cause but cannot be as active as in the past. Aurélien explains:

> The issue of blackmail for an [airport] access pass [*chantage au titre d'accès*] impacted employees and mostly activists. We have passes. And now it is a really sensitive topic because without it you do not work anymore. There is a really important presence of *Renseignements Généraux* (*RG*) [i.e. home intelligence services] on the airport compounds, and also possibly of the *Direction de la Surveillance du Territoire*[16] (DST) [general direction of surveillance. Both *RG* and *DST* agents specialize in intelligence gathering]. This is why we do not really expose our activists nowadays, because there are interrogations. We do not question our engagement but it is much more complicated today.
>
> RESEARCHER: At first you had less issues with blackmail for the pass?
> AURÉLIEN: It did not appear
> CHRISTOPHE: It really worsened after 2001, after the New York attacks. In the years 2002, 2003 and 2004 there was a huge clampdown. I do not recall the figures but 4,000 passes were withdrawn at the time on the airport compounds … (Interview, February 2014).

Aurélien means that the pass allowing access to the airport secure zone could be easily withdrawn, depriving activists of their livelihoods. It became more complicated for trade unionists to engage in activism after the 9/11 terrorist attacks.

16 Now called *Direction générale de la sécurité intérieure* since April 30, 2014. This department took over the missions of the *Direction centrale du renseignement intérieur* (itself created in 2008 and encompassing the missions of the *Direction Centrale des Renseignements Généraux* and of the *Direction de la Surveillance du Territoire*). Cf. http://www.interieur.gouv.fr/Le-ministere/DGSI Accessed May 3, 2016.

In conclusion, the institution of the waiting zone is financed by carriers sanctions. Transport companies pay a steep price for bringing inadmissible travelers. In addition to having to cover the costs of confinement and return, they are legally compelled to pay fines each time a passenger is refused entry for reasons pertaining to travel documents. Carriers sanctions and refugee protection have been mutually exclusive from the very beginning, in spite of the Schengen Convention and Annex 9 to the Chicago Convention mentioning the need for States parties to respect their obligations under the Refugee Convention. This outcome was predictable, since countries introduced sanctions against carriers in order to reduce the number of asylum seekers reaching their borders. Trade unionists at CDG refused to endorse the role of border police agents, but their actions against the carrier responsibility framework were bound to fail. Airline companies had no choice but to abide by the legal requirements in place, transferring the burden of document control to their own employees.

The Ministry of the Interior's civil servants I talked to do not see carriers sanctions as problematic for asylum claimants, for they do not think that some people may be genuine refugees. These findings support Macklin's argument that the refugee is disappearing discursively (2005). As she writes, "a significant segment of the public believes that many asylum seekers are frauds, that is, migrants with no fear of persecution who attempt to use the refugee system to circumvent otherwise restrictive entry provisions" (Macklin 2005, 2). After demonstrating that carriers sanctions, a *non-entrée* mechanism, are funding the waiting zone, next chapter will argue that the waiting zone *itself* functions as a *non-entrée* mechanism.

CHAPTER 9

The Waiting Zone: the Last Gate to Keep Asylum Seekers Away

This chapter provides evidence that the waiting zone *in itself* constitutes the ultimate gate that asylum seekers need to pass before finally reaching the regular refugee status determination system. These findings buttress the argument developed throughout this book: nowhere countries constitute *non-entrée* mechanisms *per se*. The waiting zone serves the same purpose as its predecessor, the international zone. It is one of many devices crafted by States to keep asylum claimants away from their territory. In fact, the French waiting zone constitutes the last *non-entrée* mechanism to France (and the Schengen area) when all the upstream ones (including carriers sanctions) have failed.

Interpretation and communication issues, along with unsatisfactory access to legal recourses, filter asylum claimants dramatically. It is challenging for asylum claimants to appeal against the decision refusing them entry to the territory. Observation of court hearings, statistics and interviews suggest that administrative judges embrace the executive's perspective on and narrative about those seeking international protection at French borders.

1 Interpretation and Communication Issues

OFPRA, the refugee agency, has a small unit inside ZAPI 3, at the heart of Charles de Gaulle's waiting zone. From there, OFPRA agents hear all claimants placed in the waiting zone on the grounds of asylum claims, whether located at Charles de Gaulle or in French territories overseas. Interpretation always takes place over the phone, a practice which raises complications.[1] Michaël's company occasionally provides interpretation services for OFPRA's department of asylum at the border. Michäel explains that the conditions in which interpreters work are far from ideal:

1 At the beginning of the 2000s, interpreters would come on site from time to time. This is no longer the case. OFPRA agents mentioned only one recent exception: two children aged 12 and 6 had arrived accompanied by a smuggler. An interpreter in Filipino was brought, in order to "reassure the children" (Interview with Stéphanie, Miriam and Charline, November 2013).

 | DOI:10.1163/9789004383500_014

MICHAËL:	Work conditions are not good over the phone: being an interpreter over the phone does not make sense.
RESEARCHER:	It was one of my questions.
MICHAËL:	You cannot hear anything. Do you know how they work over there? The microphone is on the table.
RESEARCHER:	I saw the desk.
MICHAËL:	You have the microphone on the table. So the claimant is here, it resonates; you do not hear the question from the protection officer [*officer de protection,* i.e. refugee agency agent tasked with hearing asylum claimants] ... it is impossible (Interview, July 2014).

These difficulties are compounded when both OFPRA agents and interpreters carry out the interview over the phone. Poor audio quality and lack of visual contact may impede understanding. Furthermore, telephone interviews may fail to create a sense of safety for the claimant. In response to my question "is there anything that could be improved regarding asylum at the border?" Jeanne, from the Ministry of the Interior, answered:

> About what can be improved, my opinion is that OFPRA should not confine itself to phone interviews; they should at least have the person on videoconferencing, so that they see him or her. There are things that you cannot hear over a phone; you will not necessarily hear that someone is tense, or maybe you will, but you will see a behavior on videoconferencing. And the person will also see to whom he or she is talking to. This is a matter on which we [Ministry of the Interior] disagree with OFPRA. But it requires means. And even when we have an asylum claim in the Reunion Island, it is them [OFPRA at CDG], over the phone. I find it problematic. Of course they introduce themselves, of course they explain who they are, but the claimant does not see who [it is].

RESEARCHER:	Yes it is difficult to trust in these conditions.
JEANNE:	or to feel that you can trust. It is a little complicated (Interview, November 2013).

While OFPRA assured me that every individual claiming asylum at the CDG border was heard in person (Interview with Stéphanie, Miriam and Charline, November 2013), Christian could not agree less with this statement. According to this experienced lawyer, many claimants in ZAPI 3 talk to OFPRA agents over the phone:

CHRISTIAN: Often, I mean always, the person is interrogated over the phone.

RESEARCHER: Not at Roissy, it is the only exception. This is what I have been told.

CHRISTIAN: It is often by phone; for all the cases I had, most of the time it was over the phone.

RESEARCHER: Really? Even those at Roissy do their OFPRA interview over the phone?

CHRISTIAN: Yes, yes, over the phone. OFPRA is not always on site. It is not true. The last case I had, it was 10 days ago, it was a homosexual from Cameroon. He had been to the infirmary just before his interview; the doctor had given him a sedative because he was really unwell. He did his phone interview; one answer out of two was off the mark [*à côté de la plaque*]. He explained that it was difficult for him to discuss his homosexuality over the phone with someone he did not know, who was not necessarily listening carefully. It is difficult by phone and the judge reproached him that. To reject his claim, his appeal, the judge said: "answers are stereotyped, conventional, not personalized, summary; his story is not credible".

RESEARCHER: Because the conditions he was in did not allow him to present his story?

CHRISTIAN: He was rather in extremely unfavorable conditions to narrate an intimate story over the phone. So this is an important critique. Try to get numbers, information. But as far as I am concerned, each time I get asylum seekers it is over the phone.

RESEARCHER: At Roissy?

CHRISTIAN: Yes, at Roissy, I insist.

RESEARCHER: I am a little surprised. I met OFPRA; they told me that at Roissy interviews with refugee agency personnel took place in person.

CHRISTIAN: They lied to you; it is not possible. If you want I can give you the file of Ambe, the Cameroonian. I have always had phone interviews (Interview, December 2013).

Claimants interviewed in person at CDG may find it challenging to present their stories. Miriam from OFPRA explained that a policeman was always sitting on a chair just outside OFPRA's office in ZAPI 3, "to make sure everything is going well" (Interview with Miriam, November 2013). But the presence of authorities may not resonate well with someone who experienced persecution at the hands of State agents, creating an unsafe environment. Those seeking international protection at Orly airport face even more adversarial conditions, having to undergo their phone interview inside the police headquarters. At the time of research, it was actually written policy that claimants be heard in such conditions. The internal regulations document, posted on the wall of the room serving as Orly's "day" waiting zone, read: "this confidential interview [with OFPRA agents] will be carried out from the premises of Orly border police, by phone" (observations, February 2014). Since the European Court of Human Rights condemned France in 2007 in the *Gebremedhin* case, asylum seekers whose story was found "manifestly unfounded" have 48 hours to appeal against this decision. They cannot be returned during this period of time. However, while this procedure may be satisfactory on paper, in practice it is extremely difficult for claimants to initiate such recourse.

2 Unsatisfactory Access to Legal Recourses against Refusal to Enter Territory on Asylum Grounds

The number of individuals passing the manifestly unfounded test fluctuates from year to year. While 38.4 percent of claimants entered France on asylum grounds in 2000, it was the case of only 4 percent of claimants in 2003.[2] In recent years admissions to the territory have increased. In 2011, 10.1 percent of asylum seekers were admitted to the territory (1,857 OFPRA hearings for 188 admissions). This figure rose to 13 percent in 2012 (1,954 hearings for 255 admissions), 16.9 percent in 2013 (1,263 hearings for 214 admissions) and 28.9 percent in 2014 (OFPRA, April 10, 2015, 64). The law changed after I collected data. Since July 29, 2015, a third party may be present at OFPRA interviews. Claimants may elect to be accompanied by a representative of an NGO (accredited by the government-cf. chapter 6) or by their counsel (CESEDA 2016, article L.231-8-1). However, it has to be noted that the law confers a limited role to third parties: the accompanying person can only intervene at the end of the interview to make observations (CESEDA 2016, art. L.723–6).

2 In 2000, OFPRA agents at the border heard 5,262 claimants, of which 2,019 were admitted to the territory. This admission figure dropped dramatically in 2003 where 5,633 claimants were heard, resulting in only 229 admissions.

Individuals whose requests to enter France on asylum grounds were rejected, face hardships in appealing their cases. Appeals against the Ministry of the Interior's decision have to be launched within 48 hours of receipt of the decision. Appeals need to be written in French and be sufficiently well formulated to meet the Administrative Court's requirements: otherwise they will be automatically rejected without any hearing. Hence, it is impossible for a non-native French speaker, not well-versed in French administrative law, to write such an appeal.

The chances of going to court are very slim for those receiving their rejection letter during the weekends, as Anafé volunteers do not provide legal aid during this time. Dorian, from the UNHCR delegation in Paris, acknowledged that this situation, albeit satisfactory on paper, was not satisfactory in practice (phone interview, January 2014). Ségolène, custody and liberty judge, went further in suggesting that the European Court of Human Rights may well condemn France for depriving asylum claimants of an effective recourse. She explained:

> Sometimes you have in front of you a person who asked to enter France on asylum grounds and who is still within the delay to appeal. Therefore, you explain to him, you say: "Sir, you asked to enter France on asylum grounds and it was turned down, but you are still within the delay to appeal this administrative decision". Then you tell him: "Sir, my decision is to keep you [in the waiting zone] and there you can appeal within 24 hours, starting from now, time of notification". How do you want these poor detainees coming from Ghana or Brazil to understand? If they had a lawyers' clinic they could go there with the decisions and the lawyer could say: "here you can do that". I believe that one day we will get condemned because these are not effective recourses.
>
> RESEARCHER: You mean by the European Court of Human Rights?
>
> SÉGOLÈNE: Yes, one day someone will say "wait, there are no effective recourses" (Interview, November 2013).

Anafé volunteers assisting detainees with their appeals find this task challenging on two accounts: it is emotionally draining and rarely successful. Raoul recounts his experience of "contagious trauma" (Coddington 2017):

> It is always said regarding asylum claims that telling is reliving, and listening is reliving with the other person too. So you go home with all these stories. When the person lived a year of atrocities, when she takes two

> hours to tell you, you are left with five minutes in your head. One year already condensed in two hours; you are left with the horror (Interview, October 2013).

Volunteers are well aware that, from a statistical standpoint, appeals are rarely successful. For example, in 2013, out of 1,346 individuals seeking authorization to enter France on asylum grounds, 1,044 were turned down after meeting with OFPRA.[3] Of the rejected 1,044, only 84 entered the territory after the Administrative Court heard their appeal (government statistics, Anafé 2015, 161).[4] Raoul continued: "So you see, it is not always easy; from a humane standpoint what we are told is difficult and when you know it is useless …" (Interview, October 2013). I observed a few hearings before the administrative judge and will now share these ethnographic findings.

3 Administrative Court Hearings: When the Judge Embraces the State's Perspective

I observed a few hearings before the Administrative Court and do not claim to have enough information to draw general conclusions. I went to the Paris Administrative Court on three different days in September 2013. Claimants were appealing the Ministry of the Interior's decision denying them the possibility of entering France on asylum grounds at CDG.[5] One case particularly struck me. An Afghan unaccompanied minor was appealing the Ministry of the Interior's decision. His court-appointed lawyer did her best to rebut the Ministry of the Interior's arguments. She argued that a legal mistake had been made: OFPRA had gone beyond the examination of the manifestly unfounded character of his claim. According to the Ministry of the Interior, the minor's answers were too vague. For example, the question "Where is your province located in Afghanistan?" should have elicited a precise response, as this information was

3 222 individuals were granted leave to enter France after meeting with OFPRA, and 80 were not heard by OFPRA.

4 Unfortunately, official statistics do not give the number of claimants launching an appeal before the administrative court. Of the 1,124 claimants who did not enter France through OFPRA (i.e. 1,044 individuals whose claim was found manifestly unfounded + 80 individuals whose claim was not assessed by OFPRA), 355 were released from the waiting zone by the liberty and custody judge, and 36 were released by the Appeal Court (i.e. the court that rules over decisions made by the liberty and custody judge). Cf. official statistics published in Anafé's 2015 report, p 161.

5 At the Administrative Court of Paris, non-waiting zone cases are also heard.

"common knowledge". His lawyer urged the administrative judge to take into account the environment in which the young man had been raised: he had not attended school, had not learned geography and did not know how to read or write. Instead, he was working in the fields with his father. The Ministry of the Interior also reproached him for not giving enough precision regarding the Taliban's mode of recruitment.

Yet, his lawyer pointed out that the UNHCR had acknowledged in a 2012 report that intimidations and threats were indeed common in the region. The counsel insisted that her young client had received death threats. Referring to recent "gruesome events" (*événements macabres*), she remarked that sending him to a province where safety was not guaranteed would violate both article 33 of the Geneva Convention and article 3 of the European Convention on Human Rights. The *ad hoc* administrator asked for the permission to speak. The judge agreed, provided he had "new elements to bring". Explaining that he had known the young man for a week, he said he did not doubt he was telling the truth. The young man had seen many of his friends disappear in the mountains and never come back. As for the Ministry of the Interior's lawyer, she attempted to discredit the minor's story, pointing out that "it was strange for the Taliban to come 15 times to his home, only to leave a threat letter".

The interpreter, Mariam, was sitting next to me during the hearing. She told me that the minor was "really persecuted" and said she knew what she was talking about, being an Afghan national herself. He recounted that he had seen two of his friends being murdered. Mariam told me that this judge was "really tough". According to what she had observed on two previous days, the judge had not released any of the claimants from the waiting zone. These observations matched those of many other actors. Before the audience even started, I heard a chosen lawyer complain that the judge had already made her decisions, prior to hearing the claimants: "Anyway, she never releases anybody".[6] This judge was also well known to Anafé volunteers and employees. Raoul contributed to the NGO's December 2013 report on asylum procedures at the border. He observed many hearings before the Administrative Court in this capacity. Raoul never saw this judge quash a single Ministry of the Interior's decisions (Interview with Raoul, October 2013). My interview with Noémie took place before I went to the Administrative Court. This is how Noémie presented her experience at the Administrative Court:

6 I use the term "chosen lawyer" to describe a lawyer who has been approached by his client or his client's family.

RESEARCHER: Have you been to the Administrative Court?

NOÉMIE: Just once. It was horrible. I saw a judge in particular, very mean, and even border officers with whom I was talking were telling me "anyways she never releases anybody, forget about it [*c'est mort*]". She did not release anyone. And I was told: "There is no chance, even with a chosen lawyer [i.e. not a court-appointed lawyer], even someone from Sri Lanka with proofs of persecution will not be set free" (Interview, September 2013).

When I observed appeals before the administrative judge, I understood that Noémie had been describing the judge whose rulings I witnessed.

Mariam, the interpreter, explained that she had been instructed by the judge not to translate counsels' sentences because it was inconveniencing the judge. Under these conditions it must be difficult for appellants to understand proceedings enough to produce articulate answers. Furthermore, the judge instilled fear, allowing claimants to talk only if they had "something new to say", interrupting them ("I told you I was not interested in hearing again what your counsel just said"). To a national of Togo, who had started explaining persecutions at home, the judge replied: "if you want to say that you belong to a political party do not bother, I read the OFPRA decision". More research would need to be done regarding the procedure before the administrative judge. Nevertheless, statistics, observations and interviews suggest that some administrative judges embrace the executive's perspective and narrative when it comes to asylum claimants at the border, leaving the latter with infinitesimal chances of entering France. The judge rejected all the appeals that I observed and the young Afghan's case was no exception. His request to enter France to seek asylum was turned down. I later learned that he had been returned to Afghanistan where his life was in danger.

4 *Refoulement* of Asylum Claimants to Countries Where Their Lives or Freedom Are at Risk

Both Anafé (Interview with Raoul) and Red Cross representatives informed me that the young Afghan national had been returned to Afghanistan, where he became victim of the Taliban. I discussed this case with Gérard, an experienced Red Cross *ad hoc* administrator:

RESEARCHER: I saw an Afghan minor who was finally sent back.

GÉRARD: Is not it the one we were following? A minor who was then identified as an adult?

RESEARCHER: I am not sure but a Red Cross *ad hoc* administrator was there.

GÉRARD: We had a case. It must be him. This minor was returned because we were taken off the case. I think that he would not have been returned had he still been considered as an isolated minor … But the police had found documents stating he was an adult. We fought the decision to take us off the case; we went before the liberty and custody judge, before the public prosecutor but it did not work. So we were no longer *ad hoc* administrator on this case. He was sent back and it is true that it did not take place in good conditions. We found his trace but it was complicated.

RESEARCHER: If we are talking about the same person, Anafé told me that he was in the hands of the Taliban.

GÉRARD: Yes, absolutely, it is him. From the moment he was considered an adult, he was returned to his country of transit, the United Arab Emirates (UAE). We contacted human rights organizations in UAE so that they could find him but we never got an answer. And Mathieu, who was *ad hoc* administrator, was in touch with the family in Germany as his mother and brother were asylum seekers in Germany … At the end the family told Mathieu—we were in contact with Anafé on this case-that they had received news from his aunt; he had been returned from Dubai. *The aunt said she had found him but he was abducted under her eyes by a group of Taliban* (Interview, December 2013).

Individuals whose claim is found manifestly unfounded by OFPRA and whose appeal to the Administrative Court is unsuccessful (or upon expiry of the delay to appeal) move from the category of "asylum seeker" to that of "inadmissible person". Once assigned to the latter, they can be sent back at anytime.[7] Anafé

7 According to Anafé, in some instances the border police may also attempt to send back claimants before the expiry of the legal delay to appeal to the administrative court. This is a serious violation of domestic and international law. It was the case at Orly around 2011 (Interview with Lise and Anne, December 2013). Cf. also Anafé's December 2013 report, p. 25.

attempts to follow individuals once they leave the waiting zone. According to the organization's findings, the case of the young Afghan is not isolated. In fact, the NGO documented how a number of failed asylum claimants experienced mistreatment once returned to their countries of origin or transit (Anafé April 2010). Worrisomely, local authorities seem to have access to information regarding the asylum claim in some cases. Anafé recommended to French border agents to refrain from forwarding information pertaining to asylum claims to authorities in countries of return (Anafé, April 2010). Anafé volunteer Noémie recounted:

> Sometimes authorities in the country of origin know that [returned] individuals sought asylum in France.
>
> RESEARCHER: But how can they know that?
>
> NOÉMIE: We do not know exactly. You were asking me how local authorities could know that a person sought asylum. Actually, when someone leaves Roissy or the waiting zone, there is a file with all his or her documents that is given to the pilot. Or, if there is an escort, the escorting officers have it. This file is not supposed to contain asylum-related documents, but sometimes it happens.
>
> RESEARCHER: Really?
>
> NOÉMIE: We do not really know but we have testimonies of persons who arrived and were imprisoned. Local authorities knew and we think that the documents were given to them.
>
> RESEARCHER: How else could they know? If the person himself or herself does not say anything ...
>
> NOÉMIE: Also, at Anafé we visit airport terminals and it is really interesting because we have the opportunity to talk to many border officers. Because there are four police stations and four holding rooms and each time you talk to different agents. We often ask them the following question: "when you return someone, are there also documents pertaining to the asylum claim in the file?" And sometimes they tell you "yes of course". Then they do some research and they tell you "no, actually no" (Interview, September 2013).

While the officers interviewed by Noémie may not be the ones directly responsible for the return of failed claimants, their answers are nevertheless a matter of concern. They indicate a widespread lack of understanding of asylum-related issues within the border police force.

Air France trade unionists shed light on the mechanisms by which local authorities may come in possession of a returnee's travel documents. Christophe and Jean told me:

CHRISTOPHE: We had problems with passports too, do you remember? [Talking to Jean] In countries where they [the police] gave passports to airline personnel, including to the pilot, when returns took place.

JEAN: They gave [the passport] to the pilot who, instead of giving it back to the individual gave it to authorities and the person was arrested with all the dangers of mistreatment.

CHRISTOPHE: People who had accepted to leave were returned. But instead of giving the passport back to the person, [the police] handed it to the pilot with instructions to give it to the police upon arrival. Some pilots were not doing this. During the flight they had the passport given back to the individual. They said: "it is none of my business, let him handle it, it is his passport after all … (Interview, February 2014).

Their statement shows that returnees' treatment depends on luck. It is highly variable and depends on the pilot's ethical compass. In June 2017 a pilot let me briefly access the Air France procedures manual intended for the company's pilots. Worringly, the manual recommends that pilots directly hand the documents of the returnee to local authorities upon arrival, buttressing the information previously gathered.

Conclusions

1 How to Render Nowhere Countries Visible?

Compartmentalized methodological and disciplinary approaches cannot grasp the diversity and vastness of exclusionary mechanisms that uphold nowhere countries. Disciplinary boundaries need to be crossed to study the border, a concept that lies at the crossroads of law, history, geography, sociology, anthropology, philosophy, psychology and political science. In order to render visible what would otherwise remain hidden, the researcher needs to adopt interdisciplinary lenses and methods. Research anchored in a unique discipline and way of collecting and analyzing data would not provide sufficient leverage to understand the issue. As Morin and Kern (1999, 1) write:

> The reductionist approach, which consists in relying on a single series of factors to regulate the totality of problems associated with the multiform crisis we are currently in the middle of, is less a solution than the problem itself. … Intelligence that is fragmented, compartmentalized, mechanistic, disjunctive, and reductionistic [*sic*] breaks the complexity of the world into disjointed pieces, splits up problems, separates that which is linked together, and renders unidimensional the multidimensional …

They continue: "We need a kind of thinking that relinks that which is disjointed and compartmentalized, that respects diversity as it recognizes unity, and that tries to discern interdependencies" (Morin and Kern 1999, 130). The present book strives to link laws and political discourses with the representations of the people governing or caught in exclusionary frameworks. Engaging both in macro and micro levels of analysis proved necessary. The processes that sustain nowhere countries are creative, incredibly complex and constantly changing, making the latter objects that would be undecipherable if not for congruent macro *and* micro approaches. The same exclusionary logic shapes laws and mental landscapes. Such an analysis at Charles de Gaulle airport revealed that most stakeholders working on or in nowhere countries lack legal consciousness and focus on their tasks, in their professional *habitus*, without questioning the consequences (Bourdieu 2000). Most seem ignorant of the position they occupy within the larger exclusion machinery: the expression *chacun dans son rôle* (everyone is in one's role) was frequently used to elude further questioning on individual's responsibility regarding other human beings' fate. Philosophers and linguists observed the role of stereotyped language

 | DOI:10.1163/9789004383500_015

in totalitarian States (Arendt 1964 and Klemperer 2000). To a lesser extent, similar processes are at work in nowhere countries. In these spaces at the margins of liberal democracies, stakeholders seem to use stereotyped language and categories to avoid facing moral dilemmas. A few stakeholders I met were distressed and expressed strong concerns regarding their own actions within this institutional exclusionary system.

2 Why Do States Create Nowhere Countries?

Having lost their power to regulate (most of) economic and financial matters in a globalized world, States have turned to the only policy domain they can still impact at home: border control. As Dauvergne (2008, 169) remarks, "migration law is being transformed as the last bastion of sovereignty". She writes (2008, 169): "as the capacity of national governments to influence policy in many areas is eroded by global forces, control efforts have been concentrated on those areas that remain, ostensibly, within the direct control of national lawmakers". Feeling their very existence under threat, States have deployed strategies to protect themselves, thereby confirming Devereux's (1994) concept of countertransference. Human beings are animated by archaic psychological, social and biological mechanisms that push them to be, at first, afraid of otherness. These profoundly primal, unconscious mechanisms, may explain why governments from opposite sides of the political spectrum, in countries far away from one another, have adopted and pursued similar exclusionary policies. In spite of their declared political differences, governments from the Left and the Right have built upon and buttressed each other's exclusionary policies. Using the sophisticated legal and legislative tools of liberal democracies, States seem to have engaged in frantic moves to justify and preserve their existence. Bauman (2004, 66) notes:

> Uncertainty and anguish born of uncertainty are globalization's staple products. State powers can do next to nothing to placate, let alone quash uncertainty. The most they can do is to refocus it on objects within reach; shift it from the objects they can do nothing about to those they can at least make a show of being able to handle and control. Refugees, asylum seekers, immigrants-the waste products of globalization-fit the bill perfectly.

Nowhere countries are the product of multiple interactions between the executive, legislative, and judicial powers, and, sometimes, activists and NGOs.

3 How to Conceptualize the Exclusion upon Which Nowhere Countries Are Established?

This book identified two forms of extra-territorial exclusion that have sustained the creation and operation of nowhere countries. Under the first configuration of extra-territoriality, State authorities consider non-citizens to be *not* physically located on the State's territory. Exclusion from rights is triggered by geography and legal absence: situated in a geographical space *construed* as non-national, some incoming people are denied access to the legal, human and refugee rights attached to sovereign territory. This is what happened to non-citizens stranded in the international zone at Paris' airports in the 1980s and early 1990s: the government instructed border authorities to disregard the applicable domestic legal framework (i.e. article 35 bis of the 1945 Ordinance) and its associated rights. Placed in a legal limbo, foreign nationals were refused the protection of the law on account of their location in a space *portrayed* as extra-territorial. Similarly, the non-citizens from the Fujian Province who arrived off the Canadian coast of British Columbia in 1999 were taken to the Esquimalt naval base, a place *depicted as* "Not-Canada". Canadian authorities declared the naval base a "port of entry", claiming that the Chinese people were still walking the tunnels of an international airport, not yet landed in Canada. This sovereign trick allowed the Canadian government to deny access to lawyers during processing at the base: migrants being assessed at a port of entry do *not* have the right to legal counsel under Canadian law. This first configuration of extra-territoriality attracted widespread criticism from human and refugee rights activists, lawyers and courts, and may have forced States to resort to a subtler configuration.

The second form of extra-territoriality (the second and the first form not being mutually exclusive) is less manifest: when physically located in spaces *deemed* extra-territorial, non-citizens are not refused legal protection. Instead, they are subjected to a less protective regime compared to that granted to foreign nationals who are not located in spaces *construed* as extra-national. Exclusion from the regular rights regime is triggered by geography *and* a legal technique. Although non-citizens receive the exclusionary status when located in a space *declared* extra-territorial, the exclusionary regime follows them well after they leave this space. Once non-citizens are assigned to the French or the Australian legal regime of exclusion, they carry it with them whenever they go. The waiting zone and the excision framework have created a particular legal space of lesser rights that always accompanies the individual, no matter his or her location. "Offshore entry persons" and "unauthorised maritime arrivals" have been banned from Australia's refugee determination process, even when entering the country's mainland at a later date. Practitioners explain that non-citizens carry the waiting zone status like a "backpack" or are in a waiting zone "bubble". Christian, a lawyer, uses both terms (Interview, December 2013).

Importantly, alternate legal regimes may be enshrined in the law or exist *de facto*, as evidenced by the Canadian case. The Chinese boat people's location on Esquimalt naval base, a space *declared* extra-territorial, triggered a less protective legal regime that was not engraved in Canadian law. While the asylum seekers were granted due process on paper, in practice their access to rights was altered by geography. The second form of exclusion from rights through extra-territoriality allows States to appear engaged in the global refugee regime while subverting it. Both configurations of extra-territoriality enable States to tailor the border to suit their immigration goals.

4 Nowhere Countries' Purpose: Prevent Asylum Seekers' Arrival

State authorities create and operate nowhere countries to transfer the obligations owed to asylum seekers under the Refugee Convention to other Nations. Nowhere countries constitute a *non-entrée* mechanism *per se*. They are also the last link in a wider network of devices designed to prevent asylum seekers' arrival. The French waiting zone (cf. chapters 8 and 9) and the Australian excised offshore place (cf. chapter 5) have served the same purpose: they have constituted the last *non-entrée* device when all the previous ones have failed to hold back claimants. Weber (2007, 87) remarks: "the need for excision as a back-up for interdiction was explained by the Immigration Minister: 'No amount of practicable surveillance over such a broad range of coastline and range of islands will be successful ... The only way to be successful is to excise these islands from the migration zone' ". Frenetic attempts to excise Australian territory denote the anxiety of Australian leaders in the face of arrivals. Tremendous efforts were deployed to create the excision policy, as it was seen as the last barrier to contain unplanned entries, when all the previous gates had failed.

France, Australia, Morocco and Canada have established spaces of lesser rights to deter and penalize the arrival of unplanned non-citizens, including asylum seekers. All countries share the same overarching goal; however, the rationale for thwarting people seeking refuge has varied slightly from one country to the next. For example, unlike French governments, Australian leaders have not questioned the fact that asylum seekers are in danger in their countries of origin. While in France asylum claimants have been characterized as economic migrants in disguise, in Australia they have been portrayed as "queue jumpers", i.e. as people trying to obtain refugee status before those waiting patiently in refugee camps, outside of Australia, for the paperwork granting entry into the country.

Non-citizens arriving to "Not-Australia" and to "Not-France" have not been subjected to the same time frames: while some asylum seekers spent years in Nauru or in Papua New Guinea, non-French nationals cannot be kept in the French waiting zone for more than 26 days. The citizenry's emotional implication has also varied greatly in Australia and in France. From the Tampa incident, Australian leaders' exclusionary policies have garnered considerable electoral support. By contrast, the issue of the waiting zone remains largely unknown to the public in France. Most passengers waiting to board their planes ignore the fact that people are detained a few kilometers or meters away from them.

5 Creating and Operating Nowhere Countries Is Costly from an Economic and Human Standpoint

Excluding non-citizens from rights is costly from both an economic and a human perspective. Transport companies and taxpayers support the financial cost of operating nowhere countries. Fines severely impact carriers' budgets, sometimes driving the latter to bankruptcy. Estimates suggest that the Australian policy of exclusion weighs taxpayers down. Precise numbers are impossible to obtain, as Australian officials have been reluctant to reveal the cost of offshore detention on Nauru and Papua New Guinea. However, analysts in the Parliamentary Library analyzed Senate estimates hearing transcripts, concluding that Australians had paid $1.6 billion to build, maintain and run the detention center on Manus Island since its re-opening in 2012 (Gartrell, August 20, 2016). The figures did not include the cost of resettlement, charter flights to and from the island, or the additional aid granted to Papua New Guinea. In 2016, it was estimated that Australian taxpayers had paid more than $1 million for each of the 2000 foreign national detained on Manus Island (Gartrell, August 20, 2016). The greatest cost of all has been in terms of human suffering. Confinement in nowhere countries has often resulted in great physical and mental hardships for detainees.

6 Nowhere Countries are Social Constructs that May Be Unmade

This book traced the recent *creation* of nowhere countries, showing how non-citizens have been excluded from rights through extra-territoriality at home. Findings deconstructed the deeply ingrained idea that less protective systems of rights, premised on extra-territoriality, are natural in liberal democracies (France, Australia and Canada) bound by human rights and refugee conventions. This analysis shed light on how some ideas become common sense and set aside different interpretations (Waitt, 2010). Public opinion nowadays views questions pertaining to asylum seeking as a matter of State security rather than as a rights issue (Wihtol de Wenden 2016). As social constructs and historical products, nowhere countries are *not* unchangeable. This book hopes to have conveyed the message that nowhere countries have been made. Hence, they could be unmade.

Appendices

APPENDIX 1

Table of Research Participants: Experts

Pseudonyms are used except when consent was explicitly given to disclose identity and when it could not be foreseen that such disclosure would be detrimental to the interviewee.

Pseudonym/name (first and last name)	Organization	Role	Sex
Agnès	Cimade	Employee	Female (F)
Anna	Hotel "Ibis" at Orly	Managerial position	F
Anne	Anafé	Employee	F
Arnaud	Border police	Agent at CDG	Male (M)
Aurélien	CFDT-Air France	Trade unionist	M
Cédric	Chaplaincy at CDG	Priest	M
Charline	OFPRA	Employee	F
Christophe	CFDT (trade union)-Air France	Trade unionist	M
Christian	Legal firm	Legal counsel	M
Clémence	Legal firm	Legal counsel	F
Clotilde	Ministry of the Interior	Employee-department administering fines to carriers	F
Danièle Lochak	University of Paris-Ouest-Nanterre la Défense	Professor Emeritus of public law	F
Dominique	Border police	High-ranking agent at CDG	M
Dominique Monget-Sarrail	Legal firm	Legal counsel in the *Amuur* case	F
Dorian	UNHCR	Employee	M
Frédéric	Legal firm	Legal counsel	M

 | DOI:10.1163/9789004383500_016

Pseudonym/name (first and last name)	Organization	Role	Sex
Georges	Red Cross or *Famille Assistance*	*Ad hoc* administrator	M
Gérard	Red Cross or *Famille Assistance*	*Ad hoc* administrator	M
Gilles	Border police	High-ranking agent at CDG	M
Guillaume	Border police	High-ranking agent at Orly	M
Henri	Border police	Agent at CDG	M
Jacques	General Inspector of places of deprivation of liberty	Inspector	M
Jean	CFDT-Air France	Ex-trade unionist	M
Jeanne	Ministry of the Interior	Employee-department reviewing asylum seekers' requests at the border	F
Jérémie	Border police	Agent at CDG	M
Joël	Translation Company	Interpreter	M
Laura	Red Cross	Former mediator	F
Léa	Ministry of Justice	Judge	F
Lise	Anafé	Employee	F
Louise	Senate	Senator and former lawyer	F
Luc	Legal firm	Legal counsel	M
Lydia	Anafé	Volunteer	F
Mathieu	Red Cross or *Famille Assistance*	*Ad hoc* administrator	M
Mariam	Paris Administrative Court	Interpreter	F
Michaël	Translation company	Company's director	M

Pseudonym/name (first and last name)	Organization	Role	Sex
Noémie	Anafé	Former volunteer	F
Miriam	OFPRA	Employee	F
Paul	Red Cross	Former mediator	M
Philippe	Border police	Agent at CDG	M
Pierre	Medical center at ZAPI 3	Doctor	M
Raphaël	Chaplaincy at CDG	Priest	M
Raoul	Anafé	Volunteer	M
Rémi Rouquette	Legal firm	Legal counsel and former lecturer in public law	M
Ségolène	Ministry of Justice	Judge	F
Serge Slama	University of Paris Ouest-Nanterre la Défense	Professor of public law	M
Simon	Border police	Agent at CDG	M
Stéphanie	OFPRA	Employee	F
Sylvie	Red Cross	Mediator-minor zone	F
Valentin	Border police	Agent at cdg	M

APPENDIX 2

Table of Research Participants: Individuals Placed under the Waiting Zone Regime[a]

Pseudonym	Geographic origin	Sex
Ajitabh	Sri Lanka	M
Alfredo	Cuba	M
Amanda	Central America	F
Amine	Algeria	M
André	Central African Republic	M
Arthur	Democratic Republic of Congo-living in France	M
Carmen	Central America	F
Cherif	Algeria	M
Françoise	Senegal	F
Gabriela	Central America	F
Hassan	Syria-born in Kuwait- descendant of Palestine refugees	M
Isabela	Nicaragua	F
Jazmin	Central America	F
José	Nicaragua	M
Joyce	Central America	F
Laurent	Senegal	M
Leïla	Morocco	F
Lola	Central America	F
Rosalita	Nicaragua	F
Veronica	Central America	F

a Appendix 2 contains the pseudonyms of all the individuals placed under the waiting zone regime that I personally met or whom I heard about over the course of my research on and at Charles de Gaulle airport. The individuals that are not mentioned in this book appear in other publication venues.

 | DOI:10.1163/9789004383500_017

APPENDIX 3

Migration Amendment (Excision from Migration Zone) Act 2001 (Australia) No. 127, 2001

An Act to excise certain Australian territory from the migration zone under the *Migration Act 1958* for purposes related to unauthorised arrivals, and for related purposes

Schedule 1—Amendment of the Migration Act 1958 3

Migration Amendment (Excision from Migration Zone) Act 2001 No. 127, 2001

An Act to excise certain Australian territory from the migration zone under the *Migration Act 1958* for purposes related to unauthorised arrivals, and for related purposes

[*Assented to 27 September 2001*]

The Parliament of Australia enacts:

1 Short title

This Act may be cited as the *Migration Amendment (Excision from Migration Zone) Act 2001*.

2 Commencement

This Act commences on the day on which it receives the Royal Assent.

3 Schedule(s)

Each Act that is specified in a Schedule to this Act is amended or repealed as set out in the applicable items in the Schedule concerned, and any other item in a Schedule to this Act has effect according to its terms.

4 Application of amendments

The amendments made by this Act apply to a visa application made after the excision time for the excised offshore place concerned.

Example: If a person becomes an offshore entry person by entering Australia at Christmas Island, then the amendments apply to any visa application made by the person after 2 pm on 8 September 2001 by legal time in the Australian Capital Territory.

 | DOI:10.1163/9789004383500_018

Schedule 1—Amendment of the Migration Act 1958

1 *Subsection 5(1)*

Insert:

excised offshore place means any of the following:

(a) the Territory of Christmas Island;
(b) the Territory of Ashmore and Cartier Islands;
(c) the Territory of Cocos (Keeling) Islands;
(d) any other external Territory that is prescribed by the regulations for the purposes of this paragraph;
(e) any island that forms part of a State or Territory and is prescribed for the purposes of this paragraph;
(f) an Australian sea installation;
(g) an Australian resources installation.

Note: The effect of this definition is to excise the listed places and installations from the migration zone for the purposes of limiting the ability of offshore entry persons to make valid visa applications.

2 *Subsection 5(1)*

Insert:

excision time, for an excised offshore place, means:

(a) for the Territory of Christmas Island—2 pm on 8 September 2001 by legal time in the Australian Capital Territory; or
(b) for the Territory of Ashmore and Cartier Islands—2 pm on 8 September 2001 by legal time in the Australian Capital Territory; or
(c) for the Territory of Cocos (Keeling) Islands—12 noon on 17 September 2001 by legal time in the Australian Capital Territory; or
(d) for any other external Territory that is prescribed by the regulations for the purposes of the definition of ***excised offshore place***—the time when the regulations commence; or
(e) for any island that forms part of a State or Territory and is prescribed by the regulations for the purposes of the definition of ***excised offshore place***—the time when the regulations commence; or
(f) for an Australian sea installation—the commencement of the *Migration Amendment (Excision from Migration Zone) Act 2001*; or
(g) for an Australian resources installation—the commencement of the *Migration Amendment (Excision from Migration Zone) Act 2001*.

3 *Subsection 5(1)*

Insert:

offshore entry person means a person who:

(a) entered Australia at an excised offshore place after the excision time for that offshore place; and

(b) became an unlawful non-citizen because of that entry.

4 *After Section 46*

Insert:

46A Visa applications by offshore entry persons

(1) An application for a visa is not a valid application if it is made by an offshore entry person who:

(a) is in Australia; and

(b) is an unlawful non-citizen.

(2) If the Minister thinks that it is in the public interest to do so, the Minister may, by written notice given to an offshore entry person, determine that subsection (1) does not apply to an application by the person for a visa of a class specified in the determination.

(3) The power under subsection (2) may only be exercised by the Minister personally.

(4) If the Minister makes a determination under subsection (2), the Minister must cause to be laid before each House of the Parliament a statement that:

(a) sets out the determination; and

(b) sets out the reasons for the determination, referring in particular to the Minister's reasons for thinking that the Minister's actions are in the public interest.

(5) A statement under subsection (4) must not include:

(a) the name of the offshore entry person; or

(b) any information that may identify the offshore entry person; or

(c) if the Minister thinks that it would not be in the public interest to publish the name of another person connected in any way with the matter concerned—the name of that other person or any information that may identify that other person.

(6) A statement under subsection (4) must be laid before each House of the Parliament within 15 sitting days of that House after:

(a) if the determination is made between 1 January and 30 June (inclusive) in a year—1 July in that year; or

(b) if the determination is made between 1 July and 31 December (inclusive) in a year—1 January in the following year.

(7) The Minister does not have a duty to consider whether to exercise the power under subsection (2) in respect of any offshore entry person whether the Minister is requested to do so by the offshore entry person or by any other person, or in any other circumstances.

[*Minister's second reading speech made in—*
House of Representatives on 18 September 2001
Senate on 20 September 2001]
(184/01)

APPENDIX 4

Migration Amendment (Excision from Migration Zone) (Consequential Provisions) Act 2001 (Australia) No. 128, 2001

An Act to make consequential provision for dealing with unauthorised arrivals in places excised from the migration zone under the *Migration Act 1958* for purposes related to unauthorised arrivals, and for related purposes

[*Assented to 27 September 2001*]

The Parliament of Australia enacts:

1 Short title

This Act may be cited as the *Migration Amendment (Excision from Migration Zone) (Consequential Provisions) Act 2001*.

2 Commencement

This Act commences, or is taken to have commenced, at the same time as the *Migration Amendment (Excision from Migration Zone) Act 2001*.

3 Schedule(s)

(1) Each Act, and each set of regulations, that is specified in a Schedule to this Act is amended or repealed as set out in the applicable items in the Schedule concerned, and any other item in a Schedule to this Act has effect according to its terms.

(2) The amendment of any regulation under subsection (1) does not prevent the regulation, as so amended, from being amended or repealed by the Governor-General.

(3) To avoid doubt, regulations amended under subsection (1) are taken to still be regulations.

4 Application of amendments

The amendment made by item 7 of Schedule 1 applies to:

(a) the institution of proceedings on or after the day on which this Act receives the Royal Assent; and

(b) the continuation, after the day on which this Act receives the Royal Assent, of proceedings that were instituted before that day, being proceedings instituted after the excision time for the excised offshore place concerned.

Example: Proceedings of the kind mentioned in section 494AA of the Migration Act are instituted, before the day on which this Act receives the Royal Assent, in relation to

 | DOI:10.1163/9789004383500_019

a person who became an offshore entry person by entering Australia at Christmas Island. Those proceedings cannot be continued after the day on which this Act receives the Royal Assent.

Schedule 1—Amendment of the Migration Act 1958

1 *Subsection 5(1) (At the End of the Definition of Immigration Detention)*

Add:

Note: See also section 198A, which provides that being dealt with under that section does not amount to ***immigration detention***.

2 *Subsection 189(1)*

After "migration zone", insert "(other than an excised offshore place)".

3 *Paragraph 189(2)(a)*

After "migration zone", insert "(other than an excised offshore place)".

4 *At the End of Section 189*

Add:

(3) If an officer knows or reasonably suspects that a person in an excised offshore place is an unlawful non-citizen, the officer may detain the person.

(4) If an officer reasonably suspects that a person in Australia but outside the migration zone:

(a) is seeking to enter an excised offshore place; and

(b) would, if in the migration zone, be an unlawful non-citizen;

the officer may detain the person.

(5) In subsections (3) and (4) and any other provisions of this Act that relate to those subsections, ***officer*** means an officer within the meaning of section 5, and includes a member of the Australian Defence Force.

5 *At the End of Paragraph 193(1)(c)*

Add ", (3) or (4)".

6 *After Section 198*

Insert:

198A Offshore entry person may be taken to a declared country

(1) An officer may take an offshore entry person from Australia to a country in respect of which a declaration is in force under subsection (3).

(2) The power under subsection (1) includes the power to do any of the following things within or outside Australia:
  (a) place the person on a vehicle or vessel;
  (b) restrain the person on a vehicle or vessel;
  (c) remove the person from a vehicle or vessel;
  (d) use such force as is necessary and reasonable.

(3) The Minister may:
  (a) declare in writing that a specified country:
    (i) provides access, for persons seeking asylum, to effective procedures for assessing their need for protection; and
    (ii) provides protection for persons seeking asylum, pending determination of their refugee status; and
    (iii) provides protection to persons who are given refugee status, pending their voluntary repatriation to their country of origin or resettlement in another country; and
    (iv) meets relevant human rights standards in providing that protection; and
  (b) in writing, revoke a declaration made under paragraph (a).

(4) An offshore entry person who is being dealt with under this section is taken not to be in ***immigration detention*** (as defined in subsection 5(1)).

(5) In this section, ***officer*** means an officer within the meaning of section 5, and includes a member of the Australian Defence Force.

7 After Section 494

Insert:

494AA Bar on certain legal proceedings relating to offshore entry persons

(1) The following proceedings against the Commonwealth may not be instituted or continued in any court:
  (a) proceedings relating to an offshore entry by an offshore entry person;
  (b) proceedings relating to the status of an offshore entry person as an unlawful non-citizen during any part of the ineligibility period;
  (c) proceedings relating to the lawfulness of the detention of an offshore entry person during the ineligibility period, being a detention based on the status of the person as an unlawful non-citizen;
  (d) proceedings relating to the exercise of powers under section 198A.

(2) This section has effect despite anything else in this Act or any other law.

(3) Nothing in this section is intended to affect the jurisdiction of the High Court under section 75 of the Constitution.

(4) In this section:

Commonwealth includes:

(a) an officer of the Commonwealth; and

(b) any other person acting on behalf of the Commonwealth.

ineligibility period means the period from the time of the offshore entry until the time when the person next ceases to be an unlawful non-citizen.

offshore entry means an entry into Australia that occurs:

(a) at an excised offshore place; and
(b) after the excision time for the offshore place concerned.

Schedule 2—Amendment of the Migration Regulations 1994

[1] *Schedule 1, Item 1127*

omit

[2] *Schedule 1, Part 4, Heading*

substitute

Part 4 Protection, Refugee and Humanitarian visas

[3] *Schedule 1, after Item 1401*

insert

1402. Refugee and Humanitarian (Class XB)

(1) Form: 842.
(2) Visa application charge: Nil.
(3) Other:
  (a) Application must be made outside Australia.
  (b) Applicant must be outside Australia.
  (c) Application by a person claiming to be a member of the family unit of a person who is an applicant for a Refugee and Humanitarian (Class XB) visa may be made at the same time and place as, and combined with, the application by that person.
(4) Subclasses:
  200 (Refugee)
  201 (In-country Special Humanitarian)
  202 (Global Special Humanitarian)
  203 (Emergency Rescue)
  204 (Woman at Risk)

447 (Secondary Movement Offshore Entry (Temporary))
451 (Secondary Movement Relocation (Temporary))

[4] *Schedule 2, after Clause 200.211*

insert

200.212

(1) The applicant, since leaving his or her home country, has not ever resided, for a continuous period of at least 7 days, in a country in which the applicant could have sought and obtained effective protection:
  (a) of the country; or
  (b) through the offices of the United Nations High Commissioner for Refugees located in that country.

(2) The Minister may waive the requirement under subclause (1) if the Minister is satisfied that it is in the public interest to do so.

[5] *Schedule 2, after Clause 202.211*

insert

202.212

(1) The applicant, since leaving his or her home country, has not ever resided, for a continuous period of at least 7 days, in a country in which the applicant could have sought and obtained effective protection:
  (a) of the country; or
  (b) through the offices of the United Nations High Commissioner for Refugees located in that country.

(2) The Minister may waive the requirement under subclause (1) if the Minister is satisfied that it is in the public interest to do so.

[6] *Schedule 2, after Clause 204.212*

insert

204.213

(1) The applicant, since leaving his or her home country, has not ever resided, for a continuous period of at least 7 days, in a country in which the applicant could have sought and obtained effective protection:
  (a) of the country; or
  (b) through the offices of the United Nations High Commissioner for Refugees located in that country.

(2) The Minister may waive the requirement under subclause (1) if the Minister is satisfied that it is in the public interest to do so.

[7] *Schedule 2, after Part 446*
insert

Subclass 447 Secondary Movement Offshore Entry (Temporary)

447.1 Interpretation

Note ***member of the family unit*** is defined in regulation 1.03.

No interpretation provisions specific to this Part.

447.2 Primary Criteria

Note The primary criteria must be satisfied by at least 1 member of a family unit. Other members of the family unit who are applicants for a visa of this subclass need satisfy only the secondary criteria.

447.21 Criteria to be satisfied at time of application

447.211 The applicant:

(a) is either:

(i) subject to persecution in the applicant's home country; or

(ii) subject to substantial discrimination, amounting to gross violation of human rights, in the applicant's home country; or

(iii) a female person who is subject to persecution or is registered as being of concern to the United Nations High Commissioner for Refugees; and

(b) is an offshore entry person.

447.22 Criteria to be satisfied at time of decision

447.221 The applicant continues to satisfy the criterion in clause 447.211.

447.222 The Minister is satisfied that there are compelling reasons for giving special consideration to granting the applicant a temporary visa, having regard to:

(a) the extent of the applicant's connection with Australia; and

(b) if the applicant continues to meet the requirement in subparagraph 447.211 (a) (i)—the degree of persecution to which the applicant is subject in the applicant's home country; and

(c) if the applicant continues to meet the requirement in subparagraph 447.211 (a) (ii)—the degree of discrimination to which the applicant is subject in the applicant's home country; and

(d) if the applicant continues to meet the requirement in subparagraph 447.211 (a) (iii)—whether the applicant has the protection of a male relative and is in danger of victimisation, harassment or serious abuse because of her sex; and

(e) whether there is any suitable country available, other than Australia, that can provide for the applicant's stay and protection from persecution, discrimination, victimisation, harassment or serious abuse; and
(f) the capacity of the Australian community to provide for the temporary stay of persons such as the applicant in Australia.

447.223 The Minister is satisfied that temporary stay in Australia would not be contrary to the interests of Australia.

447.224 Grant of the visa would not result in either:
(a) the number of Subclass 447 visas granted in a financial year exceeding the maximum number of Subclass 447 visas, as determined by Gazette Notice, that may be granted in that financial year; or
(b) the number of visas of particular classes (including Refugee and Humanitarian (Class XB) visa) granted in a financial year exceeding the maximum number of visas of those classes, as determined by Gazette Notice, that may be granted in that financial year.

447.225 The applicant satisfies public interest criteria 4001, 4002, 4003, 4004 and 4007.

447.226 If the applicant has previously been in Australia, the applicant satisfies special return criterion 5001.

447.227
(1) In relation to the family unit of the applicant, each member of the family unit who is an applicant for a Subclass 447 visa is a person who:
  (a) satisfies public interest criteria 4001, 4002, 4003, 4004 and 4007; and
  (b) if he or she has previously been in Australia—satisfies special return criterion 5001.
(2) In relation to the family unit of the applicant, each member of the family unit who is not an applicant for a Subclass 447 visa is a person who:
  (a) satisfies public interest criteria 4001, 4002, 4003 and 4004; and
  (b) satisfies public interest criterion 4007, unless the Minister is satisfied that it would be unreasonable to require the person to undergo assessment in relation to that criterion.

447.3 Secondary Criteria

Note These criteria must be satisfied by applicants who are members of the family unit of a person who satisfies the primary criteria.

447.31 Criteria to be Satisfied at Time of Application

447.311 The applicant:
(a) is a member of the family unit of a person who satisfies, or has satisfied, the criterion in clause 447.211; and
(b) is in the same country as that person.

447.32 Criteria to be satisfied at time of decision

447.321 The applicant continues to be a member of the family unit of a person who, having satisfied the primary criteria, is the holder of a Subclass 447 visa.

447.322 If the applicant has not turned 18, public interest criteria 4017 and 4018 are satisfied in relation to the applicant.

447.323 The applicant:

(a) satisfies public interest criteria 4001, 4002, 4003, 4004 and 4007; and

(b) if he or she has previously been in Australia, satisfies special return criterion 5001.

447.4 Circumstances Applicable to Grant

447.411 The applicant must be outside Australia at the time of grant.

447.5 When Visa is in Effect

447.511 Temporary visa permitting the holder:

(a) to travel to and enter Australia on 1 occasion, as specified by the Minister; and

(b) to remain in Australia until:

  (i) if the holder applies for a visa after the temporary visa is granted and before the end of 36 months from the grant—the day on which the application is finally determined; and

  (ii) in any other case—the end of the 36 months.

447.6 Conditions

447.611 The holder cannot be granted a substantive visa other than a protection visa.

447.612 Entry must be made before the date specified by the Minister for the purpose.

447.613 Condition 8502 may be imposed.

447.7 Way of Giving Evidence

447.711 Visa label affixed to a Convention travel document or valid passport.

[8] *Schedule 2, after Part 450*

insert

Subclass 451 Secondary Movement Relocation (Temporary)

451.1 Interpretation

Note ***member of the family unit*** is defined in regulation 1.03.

No interpretation provisions specific to this Part.

451.2 Primary Criteria

Note The primary criteria must be satisfied by at least 1 member of a family unit. Other members of the family unit who are applicants for a visa of this subclass need satisfy only the secondary criteria.

451.21 Criteria to be satisfied at time of application

451.211 The applicant:

(a) is either:
 (i) subject to persecution in the applicant's home country; or
 (ii) subject to substantial discrimination, amounting to gross violation of human rights, in the applicant's home country; or
 (iii) a female person who is subject to persecution or is registered as being of concern to the United Nations High Commissioner for Refugees; and

(b) is outside his or her home country and is not an offshore entry person.

451.22 Criteria to be satisfied at time of decision

451.221 The applicant continues to satisfy the criterion in clause 451.211.

451.222 The Minister is satisfied that there are compelling reasons for giving special consideration to granting the applicant a temporary visa, having regard to:

(a) the extent of the applicant's connection with Australia; and
(b) if the applicant continues to meet the requirement in subparagraph 451.211 (a) (i)—the degree of persecution to which the applicant is subject in the applicant's home country; and
(c) if the applicant continues to meet the requirement in subparagraph 451.211 (a) (ii)—the degree of discrimination to which the applicant is subject in the applicant's home country; and
(d) if the applicant continues to meet the requirement in subparagraph 451.211 (a) (iii)—whether the applicant has the protection of a male relative and is in danger of victimisation, harassment or serious abuse because of her sex; and
(e) whether there is any suitable country available, other than Australia, that can provide for the applicant's stay and protection from persecution, discrimination, victimisation, harassment or serious abuse; and
(f) the capacity of the Australian community to provide for the temporary stay of persons such as the applicant in Australia.

451.223 The Minister is satisfied that temporary stay in Australia would not be contrary to the interests of Australia.

451.224 Grant of the visa would not result in either:

(a) the number of Subclass 451 visas granted in a financial year exceeding the maximum number of Subclass 451 visas, as determined by Gazette Notice, that may be granted in that financial year; or

(b) the number of visas of particular classes (including Refugee and Humanitarian (Class XB) visa) granted in a financial year exceeding the maximum number of visas of those classes, as determined by Gazette Notice, that may be granted in that financial year.

451.225 The applicant satisfies public interest criteria 4001, 4002, 4003, 4004 and 4007.

451.226 If the applicant has previously been in Australia, the applicant satisfies special return criterion 5001.

451.227

(1) In relation to the family unit of the applicant, each member of the family unit who is an applicant for a Subclass 451 visa is a person who:
   (a) satisfies public interest criteria 4001, 4002, 4003, 4004 and 4007; and
   (b) if he or she has previously been in Australia—satisfies special return criterion 5001.

(2) In relation to the family unit of the applicant, each member of the family unit who is not an applicant for a Subclass 451 visa is a person who:
   (a) satisfies public interest criteria 4001, 4002, 4003 and 4004; and
   (b) satisfies public interest criterion 4007, unless the Minister is satisfied that it would be unreasonable to require the person to undergo assessment in relation to that criterion.

451.3 Secondary Criteria

Note These criteria must be satisfied by applicants who are members of the family unit of a person who satisfies the primary criteria.

451.31 Criteria to be satisfied at time of application

451.311 The applicant:

(a) is a member of the family unit of a person who satisfies, or has satisfied, the criterion in clause 451.211; and

(b) is in the same country as that person.

451.32 Criteria to be satisfied at time of decision

451.321 The applicant continues to be a member of the family unit of a person who, having satisfied the primary criteria, is the holder of a Subclass 451 visa.

451.322 If the applicant has not turned 18, public interest criteria 4017 and 4018 are satisfied in relation to the applicant.

451.323 The applicant:

(a) satisfies public interest criteria 4001, 4002, 4003, 4004 and 4007; and

(b) if he or she has previously been in Australia, satisfies special return criterion 5001.

451.4 Circumstances Applicable to Grant

451.411 The applicant must be outside Australia at the time of grant.

451.5 When Visa is in Effect

451.511 Temporary visa permitting the holder:

(a) to travel to and enter Australia on 1 occasion, as specified by the Minister; and

(b) to remain in Australia until:

  (i) if the holder applies for a visa after the temporary visa is granted and before the end of 60 months from the grant—the day on which the application is finally determined; and

  (ii) in any other case—the end of the 60 months.

451.6 Conditions

451.611 The holder cannot be granted a substantive visa other than a protection visa.

451.612 Entry must be made before the date specified by the Minister for the purpose.

451.613 Condition 8502 may be imposed.

451.7 Way of Giving Evidence

451.711 Visa label affixed to a Convention travel document or valid passport.

[9] ***Schedule 2, after 866.213***

insert

866.214

(1) The applicant has not held a Subclass 447 (Secondary Movement Offshore Entry (Temporary)) visa since last entering Australia.

(2) The Minister may waive the requirement under subclause (1) if the Minister is satisfied that it is in the public interest to do so.

866.215

(1) If the applicant has held a Subclass 785 (Temporary Protection) visa since last entering Australia, the applicant, since leaving his or her home country, has not ever resided, for a continuous period of at least 7 days, in a country in which the applicant could have sought and obtained effective protection:

  (a) of the country; or

  (b) through the offices of the United Nations High Commissioner for Refugees located in that country.

(2) The Minister may waive the requirement under subclause (1) if the Minister is satisfied that it is in the public interest to do so.

[10] *Schedule 2, after 866.228*

866.228A If the applicant holds a Subclass 451 (Secondary Movement Relocation (Temporary)) visa, the applicant has held that visa for the lesser of:

(a) a continuous period of 54 months; and

(b) a shorter period specified in writing by the Minister in relation to the applicant.

[11] *Transitional*

(1) The amendments made by items [1] to [10] apply to an application for a visa made after the commencement of this Act.

(2) Despite anything in items [1] to [10], item 1127 and Parts 200, 201, 202, 203 and 204 of the *Migration Regulations 1994* as they read immediately before the commencement of this Act continue to apply in relation to:

  (a) applications for Subclass 200 (Refugee), 201 (In-country Special Humanitarian), 202 (Global Special Humanitarian), 203 (Emergency Rescue) or 204 (Woman at Risk) visas made, but not finally determined within the meaning of subsection 5(9) of the *Migration Act 1958*, before the commencement of this Act; and

  (b) Subclass 200, 201, 202, 203 or 204 visas in effect on that date.

[*Minister's second reading speech made in—*
House of Representatives on 18 September 2001
Senate on 20 September 2001]
(183/01)

APPENDIX 5

Border Protection (Validation and Enforcement Powers) Act 2001 (Australia)

Border Protection (Validation and Enforcement Powers) Act 2001

No. 126, 2001
An Act to validate the actions of the Commonwealth and others in relation to the *MV Tampa* and other vessels, and to provide increased powers to protect Australia's borders, and for related purposes

Border Protection (Validation and Enforcement Powers) Act 2001

No. 126, 2001

An Act to validate the actions of the Commonwealth and others in relation to the *MV Tampa* and other vessels, and to provide increased powers to protect Australia's borders, and for related purposes

[*Assented to 27 September 2001*]

The Parliament of Australia enacts:

Part 1—Preliminary

1 *Short Title*

This Act may be cited as the *Border Protection (Validation and Enforcement Powers) Act 2001*.

2 *Commencement*

This Act commences on the day on which it receives the Royal Assent.

3 *Schedule(s)*

Each Act that is specified in a Schedule to this Act is amended or repealed as set out in the applicable items in the Schedule concerned, and any other item in a Schedule to this Act has effect according to its terms.

 | DOI:10.1163/9789004383500_020

Part 2—Validation of Certain Actions

4 *Definitions*

In this Part:

Commonwealth officer includes a person who:

(a) is in the service or employment of the Commonwealth or an authority of the Commonwealth; or

(b) holds or performs the duties of any office or position under a law of the Commonwealth; or

(c) is a member of the Australian Defence Force.

validation period means the period starting on 27 August 2001 and ending at the beginning of the day on which this Act commences.

vessel has the same meaning as in the *Migration Act 1958*.

5 *Action to Which This Part Applies*

This Part applies to any action taken during the validation period by the Commonwealth, or by a Commonwealth officer, or any other person, acting on behalf of the Commonwealth, in relation to:

(a) the *MV Tampa*; or

(b) the *Aceng*; or

(c) any other vessel carrying persons in respect of whom there were reasonable grounds for believing that their intention was to enter Australia unlawfully; or

(d) any person who was on board a vessel mentioned in paragraph (a), (b) or (c) at any time during the validation period (whether or not the action was taken while the person was on board the vessel).

6 *Action to Which This Part Applies Taken to be Lawful*

All action to which this Part applies is taken for all purposes to have been lawful when it occurred.

7 *No Proceedings in Respect of Action to Which This Part Applies*

(1) Proceedings, whether civil or criminal, may not be instituted or continued in any court, in respect of action to which this Part applies, against:

(a) the Commonwealth; or

(b) a Commonwealth officer; or

(c) any other person who acted on behalf of the Commonwealth in relation to the action.

(2) This section applies to:

(a) the institution of proceedings on or after the day on which this Act receives the Royal Assent; and

(b) the continuation, on or after the day on which this Act receives the Royal Assent, of proceedings that were instituted on or before that day.

8 *Compensation for Acquisition of Property*

(1) If:

(a) this Part would result in an acquisition of property; and

(b) any provision of this Part would not be valid, apart from this section, because a particular person has not been compensated;

the Commonwealth must pay that person:

(c) a reasonable amount of compensation agreed on between the person and the Commonwealth; or

(d) failing agreement—a reasonable amount of compensation determined by a court of competent jurisdiction.

(2) Any damages or compensation recovered, or other remedy given, in a proceeding begun otherwise than under this section must be taken into account in assessing compensation payable in a proceeding begun under this section and arising out of the same event or transaction.

(3) In this section:

acquisition of property has the same meaning as in paragraph 51(xxxi) of the Constitution.

9 *Jurisdiction of High Court*

Nothing in this Part is intended to affect the jurisdiction of the High Court under section 75 of the Constitution.

Schedule 1—Amendment of the Customs Act 1901

1 *At the End of Section 184A*

Add:

(13) In this section:

(a) a reference to the ***commander of a Commonwealth ship or Commonwealth aircraft*** includes a reference to a commissioned officer of the Australian Defence Force, and a reference to a ***member of the commander's crew*** includes, in relation to a commissioned officer of the Australian Defence Force, a reference to a person acting under the command of the commissioned officer; and

(b) ***commissioned officer of the Australian Defence Force*** means an officer within the meaning of the *Defence Act 1903*.

2 *Subsection 185(3)*

Omit "to a port, airport or other place", substitute "to a port or airport, or to another place (including, in relation to a ship, a place within the territorial sea or the contiguous zone in relation to Australia)",.

3 *Subsection 185(3A)*

Repeal the subsection, substitute:

People on detained ships or aircraft

(3AAA) If an officer detains a ship or aircraft under this section, any restraint on the liberty of any person found on the ship or aircraft that results from the detention of the ship or aircraft is not unlawful, and proceedings, whether civil or criminal, in respect of that restraint may not be instituted or continued in any court against the Commonwealth, the officer or any person assisting the officer in detaining the ship or aircraft.

Jurisdiction of High Court

(3AAB) Nothing in subsection (3AAA) is intended to affect the jurisdiction of the High Court under section 75 of the Constitution.

Powers of officers in respect of people found on detained ships or aircraft

(3A) If an officer detains a ship or aircraft under this section, the officer may:

(a) detain any person found on the ship or aircraft and bring the person, or cause the person to be brought, to the migration zone (within the meaning of the *Migration Act 1958*); or

(b) take the person, or cause the person to be taken, to a place outside Australia.

The definition of ***place outside Australia*** in subsection 4(1) does not apply for the purposes of paragraph (b).

Powers to move people

(3AA) For the purpose of moving a person under subsection (3A), an officer may, within or outside Australia:

(a) place the person on a ship or aircraft; or

(b) restrain the person on a ship or aircraft; or

(c) remove the person from a ship or aircraft.

Protection if officers etc. act in good faith

(3AB) Proceedings, whether civil or criminal, may not be instituted or continued, in respect of any action taken under subsection (3AA), against the Commonwealth, an officer or any person assisting an officer if the officer or person who took the action acted in good faith and used no more force than was authorised by subsection (3B).

4 *After Section 185A*

Insert:

185AA Searches of people on certain ships or aircraft

(1) For the purposes set out in subsection (2), a person, and the person's clothing and any property under the immediate control of the person, may, without warrant, be searched if the person:

(a) is on a ship or aircraft that has been detained under subsection 185(3); or

(b) has been placed on a ship or aircraft under subsection 185(3AA).

(2) The purpose for which a person, and the person's clothing and any property under the immediate control of the person, may be searched under this section is to find out whether the person is carrying, or there is hidden on the person, in the clothing or in the property, a weapon or other thing capable of being used to inflict bodily injury or to help the person to escape.

Note: Division 1B of Part XII provides search powers in respect of certain persons suspected of unlawfully carrying prohibited goods.

(3) If, in the course of a search under this section, a weapon or other thing referred to in subsection (2) is found, an officer:

(a) may take possession of the weapon or other thing; and

(b) may retain the weapon or other thing for such time as he or she thinks necessary for the purposes of this Act.

(4) This section does not authorise an officer, or another person conducting a search pursuant to subsection (5), to remove any of the person's clothing, or to require a person to remove any of his or her clothing, except the person's outer garments (including but not limited to the person's overcoat, coat, jacket, gloves, shoes and head covering).

(5) A search under this section of a person, and the person's clothing, must be conducted by:

(a) an officer of the same sex as the person; or

(b) in a case where an officer of the same sex as the person is not available to conduct the search—any other person who is of the same sex and:

(i) is requested by an officer; and

(ii) agrees;

to conduct the search.

(6) An action or proceeding, whether civil or criminal, does not lie against a person who, at the request of an officer, conducts a search under this section if the person acts in good faith and does not contravene subsection (7).

(7) An officer or other person who conducts a search under this section must not use more force, or subject a person to greater indignity, than is reasonably necessary in order to conduct the search.

(8) In this section, ***officer*** has the same meaning as it has in section 185.

185AB Returning persons to ships

(1) An officer, or a person assisting an officer, may return to a ship that is detained under section 185 a person who:

(a) was on the ship when it was initially detained under section 185; and

(b) later leaves the ship.

For this purpose, reasonable means, including reasonable force, may be used by the officer or another person.

(2) A person may only be returned to a ship under subsection (1) if the officer or person assisting is satisfied that it is safe to return the person to the ship.

(3) In this section, ***officer*** has the same meaning as it has in section 185.

5 At the End of Section 185B

Add:

(9) In this section, ***officer*** includes a member of the Australian Defence Force.

Schedule 2—Amendment of the Migration Act 1958

1 Subsection 5(1) (subparagraph (b)(v) of the Definition of Immigration Detention)

Repeal the subparagraph, substitute:

(v) in another place approved by the Minister in writing;

but does not include being restrained as described in subsection 245F(8A), or being dealt with under paragraph 245F(9)(b).

2 After Section 7

Insert:

7A Effect on executive power to protect Australia's borders

The existence of statutory powers under this Act does not prevent the exercise of any executive power of the Commonwealth to protect Australia's borders, including, where necessary, by ejecting persons who have crossed those borders.

3 At the End of Section 232A

Add:

Note: Sections 233B and 233C limit conviction and sentencing options for offences under this section.

4 *At the End of Section 233A*

Add:

Note: Sections 233B and 233C limit conviction and sentencing options for offences under this section.

5 *After Section 233A*

Insert the following sections:

233B No discharge of offenders without proceeding to conviction for certain offences

The court may not make an order under section 19B of the *Crimes Act 1914* in respect of a charge for an offence under section 232A or 233A, unless it is established on the balance of probabilities that the person charged was aged under 18 years at the time when the offence was alleged to have been committed.

233C Mandatory penalties for certain offences

(1) This section applies if a person is convicted of an offence under section 232A or 233A, unless it is established on the balance of probabilities that the person was aged under 18 years when the offence was committed.

(2) The court must impose a sentence of imprisonment of at least:
  - (a) 8 years, if the conviction is for a repeat offence; or
  - (b) 5 years, in any other case.

(3) The court must also set a non-parole period of at least:
  - (a) 5 years, if the conviction is for a repeat offence; or
  - (b) 3 years, in any other case.

(4) In this section:
  - (a) ***non-parole period*** has the same meaning as it has in Part 1B of the *Crimes Act 1914*; and
  - (b) a person's conviction for an offence is for a ***repeat offence*** if, on a previous occasion after the commencement of this section, a court:
    - (i) has convicted the person of another offence, being an offence against section 232A or 233A; or
    - (ii) has found, without recording a conviction, that the person had committed another such offence.

6 *At the End of Section 245B*

Add:

(11) In this section:

(a) a reference to the ***commander of a Commonwealth ship or Commonwealth aircraft*** includes a reference to a commissioned officer of the Australian Defence

Force, and a reference to a ***member of the commander's crew*** includes, in relation to a commissioned officer of the Australian Defence Force, a reference to a person acting under the command of the commissioned officer; and

(b) ***commissioned officer of the Australian Defence Force*** means an officer within the meaning of the *Defence Act 1903*.

7 *Subsection 245F(8)*

Omit "to a port or other place", substitute "to a port, or to another place (including a place within the territorial sea or the contiguous zone in relation to Australia)",.

8 *Subsection 245F(9)*

Repeal the subsection, substitute:

People on detained ships or aircraft

(8A) If an officer detains a ship or aircraft under this section, any restraint on the liberty of any person found on the ship or aircraft that results from the detention of the ship or aircraft is not unlawful, and proceedings, whether civil or criminal, in respect of that restraint may not be instituted or continued in any court against the Commonwealth, the officer or any person assisting the officer in detaining the ship or aircraft.

Jurisdiction of High Court

(8B) Nothing in subsection (8A) is intended to affect the jurisdiction of the High Court under section 75 of the Constitution.

Powers of officers in respect of people found on detained ships or aircraft

(9) If an officer detains a ship or aircraft under this section, the officer may:

(a) detain any person found on the ship or aircraft and bring the person, or cause the person to be brought, to the migration zone; or

(b) take the person, or cause the person to be taken, to a place outside Australia.

Powers to move people

(9A) For the purpose of moving a person under subsection (9), an officer may, within or outside Australia:

(a) place the person on a ship or aircraft; or

(b) restrain the person on a ship or aircraft; or

(c) remove the person from a ship or aircraft.

Protection if officers etc. act in good faith

(9B) Proceedings, whether civil or criminal, may not be instituted or continued, in respect of any action taken under subsection (9A), against the Commonwealth, an officer or any person assisting an officer if the officer or person who took the action acted in good faith and used no more force than was authorised by subsection (10).

9 *After Section 245F*

Insert:

245FA Searches of people on certain ships or aircraft

(1) For the purposes set out in subsection (2), a person, and the person's clothing and any property under the immediate control of the person, may, without warrant, be searched if the person:

(a) is on a ship or aircraft that has been detained under subsection 245F(8); or

(b) has been placed on a ship or aircraft under subsection 245F(9A).

Note: Division 13 of Part 2 provides search powers in respect of persons who are in immigration detention.

(2) The purpose for which a person, and the person's clothing and any property under the immediate control of the person, may be searched under this section is to find out whether the person is carrying, or there is hidden on the person, in the clothing or in the property, a weapon or other thing capable of being used to inflict bodily injury or to help the person to escape.

(3) If, in the course of a search under this section, a weapon or other thing referred to in subsection (2) is found, an officer:

(a) may take possession of the weapon or other thing; and

(b) may retain the weapon or other thing for such time as he or she thinks necessary for the purposes of this Act.

(4) This section does not authorise an officer, or another person conducting a search pursuant to subsection (5), to remove any of the person's clothing, or to require a person to remove any of his or her clothing, except the person's outer garments (including but not limited to the person's overcoat, coat, jacket, gloves, shoes and head covering).

(5) A search under this section of a person, and the person's clothing, must be conducted by:

(a) an officer of the same sex as the person; or

(b) in a case where an officer of the same sex as the person is not available to conduct the search—any other person who is of the same sex and:

(i) is requested by an officer; and

(ii) agrees;

to conduct the search.

(6) An action or proceeding, whether civil or criminal, does not lie against a person who, at the request of an officer, conducts a search under this section if the person acts in good faith and does not contravene subsection (7).

(7) An officer or other person who conducts a search under this section must not use more force, or subject a person to greater indignity, than is reasonably necessary in order to conduct the search.

(8) In this section, ***officer*** has the same meaning as it has in section 245F.

245FB Returning Persons to Ships

(1) An officer, or a person assisting an officer, may return to a ship that is detained under section 245F a person who:

(a) was on the ship when it was initially detained under section 245F; and

(b) later leaves the ship.

For this purpose, reasonable means, including reasonable force, may be used by the officer or another person.

(2) A person may only be returned to a ship under subsection (1) if the officer or person assisting is satisfied that it is safe to return the person to the ship.

(3) In this section, ***officer*** has the same meaning as it has in section 245F.

10 At the End of Section 245H

Add:

(8) In this section, ***officer*** means an officer within the meaning of section 5, and includes:

(a) a member of the Australian Defence Force; and

(b) any other person who is an officer within the meaning of section 245F in relation to the ship concerned.

[*Minister's second reading speech made in—*
House of Representatives on 18 September 2001
Senate on 20 September 2001]
(185/01)

APPENDIX 6

Migration Amendment (Unauthorised Maritime Arrivals and Other Measures) Act 2013

No. 35, 2013

An Act to amend the *Migration Act 1958*, and for other purposes

[*Assented to 20 May 2013*]

The Parliament of Australia enacts:

1 *Short title*

This Act may be cited as the *Migration Amendment (Unauthorised Maritime Arrivals and Other Measures) Act 2013*.

2 *Commencement*

(1) Each provision of this Act specified in column 1 of the table commences, or is taken to have commenced, in accordance with column 2 of the table. Any other statement in column 2 has effect according to its terms.

Commencement information		
Column 1	**Column 2**	**Column 3**
Provision(s)	**Commencement**	**Date/Details**
1. Sections 1 to 3 and anything in this Act not elsewhere covered by this table	The day this Act receives the Royal Assent.	20 May 2013
2. Schedule 1, items 1 to 14	A single day to be fixed by Proclamation. However, if the provision(s) do not commence within the period of 6 months beginning on the day this Act receives the Royal Assent, they commence on the day after the end of that period.	1 June 2013 (*see*F2013L00880)

 | DOI:10.1163/9789004383500_021

Commencement information		
Column 1	**Column 2**	**Column 3**
Provision(s)	**Commencement**	**Date/Details**
3. Schedule 1, items 15 and 16	The day after this Act receives the Royal Assent.	21 May 2013
4. Schedule 1, items 17 to 62	At the same time as the provision(s) covered by table item 2.	1 June 2013
5. Schedule 2	The later of: (a) immediately after the commencement of the provision(s) covered by table item 2; and (b) immediately after the commencement of section 69 of the *Maritime Powers Act 2013*. However, the provision(s) do not commence at all if the event mentioned in paragraph (b) does not occur.	27 March 2014 (paragraph (b) applies)

NOTE: This table relates only to the provisions of this Act as originally enacted. It will not be amended to deal with any later amendments of this Act.

(2) Any information in column 3 of the table is not part of this Act. Information may be inserted in this column, or information in it may be edited, in any published version of this Act.

3 *Schedule(s)*

Each Act that is specified in a Schedule to this Act is amended or repealed as set out in the applicable items in the Schedule concerned, and any other item in a Schedule to this Act has effect according to its terms.

Schedule 1—Main Amendments

Part 1—Amendments

Migration Act 1958

1 Subsection 4(5)

Omit "offshore entry persons", substitute "unauthorised maritime arrivals".

2 *Sub(1) (Note at the End of the Definition of* Excised Offshore Place*)*
Repeal the note.

3 *Subsection 5(1) (Definition of* Offshore Entry Person*)*
Repeal the definition.

4 *Subsection 5(1) (paragraphs (a) and (aa) of the Definition of* Transitory Person*)*
Omit "an offshore entry person", substitute "a person".

5 *Subsection 5(1) (subparagraph (c)(iii) of the Definition of* Transitory Person*)*
Omit "country;", substitute "country"..

6 *Subsection 5(1) (Definition of* Transitory Person*)*
Omit all the words after subparagraph (c)(iii) of the definition.

7 *Subsection 5(1)*
Insert:

unauthorised maritime arrival has the meaning given by section 5AA.

8 *After Section 5*
Insert:

5AA Meaning of *unauthorised maritime arrival*

(1) For the purposes of this Act, a person is an ***unauthorised maritime arrival*** if:

(a) the person entered Australia by sea:

(i) at an excised offshore place at any time after the excision time for that place; or

(ii) at any other place at any time on or after the commencement of this section; and

(b) the person became an unlawful non-citizen because of that entry; and

(c) the person is not an excluded maritime arrival.

Entered Australia by sea

(2) A person ***entered Australia by sea*** if:

(a) the person entered the migration zone except on an aircraft that landed in the migration zone; or

(b) the person entered the migration zone as a result of being found on a ship detained under section 245F and being dealt with under paragraph 245F(9)(a); or

(c) the person entered the migration zone after being rescued at sea.

Excluded maritime arrival

(3) A person is an ***excluded maritime arrival*** if the person:

(a) is a New Zealand citizen who holds and produces a New Zealand passport that is in force; or

(b) is a non-citizen who holds and produces a passport that is in force and is endorsed with an authority to reside indefinitely on Norfolk Island; or

(c) is included in a prescribed class of persons.

Definitions

(4) In this section:

aircraft has the same meaning as in section 245A.

ship has the meaning given by section 245A.

9 Subparagraphs 5A(3)(j)(ii) and (iii)

Omit "offshore entry person", substitute "unauthorised maritime arrival".

10 Section 46A (heading)

Repeal the heading, substitute:

46A Visa applications by unauthorised maritime arrivals

11 Subsections 46A(1) and (2)

Omit "offshore entry person", substitute "unauthorised maritime arrival".

12 Subsection 46A(2)

Omit "the person", substitute "the unauthorised maritime arrival".

13 Paragraphs 46A(5)(a) and (b)

Omit "offshore entry person", substitute "unauthorised maritime arrival".

14 Subsection 46A(7)

Omit "offshore entry person" (wherever occurring), substitute "unauthorised maritime arrival".

15 Subsection 189(2)

Omit "must detain", substitute "may detain".

16 Paragraph 189(3A)(a)

Repeal the paragraph, substitute:

(a) is a citizen of Papua New Guinea; and

17 *Subsection 198(11)*

Omit "offshore entry person", substitute "unauthorised maritime arrival".

18 *Paragraph 198AA(b)*

Omit "offshore entry persons" (wherever occurring), substitute "unauthorised maritime arrivals".

19 *Section 198AD (heading)*

Repeal the heading, substitute:

198AD Taking unauthorised maritime arrivals to a regional processing country

20 *Subsections 198AD(1) and (2)*

Omit "offshore entry person", substitute "unauthorised maritime arrival".

21 *Paragraphs 198AD(3)(a) to (c)*

Omit "offshore entry person", substitute "unauthorised maritime arrival".

22 *Subparagraph 198AD(3)(c)(i)*

Omit "the person", substitute "the unauthorised maritime arrival".

23 *Subsection 198AD(4)*

Omit "offshore entry person", substitute "unauthorised maritime arrival".

24 *Subsection 198AD(4)*

Omit "the person" (wherever occurring), substitute "the unauthorised maritime arrival".

25 *Paragraph 198AD(4)(b)*

Omit "the person's", substitute "the unauthorised maritime arrival's".

26 *Subsection 198AD(5)*

Omit "offshore entry person", substitute "unauthorised maritime arrival".

27 *Subsection 198AD(5)*

Omit "offshore entry persons", substitute "unauthorised maritime arrivals".

28 *Subsection 198AD(8)*

Omit "offshore entry person", substitute "unauthorised maritime arrival".

29 *Subsection 198AD(8)*

Omit "offshore entry persons", substitute "unauthorised maritime arrivals".

30 *Subsections 198AD(11) and 198AE(1)*

Omit "offshore entry person", substitute "unauthorised maritime arrival".

31 *After subsection 198AE(1)*

Insert:

(1A) The Minister may, in writing, vary or revoke a determination made under subsection (1) if the Minister thinks that it is in the public interest to do so.

32 *Subsection 198AE(2)*

After "subsection (1)", insert "or (1A)".

33 *At the End of Subsection 198AE(3)*

Add "or (1A)".

34 *Subsection 198AE(4)*

After "subsection (1)", insert "or varies or revokes a determination under subsection (1A)".

35 *Paragraph 198AE(4)(a)*

After "determination", insert ", the determination as varied or the instrument of revocation".

36 *Paragraph 198AE(4)(b)*

After "determination", insert ", variation or revocation".

37 *Paragraphs 198AE(5)(a) and (b)*

Omit "offshore entry person", substitute "unauthorised maritime arrival".

38 *Paragraphs 198AE(6)(a) and (b)*

After "made", insert ", varied or revoked".

39 *Subsection 198AE(7)*

After "subsection (1)", insert "or (1A)".

40 *Subsection 198AE(7)*

Omit "offshore entry person" (wherever occurring), substitute "unauthorised maritime arrival".

41 Subsection 198AE(8)

Omit "A determination under subsection (1)", substitute "An instrument under subsection (1) or (1A)".

42 Sections 198AF and 198AG

Omit "offshore entry person" (wherever occurring), substitute "unauthorised maritime arrival".

43 Section 198AH

Before "Section 198AD", insert "(1)".

44 Paragraph 198AH(a)

Omit "offshore entry person", substitute "unauthorised maritime arrival".

45 Paragraph 198AH(c)

Omit "achieved); and", substitute "achieved)".

46 Paragraphs 198AH(d) and (e)

Repeal the paragraphs.

47 At the End of Section 198AH

Add:

(2) Subsection (1) of this section applies whether or not the transitory person has been assessed to be covered by the definition of ***refugee*** in Article 1A of the Refugees Convention as amended by the Refugees Protocol.

47A At the End of Subdivision B of Division 8 of Part 2

Add:

198AI Ministerial report

The Minister must, as soon as practicable after 30 June in each year, cause to be laid before each House of Parliament a report setting out:

(a) the activities conducted under the Bali Process during the year ending on 30 June; and

(b) the steps taken in relation to people smuggling, trafficking in persons and related transnational crime to support the Regional Cooperation Framework during the year ending on 30 June; and

(c) the progress made in relation to people smuggling, trafficking in persons and related transnational crime under the Regional Cooperation Framework during the year ending on 30 June.

198AJ Reports about unauthorised maritime arrivals

(1) The Minister must cause to be laid before each House of the Parliament, within 15 sitting days of that House after the end of a financial year, a report on the following:

(a) arrangements made by regional processing countries during the financial year for unauthorised maritime arrivals who make claims for protection under the Refugees Convention as amended by the Refugees Protocol, including arrangements for:

(i) assessing those claims in those countries; and

(ii) the accommodation, health care and education of those unauthorised maritime arrivals in those countries;

(b) the number of those claims assessed in those countries in the financial year;

(c) the number of unauthorised maritime arrivals determined in those countries in the financial year to be covered by the definition of ***refugee*** in Article 1A of the Refugees Convention as amended by the Refugees Protocol.

(2) However, a report under this section need deal with a particular regional processing country in accordance with subsection (1) only so far as information provided by the country makes it reasonably practicable for the report to do so.

(3) A report under this section must not include:

(a) the name of a person who is or was an unauthorised maritime arrival; or

(b) any information that may identify such a person; or

(c) the name of any other person connected in any way with any person covered by paragraph (a); or

(d) any information that may identify that other person.

48 Sections 198C and 198D

Repeal the sections.

49 Subparagraphs 336F(3)(a)(ii) and (iii) and (4)(a)(ii) and (iii)

Omit "offshore entry person", substitute "unauthorised maritime arrival".

50 Paragraphs 336F(5)(c) to (cc)

Omit "offshore entry person", substitute "unauthorised maritime arrival".

51 Section 494AA (Heading)

Repeal the heading, substitute:

494AA Bar on certain legal proceedings relating to unauthorised maritime arrivals

52 *Paragraph 494AA(1)(a)*

Omit "offshore entry by an offshore entry person", substitute "unauthorised entry by an unauthorised maritime arrival".

53 *Paragraphs 494AA(1)(b) and (c)*

Omit "offshore entry person", substitute "unauthorised maritime arrival".

54 *Paragraph 494AA(1)(c)*

Omit "the person", substitute "the unauthorised maritime arrival".

55 *Paragraph 494AA(1)(e)*

Omit "offshore entry person", substitute "unauthorised maritime arrival".

56 *Subsection 494AA(4) (Definition of* Ineligibility Period*)*

Omit "offshore", substitute "unauthorised".

57 *Subsection 494AA(4) (Definition of* Offshore Entry*)*

Repeal the definition.

58 *Subsection 494AA(4)*

Insert:

unauthorised entry means an entry into Australia that occurs:

(a) at an excised offshore place after the excision time for that place; or

(b) at any other place on or after the commencement of section 5AA.

Part 2—Application, Transitional and Saving Provisions

59 *Definitions*

In this Part:

commencement means the commencement of this item.

Migration Act means the *Migration Act 1958*.

60 Application Provision—Subparagraph 5AA(1)(a)(i) of the Migration Act

(1) This item applies to an unauthorised maritime arrival who entered Australia by sea as mentioned in subparagraph 5AA(1)(a)(i) of the Migration Act, as inserted by this Schedule.

(2) The amendments made by items 18 to 47 of this Schedule apply in relation to the unauthorised maritime arrival only if he or she entered Australia by sea as mentioned in that subparagraph on or after 13 August 2012.

61 Application Provision—Subsection 198AE(1A) of the Migration Act

Subsection 198AE(1A) of the Migration Act, as inserted by this Schedule, applies in relation to a determination under subsection 198AE(1) of that Act that is made before or after commencement.

61A Transitional Provision—Section 198AJ of the Migration Act

Section 198AJ of the Migration Act applies to the period beginning on 13 August 2012 and ending on the first 30 June after commencement as if that period were a financial year.

62 Saving Provision

(1) This item applies to:

(a) an authorisation (the ***access authorisation***) under section 336D of the Migration Act; or

(b) an authorisation (the ***disclosure authorisation***) under section 336F of the Migration Act;

that was in force immediately before commencement.

Access authorisation

(2) The access authorisation is taken, after commencement, to authorise access to identifying information relating to unauthorised maritime arrivals to the extent that, immediately before commencement, the authorisation authorised access to identifying information relating to offshore entry persons.

Disclosure authorisation

(2) The disclosure authorisation is taken, after commencement, to authorise the disclosure of identifying information relating to unauthorised maritime arrivals to the extent that, immediately before commencement, the authorisation authorised the disclosure of identifying information relating to offshore entry persons.

References to offshore entry person

(3) Any reference in the access authorisation or disclosure authorisation to an offshore entry person is taken, after commencement, to be a reference to an unauthorised maritime arrival.

Schedule 2—Contingent Amendments

Migration Act 1958

1 *Paragraph 5AA(2)(b)*

After “section 245F”, insert “(as in force before the commencement of section 69 of the *Maritime Powers Act 2013*)”.

2 *Paragraph 5AA(2)(b)*

After “paragraph 245F(9)(a)”, insert “(as in force before that commencement)”.

3 *After paragraph 5AA(2)(b)*

Insert:

(ba) the person entered the migration zone as a result of being on a vessel detained under section 69 of the *Maritime Powers Act 2013* and being dealt with under paragraph 72(4)(a) of that Act; or

4 *Subsection 5AA(4) (at the End of the Definition of Ship)*

Add “(as in force before the commencement of section 69 of the *Maritime Powers Act 2013*)”.

5 *Subsection 5AA(4)*

Insert:

vessel has the same meaning as in the *Maritime Powers Act 2013*.

[*Minister's second reading speech made in—*
House of Representatives on 31 October 2012
Senate on 5 February 2013]
(192/12)

APPENDIX 7

CESEDA (September 2016) (France)

Chapitre Ier: Conditions Du Maintien En Zone D'attente

Article L221-1

Modifié par LOI n°2015–925 du 29 juillet 2015—art. 13

L'étranger qui arrive en France par la voie ferroviaire, maritime ou aérienne et qui n'est pas autorisé à entrer sur le territoire français peut être maintenu dans une zone d'attente située dans une gare ferroviaire ouverte au trafic international figurant sur une liste définie par voie réglementaire, dans un port ou à proximité du lieu de débarquement ou dans un aéroport, pendant le temps strictement nécessaire à son départ.

Le présent titre s'applique également à l'étranger qui demande à entrer en France au titre de l'asile, le temps strictement nécessaire pour vérifier si l'examen de sa demande relève de la compétence d'un autre Etat en application du règlement (UE) n° 604/2013 du Parlement européen et du Conseil, du 26 juin 2013, établissant les critères et mécanismes de détermination de l'Etat membre responsable de l'examen d'une demande de protection internationale introduite dans l'un des Etats membres par un ressortissant de pays tiers ou un apatride, ou en application d'engagements identiques à ceux prévus par le même règlement, si sa demande n'est pas irrecevable ou si elle n'est pas manifestement infondée.

Lorsque l'Office français de protection des réfugiés et apatrides, dans le cadre de l'examen tendant à déterminer si la demande d'asile n'est pas irrecevable ou manifestement infondée, considère que le demandeur d'asile, notamment en raison de sa minorité ou du fait qu'il a été victime de torture, de viol ou d'une autre forme grave de violence psychologique, physique ou sexuelle, nécessite des garanties procédurales particulières qui ne sont pas compatibles avec le maintien en zone d'attente, il est mis fin à ce maintien. L'étranger est alors muni d'un visa de régularisation de huit jours. Dans ce délai, l'autorité administrative compétente lui délivre, à sa demande, une attestation de demande d'asile lui permettant d'introduire cette demande auprès de l'office.

Le maintien en zone d'attente d'un mineur non accompagné, le temps strictement nécessaire à l'examen tendant à déterminer si sa demande n'est pas irrecevable ou manifestement infondée, n'est possible que de manière exceptionnelle et seulement dans les cas prévus aux 1° et 2° du I, au 1° du II et au 5° du III de l'article L. 723-2.

Les dispositions du présent titre s'appliquent également à l'étranger qui se trouve en transit dans une gare, un port ou un aéroport si l'entreprise de transport qui devait

 DOI:10.1163/9789004383500_022

l'acheminer dans le pays de destination ultérieure refuse de l'embarquer ou si les autorités du pays de destination lui ont refusé l'entrée et l'ont renvoyé en France.

Le présent titre s'applique également à l'étranger qui arrive en Guyane par la voie fluviale ou terrestre.

Un décret en Conseil d'Etat fixe les modalités d'application du présent article. Il précise les modalités de prise en compte de la vulnérabilité du demandeur d'asile et, le cas échéant, de ses besoins particuliers.

NOTA:

Conformément à l'article 35 III de la loi n° 2015–925 du 29 juillet 2015, l'article L. 213-8-1 du code de l'entrée et du séjour des étrangers et du droit d'asile, dans sa rédaction résultant de la présente loi, s'applique aux demandes d'asile présentées à compter du 1er novembre 2015 (Décret n° 2015-1364 du 28 octobre 2015, article 4).

Article L221-2

Modifié par LOI n°2011–672 du 16 juin 2011—art. 10

La zone d'attente est délimitée par l'autorité administrative compétente. Elle s'étend des points d'embarquement et de débarquement à ceux où sont effectués les contrôles des personnes. Elle peut inclure, sur l'emprise, ou à proximité, de la gare, du port ou de l'aéroport ou à proximité du lieu de débarquement, un ou plusieurs lieux d'hébergement assurant aux étrangers concernés des prestations de type hôtelier. Dans ces lieux d'hébergement, un espace permettant aux avocats de s'entretenir confidentiellement avec les étrangers est prévu. A cette fin, sauf en cas de force majeure, il est accessible en toutes circonstances sur demande de l'avocat.

Lorsqu'il est manifeste qu'un groupe d'au moins dix étrangers vient d'arriver en France en dehors d'un point de passage frontalier, en un même lieu ou sur un ensemble de lieux distants d'au plus dix kilomètres, la zone d'attente s'étend, pour une durée maximale de vingt-six jours, du ou des lieux de découverte des intéressés jusqu'au point de passage frontalier le plus proche.

La zone d'attente s'étend, sans qu'il soit besoin de prendre une décision particulière, aux lieux dans lesquels l'étranger doit se rendre soit dans le cadre de la procédure en cours, soit en cas de nécessité médicale.

Sont matériellement distincts et séparés les locaux qui ne relèvent pas de l'administration pénitentiaire et qui sont soit des zones d'attente, soit des zones de rétention mentionnées à l'article L. 551-1.

Article L221-2-1

Créé par Ordonnance n° 2014–464 du 7 mai 2014—art. 6

Le dernier alinéa de l'article L. 221–2 n'est pas applicable à Mayotte pendant cinq ans à compter de la publication de l'ordonnance n° 2014–464 du 7 mai 2014 portant extension et adaptation à Mayotte du code de l'entrée et du séjour des étrangers et du droit d'asile (partie législative).

Lorsque le lieu d'hébergement prévu à l'article L. 221–2 est un lieu de rétention tel que mentionné à l'article L. 551-1, les étrangers maintenus en zone d'attente et les étrangers placés en rétention administrative dans le même lieu demeurent régis respectivement par les dispositions des livres II et V.

Article L221-3

Modifié par Loi n°2007-1631 du 20 novembre 2007—art. 25 JORF 21 novembre 2007

Le maintien en zone d'attente est prononcé pour une durée qui ne peut excéder quatre jours par une décision écrite et motivée d'un agent relevant d'une catégorie fixée par voie réglementaire.

Cette décision est inscrite sur un registre mentionnant l'état civil de l'intéressé et la date et l'heure auxquelles la décision de maintien lui a été notifiée. Elle est portée sans délai à la connaissance du procureur de la République. Lorsque la notification faite à l'étranger mentionne que le procureur de la République a été informé sans délai de la décision de maintien en zone d'attente, cette mention fait foi sauf preuve contraire.

Article L221-4

Modifié par LOI n°2015–925 du 29 juillet 2015—art. 13

L'étranger maintenu en zone d'attente est informé, dans les meilleurs délais, qu'il peut demander l'assistance d'un interprète et d'un médecin, communiquer avec un conseil ou toute personne de son choix et quitter à tout moment la zone d'attente pour toute destination située hors de France. Il est également informé des droits qu'il est susceptible d'exercer en matière de demande d'asile. Ces informations lui sont communiquées dans une langue qu'il comprend. Mention en est faite sur le registre mentionné au deuxième alinéa de l'article L. 221–3, qui est émargé par l'intéressé.

En cas de maintien simultané en zone d'attente d'un nombre important d'étrangers, la notification des droits mentionnés au premier alinéa s'effectue dans les meilleurs délais, compte tenu du nombre d'agents de l'autorité administrative et d'interprètes disponibles. De même, dans ces mêmes circonstances particulières, les droits notifiés s'exercent dans les meilleurs délais.

Lorsque l'étranger ne parle pas le français, il est fait application de l'article L. 111–7.

Article L221-5

Modifié par Loi n°2006–911 du 24 juillet 2006—art. 48 JORF 25 juillet 2006

Lorsqu'un étranger mineur non accompagné d'un représentant légal n'est pas autorisé à entrer en France, le procureur de la République, avisé immédiatement par l'autorité administrative, lui désigne sans délai un administrateur ad hoc. Celui-ci assiste le mineur durant son maintien en zone d'attente et assure sa représentation dans le cadre des procédures administratives et juridictionnelles relatives à ce maintien.

Il assure également la représentation du mineur dans toutes les procédures administratives et juridictionnelles afférentes à son entrée en France.

L'administrateur ad hoc est désigné par le procureur de la république compétent sur une liste de personnes morales ou physiques dont les modalités de constitution sont fixées par décret en conseil d'Etat. Ce décret précise également les conditions de leur indemnisation.

Article L221-6

Créé par LOI n°2016–274 du 7 mars 2016—art. 44

Sous réserve de ne pas porter atteinte à la dignité des personnes et aux exigences de sécurité et de bon fonctionnement de la zone d'attente, les journalistes titulaires de la carte d'identité professionnelle mentionnée à l'article L. 7111–6 du code du travail peuvent être autorisés à y accéder dans des conditions fixées par décret en Conseil d'Etat.

Les prises d'images et de son des étrangers, des personnels et des intervenants dans les zones d'attente, de même que leur diffusion, ne sont autorisées qu'avec leur accord préalable. Elles se déroulent dans le respect de l'anonymat patronymique et physique des mineurs et, sauf accord contraire exprès, des majeurs.

Section 1: Décision Du Juge Des Libertés Et De La Détention

Article L222-1

Modifié par LOI n°2016–274 du 7 mars 2016—art. 55

Le maintien en zone d'attente au-delà de quatre jours à compter de la décision initiale peut être autorisé, par le juge des libertés et de la détention statuant sur l'exercice effectif des droits reconnus à l'étranger, pour une durée qui ne peut être supérieure à huit jours.

Article L222-2

Modifié par Loi n°2007-1631 du 20 novembre 2007—art. 26 JORF 21 novembre 2007

A titre exceptionnel ou en cas de volonté délibérée de l'étranger de faire échec à son départ, le maintien en zone d'attente au-delà de douze jours peut être renouvelé, dans les conditions prévues au présent chapitre, par le juge des libertés et de la détention, pour une durée qu'il détermine et qui ne peut être supérieure à huit jours.

Toutefois, lorsque l'étranger dont l'entrée sur le territoire français a été refusée dépose une demande d'asile dans les six derniers jours de cette nouvelle période de maintien en zone d'attente, celle-ci est prorogée d'office de six jours à compter du jour de la demande. Cette décision est mentionnée sur le registre prévu à l'article L. 221–3 et portée à la connaissance du procureur de la République dans les conditions prévues au même article. Le juge des libertés et de la détention est informé immédiatement de cette prorogation. Il peut y mettre un terme.

Lorsqu'un étranger dont l'entrée sur le territoire français au titre de l'asile a été refusée dépose un recours en annulation sur le fondement de l'article L. 213–9 dans les quatre derniers jours de la période de maintien en zone d'attente fixée par la dernière décision de maintien, celle-ci est prorogée d'office de quatre jours à compter du dépôt du recours. Cette décision est mentionnée sur le registre prévu à l'article L. 221–3 et portée à la connaissance du procureur de la République dans les conditions prévues au même article. Le juge des libertés et de la détention est informé immédiatement de cette prorogation. Il peut y mettre un terme.

Article L222-3

Modifié par LOI n°2011–672 du 16 juin 2011—art. 12
Modifié par LOI n°2011–672 du 16 juin 2011—art. 13

L'autorité administrative expose dans sa saisine les raisons pour lesquelles l'étranger n'a pu être rapatrié ou, s'il a demandé l'asile, admis, et le délai nécessaire pour assurer son départ de la zone d'attente.

Le juge des libertés et de la détention statue dans les vingt-quatre heures de sa saisine ou, lorsque les nécessités de l'instruction l'imposent, dans les quarante-huit heures de celle-ci par ordonnance, après audition de l'intéressé, ou de son conseil s'il en a un, ou celui-ci dûment averti.

L'existence de garanties de représentation de l'étranger n'est pas à elle seule susceptible de justifier le refus de prolongation de son maintien en zone d'attente.

L'étranger peut demander au juge des libertés et de la détention qu'il lui soit désigné un conseil d'office. Le mineur est assisté d'un avocat choisi par l'administrateur ad hoc ou, à défaut, commis d'office. L'étranger ou, dans le cas du mineur mentionné à l'article L. 221–5, l'administrateur ad hoc peut également demander au juge des libertés et de la détention le concours d'un interprète et la communication de son dossier.

A peine d'irrecevabilité, prononcée d'office, aucune irrégularité antérieure à l'audience relative à la première prolongation du maintien en zone d'attente ne peut être soulevée lors de l'audience relative à la seconde prolongation.

Article L222-4

Modifié par LOI n°2011–672 du 16 juin 2011—art. 15

Le juge des libertés et de la détention statue au siège du tribunal de grande instance. Toutefois, si une salle d'audience attribuée au ministère de la justice lui permettant de statuer publiquement a été spécialement aménagée sur l'emprise ferroviaire, portuaire ou aéroportuaire, il statue dans cette salle.

En cas de nécessité, le président du tribunal de grande instance peut décider de tenir une seconde audience au siège du tribunal de grande instance, le même jour que celle qui se tient dans la salle spécialement aménagée.

Par décision du juge prise sur une proposition de l'autorité administrative à laquelle l'étranger dûment informé dans une langue qu'il comprend ne s'est pas opposé, l'audience peut également se dérouler avec l'utilisation de moyens de télécommunication audiovisuelle garantissant la confidentialité de la transmission. Il est alors dressé, dans chacune des deux salles d'audience ouvertes au public, un procès-verbal des opérations effectuées.

Sous réserve de l'application de l'article 435 du code de procédure civile, le juge des libertés et de la détention statue publiquement.

L'étranger est maintenu à disposition de la justice dans des conditions fixées par le procureur de la République pendant le temps strictement nécessaire à la tenue de l'audience et au prononcé de l'ordonnance.

Article L222-5

Modifié par LOI n°2011–672 du 16 juin 2011—art. 16

Si l'ordonnance met fin au maintien en zone d'attente, elle est immédiatement notifiée au procureur de la République. A moins que le procureur de la République n'en dispose autrement, l'étranger est alors maintenu à la disposition de la justice pendant un délai de six heures à compter de la notification de l'ordonnance au procureur de la République.

Section 2: Voies De Recours

Article L222-6

Modifié par LOI n°2011–672 du 16 juin 2011—art. 16

L'ordonnance est susceptible d'appel devant le premier président de la cour d'appel ou son délégué. Celui-ci est saisi sans forme et doit statuer dans les quarante-huit heures de sa saisine. Par décision du premier président de la cour d'appel ou de son délégué, prise sur une proposition de l'autorité administrative à laquelle l'étranger dûment informé dans une langue qu'il comprend ne s'est pas opposé, l'audience peut se dérouler avec l'utilisation de moyens de télécommunication audiovisuelle dans les conditions prévues au troisième alinéa de l'article L. 222–4. Le droit d'appel appartient à l'intéressé, au ministère public et au représentant de l'Etat dans le département. L'appel n'est pas suspensif.

Toutefois, le ministère public peut demander au premier président de la cour d'appel ou à son délégué de déclarer son recours suspensif. Dans ce cas, l'appel, accompagné de la demande, est formé dans un délai de six heures à compter de la notification de l'ordonnance au procureur de la République et transmis au premier président de la cour d'appel ou à son délégué. Celui-ci décide, sans délai, s'il y a lieu, au vu des pièces du dossier, de donner à cet appel un effet suspensif. Il statue par une ordonnance motivée rendue contradictoirement qui n'est pas susceptible de recours. L'intéressé est maintenu à la disposition de la justice jusqu'à ce que cette ordonnance soit rendue et, si elle donne un effet suspensif à l'appel du ministère public, jusqu'à ce qu'il soit statué sur le fond.

Section 3: Dispositions Communes

Article L222-7

Sont à la charge de l'Etat et sans recours contre l'étranger, dans les conditions prévues pour les frais de justice criminelle, correctionnelle ou de police, les honoraires et indemnités des interprètes désignés pour l'assister au cours de la procédure juridictionnelle de maintien en zone d'attente prévue par le présent titre.

Article L222-8

Créé par LOI n°2011–672 du 16 juin 2011—art. 14

En cas de violation des formes prescrites par la loi à peine de nullité ou d'inobservation des formalités substantielles, toute juridiction, y compris la Cour de cassation, qui est saisie d'une demande d'annulation ou qui relève d'office une telle irrégularité ne peut prononcer la mainlevée de la mesure de maintien en zone d'attente que lorsque celle-ci a eu pour effet de porter atteinte aux droits de l'étranger.

Chapitre III: Contrôle Des Droits Des Étrangers Maintenus En Zone D'attente

Article L223-1

Modifié par LOI n°2011–672 du 16 juin 2011—art. 67

Pendant toute la durée du maintien en zone d'attente, l'étranger dispose des droits qui lui sont reconnus à l'article L. 221–4. Le procureur de la République ainsi que, à l'issue des quatre premiers jours, le juge des libertés et de la détention peuvent se rendre sur place pour vérifier les conditions de ce maintien et se faire communiquer le registre mentionné à l'article L. 221–3. Le procureur de la République visite les zones d'attente chaque fois qu'il l'estime nécessaire et au moins une fois par an. Tout administrateur ad hoc désigné en application des dispositions de l'article L. 221–5 doit, pendant la durée du maintien en zone d'attente du mineur qu'il assiste, se rendre sur place.

Un décret en Conseil d'Etat détermine les conditions d'accès du délégué du haut-commissariat des Nations unies pour les réfugiés ou de ses représentants ainsi que des associations humanitaires aux zones d'attente.

Chapitre IV: Sortie De La Zone D'attente

Article L224-1

Modifié par LOI n°2015–925 du 29 juillet 2015—art. 13

Si le maintien en zone d'attente n'est pas prolongé au terme du délai fixé par la dernière décision de maintien, l'étranger est autorisé à entrer en France sous le couvert d'un visa de régularisation de huit jours. Il devra avoir quitté ce territoire à l'expiration de ce délai, sauf s'il obtient une autorisation provisoire de séjour ou un récépissé de demande de carte de séjour ou une attestation de demande d'asile lui permettant d'introduire sa demande d'asile.

NOTA:

Conformément à l'article 35 III de la loi n° 2015–925 du 29 juillet 2015, l'article L. 213-8-1 du code de l'entrée et du séjour des étrangers et du droit d'asile, dans sa rédaction résultant de la présente loi, s'applique aux demandes d'asile présentées à compter du 1er novembre 2015 (Décret n° 2015-1364 du 28 octobre 2015, article 4).

Article L224-2

Si le départ de l'étranger ne peut être réalisé à partir de la gare, du port ou de l'aéroport dont dépend la zone d'attente dans laquelle il est maintenu, l'étranger peut être transféré vers toute zone d'attente d'une gare, d'un port ou d'un aéroport à partir desquels son départ peut effectivement avoir lieu.

En cas de nécessité, l'étranger peut également être transféré dans une zone d'attente dans laquelle les conditions requises pour son maintien, prévues au présent titre, sont réunies.

Article L224-3

Lorsque la décision de transfert doit intervenir dans le délai de quatre jours à compter de la décision initiale de maintien en zone d'attente, elle est prise dans les conditions prévues à l'article L. 221–3.

Lorsque le transfert est envisagé alors que le délai de quatre jours à compter de la décision initiale de maintien est expiré, l'autorité administrative en informe le juge des libertés et de la détention au moment où elle le saisit dans les conditions prévues au chapitre II du présent titre.

Article L224-4

Dans les cas où la prolongation ou le renouvellement du maintien en zone d'attente ont été accordés, l'autorité administrative informe le juge des libertés et de la détention ainsi que le procureur de la République de la nécessité de transférer l'étranger dans une autre zone d'attente et procède à ce transfert.

La prolongation ou le renouvellement du maintien en zone d'attente ne sont pas interrompus par le transfert de l'étranger dans une autre zone d'attente.

L'autorité administrative avise immédiatement de l'arrivée de l'étranger dans la nouvelle zone d'attente le juge des libertés et de la détention et le procureur de la République territorialement compétent.

References

Agamben, Giorgio. 1998. *Homo Sacer: Sovereign Power and Bare Life.* Stanford, CA: Stanford University Press.

Agamben, Giorgio. 1999. *Remnants of Auschwitz: The witness and the archive.* New York: Zone Books.

Agamben, Giorgio. 2005. *State of Exception.* Chicago: The University of Chicago Press.

Agier, Michel. 2002. *Aux bords du monde, les réfugiés* [Refugees, at the edges of the world]. Paris: Flammarion.

Agier, Michel. 2008. *Gérer les indésirables: des camps de réfugiés au gouvernement humanitaire* [Managing the undesirable: from refugee camps to humanitarian government]. Paris: Flammarion.

Agier, Michel. 2010. *Le couloir des exilés, être étranger dans un monde commun* [The corridor of exiles, to be a foreigner in a common world]. Bellecombe-en-Bauges: Éditions du Croquant.

Anafé. 1993. *Frontières du droit, frontières des droits: l'introuvable statut de la "zone internationale"* [Borders of law, borders of rights: the impossible status of the 'international zone']. Paris: L'Harmattan.

Anafé, April 2001. *Bilan des visites en zone d'attente à Roissy, campagne de novembre 2000 à mars 2001* [Summary of visits in Roissy's waiting zone, observations from November 2000 to March 2001]. Available at: http://www.gisti.org/doc/actions/2001/zone-attente/visites/index.html. Accessed January 22, 2016.

Anafé, March 2003. *Violences policières en zone d'attente* [Police violence in the waiting zone]. Available at: http://www.anafe.org/IMG/pdf/violences_mars_2003.pdf Accessed September 6, 2016.

Anafé. December 2007. *Une France inaccessible. Rapport de visites en aérogares. Zone d'attente de Roissy-Charles de Gaulle* [An inaccessible France. Report of terminal visits. Waiting zone of Roissy-Charles de Gaulle]. Available at: http://www.anafe.org/IMG/pdf/anafe-rapport-aerogares-dec-07.pdf. Accessed February 29, 2016.

Anafé, April 2010. *De l'autre côté de la frontière-Suivi des personnes refoulées* [On the other side of the border-following returnees]. Available at: http://www.anafe.org/IMG/pdf/suivi_des_refoules_-_rapport_anafe_-_avril_2010_reedite_en_2012.pdf. Accessed April 25, 2016.

Anafé, September 2011. *A la frontière de l'inacceptable. Malmenés, enfermés et privés de leurs droits dans les zones d'attente d'Orly, de province et d'outre-mer. Bilan 2009–2010* [At the border of the inacceptable. Mistreated, locked up and deprived of their rights in the waiting zones of Orly, provinces and overseas. 2009–2010 report]. Available at: http://www.anafe.org/spip.php?article103 Accessed April 4, 2016.

Anafé. December 2012. *Zones d'ombre à la frontière, rapport annuel 2011, observations et interventions de l'Anafé dans les zones d'attente* [Shadow zones at the border, annual report 2011, observations and interventions of Anafé in waiting zones]. Available at: http://www.anafe.org/spip.php?article109 Accessed September 16, 2015.

Anafé. January 2013. *Guide théorique et pratique: la procédure en zone d'attente* [Theoretical and practical guide: proceedings in the waiting zone]. Available at:http://www.anafe.org/spip.php?article245 Accessed September 16, 2015.

Anafé, December 2013. *Le dédale de l'asile à la frontière, comment la France ferme ses portes aux exilés. Rapport d'observations 2013* [The maze of asylum at the border, how France closes its doors to exiles. Observation report 2013]. Available at: http://www.anafe.org/IMG/pdf/anafe_ta_dec2013_web.pdf Accessed September 6, 2016.

Anafé. October 2014. *Analyse du projet de réforme de l'asile. Dispositions relatives à l'examen des demandes d'asile à la frontière* [Analysis of the asylum reform project. Measures regarding the assessment of asylum claims at the border]. Available at: http://www.anafe.org/IMG/pdf/analyse_reforme_asile_za_-_211014.pdf Accessed August 14, 2016.

Anafé, August 2015. *Les personnes maintenues en zone d'attente face aux procédures administratives et judiciaires* [Detainees in waiting zone and administrative and judicial proceedings]. Available at : http://www.anafe.org/spip.php?article279 Accessed August 26, 2016.

Anafé. November 2015. *Des zones d'atteintes aux droits, rapport d'observations dans les zones d'attente, Rapports d'activité et financier* [Zones of right infringement, report of observations in the waiting zones, financial and activity reports]. Available at: http://www.anafe.org/spip.php?article317 Accessed March 2, 2016.

Anafé. February 2016. *Dans les coulisses de Roissy: l'enfermement des étrangers en aérogare. Rapport de visites des aérogares de Roissy-Charles de Gaulle* [Behind the scenes of Roissy: confinement of non-citizens in airport terminals. Report of visits at Roissy-Charles de Gaulle's terminals]. Available at: http://www.anafe.org/spip.php?article322. Accessed March 1, 2016.

Anafé and Gadem. June 2017. *Privés de liberté en 'zone de transit'. Des aéroports français aux aéroports marocains* [Deprived of liberty in 'transit zone'. From French airports to Moroccan airports]. Available at: http://www.anafe.org/IMG/pdf/rapport_za_maroc_-_anafe-gadem_complet.pdf Accessed March 6, 2019.

Anafé et al. January 28, 1992. "Letter to the President of the Constitutional Council, Robert Badinter".

Arendt, Hannah. 1964. *Eichmann in Jerusalem: A Report on the Banality of Evil.* New York: Viking.

Arendt, Hannah. 1968. *The Origins of Totalitarianism.* New York: Harvest, Harcourt.

Australian Department of Immigration and Citizenship. 2009. *Refugee and Humanitarian Issues. Australia's Response.* Available at: https://www.dss.gov.au/sites/default/files/documents/01_2014/refugee-humanitarian-issues-june09_access.pdf Accessed January 9, 2019.

Australian Department of Immigration and Multicultural and Indigenous Affairs (DIMIA). 2001. *Refugee and Humanitarian Issues: Australia's Response.*

Australian Department of Immigration and Multicultural and Indigenous Affairs (DIMIA). August 6, 2002. *Response to the Senate Legal and Constitutional Committee inquiry into the Migration Legislation Amendment (Further Border Protection) Bill 2002 and related matters. Questions on Notice* Available at: https://www.aph.gov.au/Parliamentary_Business/Committees/Senate/Legal_and_Constitutional_Affairs/Completed_inquiries/2002–04/mig_bp/qon/index Accessed January 18, 2019.

Australian Department of Immigration and Multicultural and Indigenous Affairs (DIMIA). August 21, 2002. *Letter from Department of Immigration and Multicultural and Indigenous Affairs to the Senate Legal and Constitutional References Committee, Attachment A (responses to questions on notice arising from the Inquiry into the Migration Legislation (Further Border Protection Measures) Bill 2002 hearing on 6 August 2002).* Available at: https://www.aph.gov.au/Parliamentary_Business/Committees/Senate/Legal_and_Constitutional_Affairs/Completed_inquiries/2002–04/mig_bp/qon/index Accessed January 18, 2019.

Australian Department of Immigration and Multicultural and Indigenous Affairs (DIMIA). 2004. *Fact Sheet 74a, Boat Arrival Details (on Australian Mainland).* Available at: http://www.sievx.com/articles/psdp/DIMIA74a_boatarrivals.pdf Accessed April 23, 2019.

Australian Department of Immigration and Multicultural and Indigenous Affairs (DIMIA). 23 May 2005. *Fact sheet 76, Offshore Processing Arrangements.* Available at: http://web.archive.org/web/20051025182708/ http://www.immi.gov.au/facts/76offshore.htm Accessed 29 August 2012.

Australian Government. 2006. *Explanatory Memorandum. Migration Amendment (Designated Unauthorised Arrivals) Bill 2006.* Available at: https://www.legislation.gov.au/Details/C2006B00068/Download Accessed February 20, 2019.

Australian Government. 2012. *Report of the Expert Panel on Asylum Seekers (2012).* Available at: http://apo.org.au/node/30608 Accessed January 21, 2019.

Australian Government. 2018. *Australia's offshore Humanitarian Program: 2017–2018.* Available at: https://www.homeaffairs.gov.au/research-and-stats/files/australia-offshore-humanitarian-program-2017–18.pdf Accessed February 26, 2019.

Australian Government. February 2019. *Social Security Guide.* Available at: http://guides.dss.gov.au/guide-social-security-law/9/1/2/120 Accessed February 28, 2019.

Australian Human Rights Commission. 2005. *Questions and Answers About Refugees and Asylum Seekers. Face the facts 2005.* Available at: https://www.humanrights.gov.au/publications/questions-and-answers-about-refugees-asylum-seekers Accessed January 9, 2019.

Australian Parliament. 2001. *Border Protection (Validation and Enforcement Powers) Act 2001. An Act to validate the actions of the Commonwealth and others in relation to the MV Tampa and other vessels, and to provide increased powers to protect Australia's borders, and for related purposes.* Available at: https://www.legislation.gov.au/Details/C2004A00886 Accessed October 30, 2018.

Australian Parliament. 2001. *Migration Amendment (Excision from Migration Zone) Act 2001. An Act to excise certain Australian territory from the migration zone under the Migration Act 1958 for purposes related to unauthorised arrivals, and for related purposes.* Available at: https://www.legislation.gov.au/Details/C2004A00887 Accessed April 23, 2019.

Australian Parliament. 2001. *Migration Amendment (Excision from Migration Zone) (Consequential Provisions) Act 2001. An Act to make consequential provision for dealing with unauthorised arrivals in places excised from the migration zone under the Migration Act 1958 for purposes related to unauthorised arrivals, and for related purposes.* Available at: https://www.legislation.gov.au/Details/C2004A00888 Accessed April 23, 2019.

Australian Parliament. 2002. *Migration Legislation Amendment (Transitional Movement) Act 2002.* Available at: https://www.legislation.gov.au/Details/C2004A00947 Accessed March 13, 2019.

Australian Parliament. 2002. *Migration Legislation Amendment (Further Border Protection Measures) Bill 2002* [No. 2]. Bills Digest No. 149. 2002–03.

Australian Parliament. 2013. *Migration Amendment (Unauthorised Maritime Arrivals and Other Measures) Act 2013.*

Australian Parliament. 2014. *Migration and Maritime Powers Legislation Amendment (Resolving the Asylum Legacy Caseload) Act 2014.* Available at: https://www.legislation.gov.au/Details/C2014A00135 Accessed September 30, 2019.

Australian Senate. August 22, 2002. Senate Legal and Constitutional Legislation Committee. *Inquiry into the Migration Legislation Amendment (Further Border Protection Measures) Bill 2002. Response to Questions on Notice arising from 6 August 2002 Hearing.*

Australian Senate. October 21, 2002. Senate Legal and Constitutional References Committee. *Report, Inquiry into the Migration Legislation Amendment (Further Border Protection Measures) Bill 2002.* Available at: https://www.aph.gov.au/Parliamentary_Business/Committees/Senate/Legal_and_Constitutional_Affairs/Completed_inquiries/2002–04/mig_bp/report/contents Accessed February 21, 2019.

Australian Senate. October 23, 2002. *Select Committee for an inquiry into a Certain Maritime Incident.* Available at: https://www.aph.gov.au/Parliamentary_Business/Committees/Senate/Former_Committees/maritimeincident/index Accessed January 28, 2019.

Australian Senate. June 13, 2006. Senate Standing Committee on Legal and Constitutional Affairs. *Report, Inquiry into the provisions of the Migration Amendment (Designated Unauthorised Arrivals) Bill 2006*. Available at:https://www.aph.gov.au/Parliamentary_Business/Committees/Senate/Legal_and_Constitutional_Affairs/Completed_inquiries/2004–07/migration_unauthorised_arrivals/report/index Accessed February 20, 2019.

Australian Senate. December 2014. Senate Legal and Constitutional Affairs References Committee. *Report, Inquiry into the Incident at the Manus Island Detention Centre from 16 February to 18 February 2014*. Available at: http://static.guim.co.uk/ni/1418272553524/Manus-Island-report-.pdf Accessed April 8, 2019.

Australian Senate. February 2015. Senate Legal and Constitutional Affairs Legislation Committee. *Report, Inquiry into the Migration Amendment (Protecting Babies Born in Australia) Bill 2014*. Available at: https://www.aph.gov.au/Parliamentary_Business/Committees/Senate/Legal_and_Constitutional_Affairs/Protecting_Babies/Report Accessed September 29, 2019.

Babbie, Earl R. and Lucia Benaquisto. 2009. *Fundamentals of social research.*
Toronto: Nelson Education.

Bacon, Lucie. 2013. "Jeux d'acteurs en zone d'attente: des interactions à géométrie variable. Zoom sur l'Anafé, la Croix-Rouge française, la police aux frontières et les juges des libertés et de la détention dans la zone d'attente de Roissy-Charles-de-Gaulle" ["Actors' games in the waiting zone: multifaceted interactions. Focus on Anafé, the French Red Cross, the border police and the liberty and custody judges in Roissy Charles de Gaulle's waiting zone"]. Masters' thesis, CNRS. Available at: https://dumas.ccsd.cnrs.fr/dumas-00865894/document Accessed April 16, 2019.

Balme, Richard. 2006. "Convergences, fragmentation et majorités cycliques dans l'opinion publique" ["Convergences, fragmentation and cyclical majorities in public opinion"]. In *La France en mutation 1980–2005* [France undergoing changes 1980–2005] edited by Pepper D. Culpepper, Peter A. Hall and Bruno Palier, *chapter 10, 375–422*. Paris: Presses de Sciences Po.

Barnett, Laura. 2002. "Global governance and the Evolution of the International Refugee Regime". *International Journal of Refugee Law* 14 (2/3): 238–262.

Barnett, Michael and Raymond Duvall. 2005. "Power in international politics". *International Organization* 59 (1): 39–75.

Basaran, Tugba. 2011. *Security, Law and Borders: At the Limits of Liberties.* London: Routledge.

Bauder, Harald. 2013. *Why We Should Use the Term Illegalized Immigrant.* (RCIS Research Brief No. 2013/1). Toronto: Ryerson Centre for Immigration and Settlement.

Bauman, Zygmunt. 2004. *Wasted Lives, modernity and its outcasts.* Cambridge: Polity.

Belcher, Oliver and Lauren Martin. 2013. "Ethnographies of closed doors: conceptualising openness and closure of US immigration and military institutions". *Area* 45(4), 403–410.

Belguendouz, Abdelkrim. 2003. "Le Maroc, vaste zone d'attente?" ["Morocco, vast waiting zone?"] *Plein Droit*, 2003/2, no. 57 (35–40). Available at: https://www.cairn.info/revue-plein-droit-2003-2-page-35.htm Accessed March 6, 2019.

Bernard, Philippe. January 21, 1992. " 'L'amendement Marchand' à nouveau devant les parlementaires. Des demandeurs d'asile contestent 'la zone internationale' prévue par le Ministère de l'Intérieur" ["The 'Marchand amendment' before parliamentarians again. Asylum seekers contest the 'international zone' planned by the Ministry of the Interior"]. *Le Monde.*

Bigo, Didier, Sergio Carrera, and Elspeth Guild. September 2009. *The Challenge Project: Final Policy Recommendations on the Changing Landscape of European Liberty and Security.* Research Paper n°16.

Bosniak, Linda. 2007. "Being Here: Ethical Territoriality and the Rights of Immigrants", *Theoretical Inquiries in Law* 8: 389–90.

Bourdieu, Pierre. 2000. *Esquisse d'une théorie de la Pratique* [Outline of a theory of practice]. Paris: Editions du Seuil.

Bourguet, Christian. 1992. "La notion de frontière dans les aéroports ou 'le pays de nulle part' " ["The notion of border in airports or 'the nowhere country' "]. *Autres Temps. Les cahiers du christianisme social* 33–34: 24–31.

Butler, Judith. 2004. *Precarious Life: The Powers of Mourning and Violence.* London/New York: Verso.

Caloz-Tschopp, Marie-Claire. 1993. "La zone internationale et le droit d'asile en Europe. Les limites d'une communauté d'Etats … de droit et l'exercice de la démocratie radicale" ["The international zone and the right to seek asylum in Europe. The limits of a community of states … based on the rule of law and the exercise of radical democracy"]. In *Frontières du droit, frontières des droits: l'introuvable statut de la "zone internationale"* [Borders of law, borders of rights: the impossible status of the "international zone"] edited by Anafé, 17–27. Paris: L'Harmattan.

Caloz-Tschopp, Marie-Claire. 2004. *Les Etrangers aux frontières de l'Europe et le spectre des camps* [Foreign nationals at Europe's borders and the camps' spectre]. Paris: La dispute.

CESEDA (*Code de l'entrée et du séjour des étrangers et du droit d'asile*) [Code on the Entry and Residency of Foreign Nationals and the Right to Asylum.]. 2016. Available at: http://www.legifrance.gouv.fr/affichCode.do?cidTexte=LEGITEXT000006070158. Accessed July 30, 2016.

Clochard, Olivier, et al. 2003. "Zones d'attente et demande d'asile à la frontière: le renforcement des contrôles migratoires ?" ["Waiting zones and asylum claims at the border: the reinforcement of migration controls ?"] *Revue européenne des migrations internationales* 19 (2) : 1–23.

Clochard, Olivier. 2007. "Le jeu des frontières dans l'accès au statut de réfugié, une géographie des politiques européennes d'asile et d'immigration" ["Border games in the access to refugee status, a geography of European policies of asylum and immigration"]. PhD diss., University of Poitiers. Available at: https://tel.archives-ouvertes.fr/tel-00550193/document Accessed September 6, 2016.

CNN. September 1, 2001. "U.N. questions Australian refugee deal". Available at: http://edition.cnn.com/2001/WORLD/asiapcf/auspac/09/01/aust.boat.people/index.html Accessed January 28, 2019.

Coddington, Kate. 2017. "Contagious trauma: Reframing the spatial mobility of trauma within advocacy work". *Emotion, Space and Society* 24: 66–73.

Cohendet, Marie-Anne. 1993. *La cohabitation, leçons d'une experience* [Coexistence, lessons from an experience]. Paris: Presses Universitaires de France.

Coleman, David. February 3, 2019. Australian Minister for Immigration, Citizenship and Multicultural Affairs. Press conference "Asylum seeker children off Nauru". Available at: https://minister.homeaffairs.gov.au/davidcoleman/Pages/press-conference-sydney-20190203.aspx Accessed February 26, 2019.

Colombani, Jean-Marie and Hugues Portelli. 1995. *Le double septennat de François Mitterrand, dernier inventaire* [The double seven-year presidency of Francois Mitterrand, last review]. Paris: Grasset & Fasquelle.

Committee on the Rights of the Child. June 4, 2004. *Consideration of Reports Submitted by States Parties Under article 44 of the Convention, Concluding Observations of the Committee on the Rights of the Child: France. 36th session. Unedited version. CRC/C/15/Add.240.*

Committee on the Rights of the Child. 2006. *General Assembly Official Records, Sixty-first session supplement no. 41 (A/61/41)*. Available at: http://www.crin.org/en/docs/Report_CRC_GA61_Eng.pdf Accessed September 7, 2016.

Coomans, Fons and Menno T. Kamminga, ed. 2004. *Extraterritorial applications of Human Rights Treaties.* Antwerp: Intersentia.

Coombs, Moira. August 2005. *Parliament of Australia, Department of Parliamentary Services. Research Note No. 5 of 2005–2006*. Available at: https://www.aph.gov.au/binaries/library/pubs/rn/2005–06/06rn05.pdf Accessed February 21, 2019.

Council of Europe. November 4, 1950. *Convention for the Protection of Human Rights and Fundamental Freedoms.* Available at: http://www.echr.coe.int/Documents/Convention_ENG.pdf. Accessed May 23, 2016.

Council of Europe: European Commission of Human Rights. October 18, 1993. *Barir and Amuur against France*. Available at (only in French): http://demo.eurocases.eu/Doc/CourtAct/4564696 Accessed September 6, 2016.

Council of Europe: European Committee for the Prevention of Torture and Inhuman or Degrading Treatment or Punishment. 2003. *Rapport au Gouvernement de la République française relatif à la visite effectuée en France par le Comité européen pour la prévention de la torture et des peines ou traitements inhumains ou dégradants (CPT) du 17 au 21 juin 2002* [Report to the government of the French Republic regarding the European Committee for the Prevention of Torture and Inhuman or Degrading Treatment or Punishment's visit to France from June 17 to 21 2002] CPT/Inf (2003) 40.

Council of Europe: European Committee for the Prevention of Torture and Inhuman or Degrading Treatment or Punishment. 2007. *Rapport au Gouvernement de la République française relatif à la visite effectuée en France par le Comité européen pour la prévention de la torture et des peines ou traitements inhumains ou dégradants (CPT) du 27 septembre au 9 octobre 2006* [Report to the government of the French Republic regarding the European Committee for the Prevention of Torture and Inhuman or Degrading Treatment or Punishment's visit to France from September 27 to October 9 2006] CPT/Inf (2007) 44.

Council of Europe: European Court of Human Rights. June 25, 1996. *Amuur v. France*, Available at: http://www.unhcr.org/refworld/docid/3ae6b76710.html Accessed February 21, 2013.

Council of Europe: European Court of Human Rights. April 26, 2007. *Gebremedhin v. France*, Available at: https://www.refworld.org/cases,ECHR,46441fa02.html Accessed April 30, 2019.

Council of Europe: European Court of Human Rights. January 19, 2012. *Popov v. France*. Available at: http://www.refworld.org/docid/4f1990b22.html Accessed May 26, 2016.

Council of Europe: European Court of Human Rights Press Unit. June 2014. *Migrants in detention, factsheet*. Available at: http://www.echr.coe.int/Documents/FS_Migrants_detention_ENG.pdf Accessed 16 September 2015.

Council of Europe: Parliamentary Assembly. 1988. *Recommendation 1088*.

Coutin, Susan B. and Véronique Fortin. 2015. "Legal ethnographies and ethnographic law". In *The handbook of law and society* edited by Sarat, Austin and Patricia Ewick, *chapter 5, 96–109*. Chichester, West Sussex, UK; Malden, MA: Wiley-Blackwell.

Crépeau, François. 1995. *Droit d'asile: de l'hospitalité aux contrôles migratoires* [Right to asylum: from hospitality to migratory controls]. Bruxelles: Bruylant.

Cresson, Edith. January 16, 1992. *Letter of the Prime Minister to the President of the Domestic Human Rights Commission*.

Créteil Court of First Instance [*Tribunal de Grande Instance de Créteil*]. March 31, 1992. *Ruling*.

Dauvergne, Catherine. 2008. *Making People Illegal: What Globalization Means for Migration and the Law*. Cambridge: Cambridge University Press.

Dauvergne, Catherine. 2016. *The New Politics of Immigration and the End of Settler Societies.* New York: Cambridge University Press.
Dean, Mitchell. 2002. "Liberal government and authoritarianism", *Economy and Society* 31 (1): 37–61.
Declaration of States Parties to the 1951 Convention and/or its 1967 Protocol Relating to the Status of Refugees at the invitation of the Government of Switzerland and of the UNHCR at the occasion of the 50th anniversary of the 1951 Refugee Convention. Available at: http://www.unhcr.org/419c74d64.pdf Accessed October 14, 2018.
Del Mundo, Fernando. June 18, 2002. "The number of refugees of concern to the UN refugee agency remained unchanged in 2001 at 12 million, according to a report released today". *UNHCR*. Available at: https://www.unhcr.org/en-lk/news/latest/2002/6/3d0f6dcb5/2001-global-refugee-statistics.html Accessed April 1, 2019.
De Loisy, Anne. 2005. *Bienvenue en France! Six mois d'enquête clandestine dans la zone d'attente de Roissy* [Welcome to France! Six months of undercover investigation in Roissy's waiting zone]. Paris: Le Cherche Midi.
Del Valle Galvez, Alejandro. 2005. "Las zonas internacionales o zonas de tránsito de los aeropuertos, ficción liminar fronteriza" ["International zones or airport transit zones, fiction of the border"]. Revista Electrónica de estudios internacionales 9: 1–18.
De Schutter, Olivier et al. 2012. "Commentary to the Maastricht Principles on Extraterritorial Obligations of States in the area of Economic, Social and Cultural Rights". *Human Rights Quarterly* 34: 1084–1169.
Devereux, Georges. 1994. *De l'angoisse à la méthode dans les sciences du comportement* [From Anxiety to Method in the Behavioral Sciences]. Flammarion, Champs Essai.
Duhamel, Eric and Olivier Forcade. 2005. *Histoire et vie politique en France depuis 1945. Des années essentielles de mutation et de modernisation du système politique français* [History and political life in France since 1945. Crucial years of transformation and modernization of the French political system]. Paris: Armand Colin.
Dupont, Alan. 2002. "Refugees and Illegal migrants in the Asia-Pacific region" In *Refugees and the Myth of the Borderless World*, published by the Department of International Relations at the Australian National University, 9–15. Canberra: Australia. Available at: https://openresearch-repository.anu.edu.au/bitstream/1885/41143/3/Keynotes-2.PDF Accessed January 12, 2019.
Eck, Jean-François. 2004. *Histoire de l'économie française depuis 1945. 7e édition* [History of French economy since 1945. 7th edition]. Paris : Armand Colin.
Edwards, Alice. 2003. "Tampering with Refugee Protection: The Case of Australia". *International Journal of Refugee Law* 15 (2): 192–211.
Elliott, Elizabeth and Gunasekera, Hasantha. October 16–18, 2015. *The health and well-being of children in immigration detention. Report to the Australian Human Rights Commission. Monitoring Visit to Wickham Point Detention Centre, Darwin, NT.*

Available at: https://www.humanrights.gov.au/sites/default/files/document/publication/Health%20and%20well-being%20of%20children%20in%20immigration%20detention%20report.pdf Accessed April 7, 2019.

European Commission and the European Migration Network (EC-EMN). December 13, 2012. *Ad-Hoc Query on implementing Council Directive 2001/51/EC.* Available at: http://ec.europa.eu/dgs/home-affairs/what-we do/networks/european_migration_network/reports/docs/ad-hoc-queries/eu-acquis/436_emn_ad-hoc_query_on_implementing_council_directive_200151ec_5november2012_wider_dissemination_en.pdf Accessed May 23, 2016.

European Parliament. December 2007. *The conditions in centres for third country nationals (detention camps, open centres as well as transit centres and transit zones) with a particular focus on provisions and facilities for persons with spécial needs in the 25 EU members states.* IP/C/LIBE/IC/2006-181.

European Union. 19 June 1990. *Convention Implementing the Schengen Agreement of 14 June 1985 between the Governments of the States of the Benelux Economic Union, the Federal Republic of Germany and the French Republic, on the Gradual Abolition of Checks at their Common Borders ("Schengen Implementation Agreement").* Available at: http://www.refworld.org/docid/3ae6b38a20.html Accessed May 18, 2016.

European Union: Council of the European Union. 30 November 1992. *Conclusions on Countries in Which There is Generally No Serious Risk of Persecution ("London Resolution").* Available at: http://www.refworld.org/docid/3f86c6ee4.html Accessed 9 July 2016.

European Union: Council of the European Union. 30 November 1992. *Council Resolution of 30 November 1992 on a Harmonized Approach to Questions Concerning Host Third Countries ("London Resolution").* Available at: http://www.refworld.org/docid/3f86c3094.html Accessed July 9, 2016.

European Union: Council of the European Union. 30 November 1992. *Council Resolution of 30 November 1992 on Manifestly Unfounded Applications for Asylum ("London Resolution").* Available at: http://www.refworld.org/docid/3f86bbcc4.html. Accessed 9 July 2016.

European Union: Council of the European Union. June 28, 2001. *Directive 2001/51/EC of 28 June 2001 supplementing the provisions of Article 26 of the Convention implementing the Schengen Agreement of 14 June 1985.* Available at: http://eur-lex.europa.eu/LexUriServ/LexUriServ.do?uri=OJ:L:2001:187:0045:0046:EN:PDF. Accessed May 23, 2016.

European Union: Council of the European Union. June 26, 2013. *Directive 2013/33/EU of the European Parliament and of the Council of June 26, 2013 laying down standards for the reception of applicants for international protection.* Available at: http://eur-lex.europa.eu/legal-content/en/TXT/?uri=celex%3A32013L0033 Accessed September 7, 2016.

European Union: Council of the European Union. June 26, 2013. *Directive 2013/32/EU of the European Parliament and of the Council of 26 June 2013 on common procedures for granting and withdrawing international protection (recast)*, Available at: http://www.refworld.org/docid/51d29b224.html Accessed August 14, 2016.

Faye, Olivier and Pascual, Julia. April 15, 2019. "Les ONG ont sauvé l'honneur de l'Europe en Méditerannée" ["NGOs saved Europe's honor in the Mediterranean Sea"]. *Le Monde.*

Feik, Nick. November 2, 2012. "This is Not-Australia". *The Monthly.* Available at: https://www.themonthly.com.au/blog/nick-feik/2012/11/05/1352084425/not-australia Accessed April 4, 2019.

Feller, Erika. 1989. "Carrier Sanctions and International Law". *International Journal of Refugee Law* 1 (1).

Fernandez, Alexandre. 2001. *L'économie française depuis 1945* [*French economy since 1945*]. Paris: Hachette.

Foster, Michelle and Jason Pobjoy, 2011. "A Failed Case of Legal Exceptionalism? Refugee Status Determination in Australia's 'Excised Territory' ". *International Journal of Refugee Law* 23 (4): 583–631.

France 3. December 12, 2013. "*Roissy Charles de Gaulle, embarquement immediat*" ["Roissy Charles de Gaulle, immediate boarding"]. Available at: https://www.youtube.com/watch?v=ygDkYHo4Ffk. Accessed January 30, 2015.

French Constitution of October 4, 1958. Available at: http://www.conseil-constitutionnel.fr/conseil-constitutionnel/francais/la-constitution/la-constitution-du-4-octobre-1958/texte-integral-de-la-constitution-du-4-octobre-1958-en-vigueur.5074.html#titre8.

French Constitutional Council [*Conseil Constitutionnel*]. July 25, 1991. *Decision n°91–294 DC of July 25, 1991.* Available at: http://www.conseil-constitutionnel.fr/conseil-con..decision-n-91-294-dc-du-25-juillet-1991.8764.html. Accessed May 23, 2016.

French Constitutional Council [*Conseil Constitutionnel*]. February 25, 1992. *Decision N° 92–307 DC of February 25, 1992.* Available at: http://www.conseil-constitutionnel.fr/conseil-con..decision-n-92-307-dc-du-25-fevrier-1992.8818.html Accessed May 24, 2016.

French Counsel of State [*Conseil d'Etat*]. January 27, 1984. Case of *Eksir.*

French Final Court of Appeal [*Cour de Cassation*]. October 28, 1987. *Case of Procureur Général de Paris et Youssef.*

French Final Court of Appeal [*Cour de Cassation*]. March 25, 2009. *Ruling.*

French government. 2003. *Réponse du Gouvernement de la République française au rapport du Comité européen pour la prevention de la torture et des peines ou traitements inhumains ou dégradants (CPT) relatif à sa visite effectuée en France du 17 au 21 juin 2002* [Response of the Government of the French Republic to the European Committee for the Prevention of Torture and Inhuman or Degrading Treatment or Punishment's report regarding the Committee's visit to France from June 17 to 21 2002]. CPT/Inf (2003) 41.

French Minister of Immigration. May 27, 2009. *Arrêté du 27 mai 2009 fixant la liste des associations humanitaires habilitées à proposer des représentants en vue d'accéder en zone d'attente* [Order of May 27, 2009 establishing the list of humanitarian organizations entitled to suggest representatives to access the waiting zone]. Available at https://www.legifrance.gouv.fr/affichTexte.do?cidTexte=LEGITEXT000020716150 Accessed September 16, 2016.

French Minister of the Interior. May 30, 2006. *Arrêté du 30 mai 2006 fixant la liste des associations humanitaires habilitées à proposer des représentants en vue d'accéder en zone d'attente* [Order of May 30, 2006 establishing the list of humanitarian organizations entitled to suggest representatives to access the waiting zone]. Available at https://www.legifrance.gouv.fr/affichTexte.do?cidTexte=JORFTEXT000000790911&categorieLien=cid Accessed September 16, 2016.

French Minister of the Interior. July 6, 2012. *Circulaire Valls. Objet: mise en oeuvre de l'assignation à residence prévue à l'article L.561–2 du CESEDA, en alternative au placement des familles en rétention administrative sur le fondement de l'article L.551-1 du même code* [Executive Order Valls. Object: implementation of compulsory residence orders according to article L561-2 of CESEDA, to replace the placement of families in administrative detention according to article L.551-1 of the same code].

French Ministry of the Interior and French Red Cross. October 6, 2003. *Convention between the Ministry of the Interior and the French Red Cross.*

French National Assembly. December 19, 1991. Minutes from parliamentary debates.

French National Assembly. January 21, 1992. Minutes from parliamentary debates.

French National Assembly. 24 June 2009. *Rapport d'information sur les centres de rétention administrative et les zones d'attente n° 1776* [Information Report on centres of administrative detention and waiting zones n°1776].

French National Assembly, Law commission. September 8, 2010. *Commission des lois constitutionnelles, de la legislation et de l'administration générale de la République* [Commission of constitutional laws, legislation and general administration of the Republic], *audition, ouverte à la presse, de M. Eric Besson, Ministre de l'immigration, de l'intégration, de l'identité nationale et du développement solidaire, sur le projet de loi relatif à l'immigration, à l'intégration et à la nationalité* [hearing, open to the press, of M. Eric Besson, Minister of immigration, integration, national identity and of development, on the bill regarding immigration, integration and citizenship], *Compte-rendu n°85* [report n°85]. Available at: http://www.assemblee-nationale.fr/13/cr-cloi/09-10/c0910085.asp. Accessed August 10, 2016.

French National Assembly. *Fiches de synthèse n°24: les commissions permanentes* [Summary sheet n°24: permanent commissions]. Available at: http://www2.assemblee-nationale.fr/decouvrir-l-assemblee/role-et-pouvoirs-de-l-assemblee-nationale/les-organes-de-l-assemblee-nationale/les-commissions-permanentes Accessed January 22, 2016.

French National Assembly. *Règlement de l'Assemblée Nationale* [Regulation manual of the National Assembly]. Available at: http://www.assemblee-nationale.fr/connaissance/reglement.asp Accessed August 31, 2016.

French Parliament. Law of February 26, 1992. *Loi no 92–190 du 26 février 1992 portant modification de l'ordonnance no 45–2658 du 2 novembre 1945 modifiée, relative aux conditions d'entrée et de séjour des étrangers en France* [Law n°92–190 of February 26, 1992 modifying the Ordinance n°45–2658 of November 2, 1945 on conditions of entry and residency of foreign nationals in France]. Available at: https://www.legifrance.gouv.fr/affichTexte.do?cidTexte=JORFTEXT000000161548&categorieLien=id. Accessed May 23, 2016.

French Parliament. Law of July 6, 1992. *Loi n° 92–625 du 6 juillet 1992 sur la zone d'attente des ports et des aéroports et portant modification de l'ordonnance n°45–2658 du 2 novembre 1945 relative aux conditions d'entrée et de séjour des étrangers en France* [Law n°92–625 of July 6, 1992 on the waiting zone of ports and airports modifying Ordinance n°45–2658 of November 2, 1945 regarding conditions of entry and residency of foreign nationals in France]. Available at: https://www.legifrance.gouv.fr/affichTexte.do?cidTexte=JORFTEXT000000175480&categorieLien=id. Accessed May 24, 2016.

French Parliament. Law of March 4, 2002. *Loi n° 2002–305 du 4 mars 2002 relative à l'autorité parentale* [Law n°2002–305 of March 4, 2002 regarding parental authority]. Available at: https://www.legifrance.gouv.fr/affichTexte.do?cidTexte=JORFTEXT000000776352&categorieLien=id Accessed September 7, 2016.

French Parliament. Law of November 26, 2003. *Loi n°2003-1119 du 26 novembre 2003 relative à la maîtrise de l'immigration, au séjour des étrangers en France et à la nationalité* [Law n°2003-1119 of November 26, 2003 regarding the control of immigration, the residency of foreign nationals in France and citizenship]. Available at: https://www.legifrance.gouv.fr/affichTexte.do?cidTexte=JORFTEXT000000795635&categorieLien=id. Accessed August 10, 2016.

French Parliament. Law of October 30, 2007. *Loi n° 2007-1545 du 30 octobre 2007 instituant un Contrôleur général des lieux de privation de liberté* [Law n°2007-1545 of October 30, 2007 establishing a General inspector of places of deprivation of liberty]. Available at: https://www.legifrance.gouv.fr/affichTexte.do?cidTexte=JORFTEXT000000279700 Accessed September 7, 2016.

French Parliament. Law of June 16, 2011. *Loi n°2011–672 du 16 juin 2011 relative à l'immigration, à l'intégration et à la nationalité* [Law n°2011–672 of June 16, 2011 regarding immigration, integration and citizenship]. Available at: https://www.legifrance.gouv.fr/affichTexte.do?categorieLien=id&cidTexte=JORFTEXT000024191380. Accessed August 10, 2016.

French Parliament. Law of March 7, 2016. *Loi n°2016-274 du 7 mars 2016 relative au droit des étrangers en France* [Law n°2016-274 of March 7, 2016 regarding non-citizens'rights in France]. Available at: https://www.legifrance.gouv.fr/affichTexteArticle.do;jsessionid=0DA281A6E9B12B4499CD7488A669C966.tplgfr41s_3?cidTexte=JORFTEXT000032164264&idArticle=LEGIARTI000032165669&dateTexte=20160308. Accessed September 14, 2016.

French Prime Minister. May 27, 1982. *Décret n°82–442 du 27 mai 1982 pris pour l'application des articles 5, 5-1 et 5-3 de l'ordonnance n°45–2658 du 2 novembre 1945 modifiée relative aux conditions d'entrée et de séjour des étrangers en France, en ce qui concerne l'admission sur le territoire français* [Decree n°82-442 of May 27, 1982 taken to implement articles 5, 5-1 and 5-3 of the modified ordinance n°45-2658 of November 2, 1945 regarding the conditions of entry and residency of foreign nationals in France, pertaining to admission to French territory].

French Red Cross. December 2011. "Regards sur le parcours des mineurs isolés étrangers maintenus en zone d'attente de Roissy Charles de Gaulle en 2010 à travers la mission d'administrateur ad hoc de la Croix-Rouge française" ["Outlooks on the itinerary of foreign unaccompanied minors held in Roissy Charles de Gaulle's waiting zone in 2010 through the Red Cross mission of *ad hoc* administrator"]. *Repères* 9: 1–40.

French Red Cross. 2013. *Rapport de la mission d'assistance humanitaire de la Croix-Rouge française auprès des étrangers en zone d'attente, année 2012* [Report of the humanitarian mission of the French Red Cross with foreign nationals in the waiting zone, year 2012].

French Red Cross. January 2013. *Bilan d'activité: mineurs isolés étrangers, 2011*. [Activity report: foreign unaccompanied minors, 2011].

French Senate. January 16, 1992. *Minutes from parliamentary debates.*

French Senate. January 22, 1992. *Minutes from parliamentary debates.*

Gammeltoft-Hansen, Thomas. 2011. *Access to asylum: international refugee law and the globalisation of migration control.* Cambridge: Cambridge University Press.

Gartrell, Adam. August 20, 2016. "Manus Island bill $2 billion and counting. $1 million for each detainee". *The Sydney Morning Herald*. Available at: https://www.smh.com.au/politics/federal/manus-island-bill-2-billion-and-counting--1-million-for-each-detainee-20160820-gqx8do.html Accessed April 28, 2019.

General inspector of places of deprivation of liberty (CGLPL) [*Contrôleur général des lieux de privation de liberté*]. January 2009. *Rapport de visite, zone d'attente de Roissy-Charles-de-Gaulle 27–28 janvier 2009* [Visit report, waiting zone of Roissy-Charles-de-Gaulle 27–28 January 2009]. Available at: http://www.cglpl.fr/2010/rapport-de-visite-de-la-zone-dattente-de-roissy-charles-de-gaulle/ Accessed May 26, 2016.

General inspector of places of deprivation of liberty (CGLPL) [*Contrôleur général des lieux de privation de liberté*]. December 2013. *Rapport de visite: zone d'attente de l'aéroport de Roissy-Charles-de-Gaulle du 10 au 12 décembre 2013* [Visit report: waiting zone of Roissy-Charles-de-Gaulle airport December 10–12, 2013]. Available at: http://www.cglpl.fr/2015/rapport-de-la-deuxieme-visite-de-la-zone-dattente-de-laeroport-de-roissy-charles-de-gaulle-val-doise/ Accessed March 14, 2016.

Genevois, Bruno. 1992. "L'entrée des étrangers en France: le rappel des exigences constitutionnelles. A propos de la décision du Conseil Constitutionnel n° 92–307 du 25 février 1992" ["Entry of foreign nationals to France: a reminder of constitutional requirements. About the Constitutional Council decision n°92–307 of February 25, 1992"]. *Revue française de droit administratif* 8 (2), March-April 1992.

Gibney, Mark, and Sigrun Skogly. 2002. "Transnational Human Rights Obligations". *Human Rights Quarterly.* 24: 781–98.

Gibney, Mark and Sigrun Skogly, ed. 2010. *Universal Human Rights and extraterritorial obligations.* University of Pennsylvania Press.

Gibney, Matthew J. 2004. *The Ethics and Politics of Asylum, Liberal Democracy and the Response to Refugees.* Cambridge University Press.

Gil-Robles, Alvaro. 19 September 2001. *Recommendation of the Commissioner for Human Rights concerning the rights of aliens wishing to enter a Council of Europe member State and the enforcement of expulsion orders.* CommDH (2001)19.

Gil-Robles, Alvaro. February 15, 2006. *Report by Mr Alvaro Gil-Robles, Commissioner for Human Rights, on the effective respect for human rights in France following his visit from 5 to 21 September 2005.* CommDH (2006)2.

Gisti, January 1989. "Une frontière bien gardée" ["A well policed border"]. *Plein Droit* 6.

Gondek, Michal. 2009. *The Reach of Human Rights in a Globalizing World: Extraterritorial Application of Human Rights Treaties.* Intersentia.

Gregory, Derek. 2007. "Vanishing Points: Law, Violence, and Exception in the Global War Prison" In *Violent geographies: fear, terror and political violence*, edited by Derek Gregory and Allan Pred, 205–236. New York: Routledge.

Grunberg, Gérard. 2006. "L'adaptation du système des partis (1965–2006)" ["The adaptation of the party system (1965–2006)"]. In *La France en mutation 1980–2005* [France undergoing changes 1980–2005] edited by Pepper D. Culpepper, Peter A. Hall and Bruno Palier, *chapter 12, 449–476.* Paris: Presses de Sciences Po.

Gueslin, André. 1992. *L'Etat, l'économie et la société française, XIXe–XX siècle* [French State, economy and society, XIX–XX century]. Paris: Hachette.

Guiraudon, Virginie. 2000. "Analyse comparative des droits des étrangers depuis les années 1970" ["Comparative analysis of foreigner's rights since the 1970s"]. In *Les politiques d'immigration en Europe, Allemagne, France, Pays Bas* [Immigration policies in Europe, Germany, France and The Netherlands]. Paris: L'Harmattan.

Guiraudon, Virginie. 2005. "Immigration Politics and Policies". In *Developments in French Politics 3* edited by Alistair Cole, Patrick Le Galès and Jonah Levy, 154–169. New York: Palgrave Macmillan.

Guiraudon, Virginie, 2006 a. "L'intégration des immigrés ou la politique de l'esquive. Réformer sans changer de modèle?" ["The integration of immigrants or the policy of elusion. Reforming without changing the model of reference?"]. In *La France en mutation 1980–2005*. [France undergoing changes 1980–2005], edited by Pepper D. Culpepper, Peter A. Hall and Bruno Palier, 265–299. Paris: Sciences Po Les Presses.

Guiraudon, Virginie. 2006 b. "Enlisting Third Parties in Border Control: a Comparative Study of its Causes and Consequences". In *Borders and Security Governance, managing borders in a globalized world*, edited by Marina Caparini and Otwin Marenin, Geneva Centre for the Democratic Control of Armed Forces (DCAF).

Harrap's Unabridged Dictionary, 2007. Volume 2, French-English. Edinburgh: Chambers Harrap's Publishers.

Hathaway, James C. 1992. "The Emerging Politics of Non-Entrée". 91 *Refugees* 40.

Hathaway, James C. 2005. *The Rights of Refugees Under International Law*. Cambridge: Cambridge University Press.

Hathaway, James C. and Thomas Gammeltoft-Hansen, 2015. "*Non-Refoulement* in a World of Cooperative Deterrence". *Columbia Journal of Transnational Law* 53 (2): 235–84.

Herbert, Steve. 2000. "For ethnography". *Progress in Human Geography*. 24 (4): 550–568.

Hindess, Barry. 2001. "The Liberal Government of Unfreedom". *Alternatives* 26: 93–111.

Human Rights Law Center, April 17, 2015. *Australian Migration Law Amendments: What this means for asylum seeker children*. Available at: https://www.hrlc.org.au/news/australian-migration-law-amendments-what-this-means-for-asylum-seeker-children?rq=caseload%20 Accessed April 4, 2019.

Human Rights Watch (HRW). 2002. "*By invitation only": Australian asylum policy*. Available at: https://www.hrw.org/report/2002/12/10/invitation-only/australian-asylum-policy Accessed April 30, 2019.

Human Rights Watch (HRW). October 2009. *Lost in Transit, Insufficient Protection for Unaccompanied Migrant Children at Roissy Charles de Gaulle*. Available at: https://www.hrw.org/report/2009/10/29/lost-transit/insufficient-protection-unaccompanied-migrant-children-roissy-charles. Accessed March 14, 2016.

Human Rights Watch (HRW). April 8, 2014. *France: Unaccompanied Children Detained at Borders. 500 a Year Held in Transit Zones*. Available at: https://www.hrw.org/news/2014/04/08/france-unaccompanied-children-detained-borders. Accessed September 16, 2015.

Human Rights Watch (HRW). March 15, 2016. "EU: Turkey Mass-Return Deal Threatens Rights". Available at: https://www.hrw.org/news/2016/03/15/eu-turkey-mass-return-deal-threatens-rights Accessed September 19, 2016.

Human Rights Watch (HRW) and Amnesty International. August 2, 2016. "Australia: Appalling Abuse, Neglect of Refugees on Nauru. Investigation on Remote Pacific Island Finds Deliberate Abuse Hidden Behind Wall of Secrecy". Available at: https://www.hrw.org/news/2016/08/02/australia-appalling-abuse-neglect-refugees-nauru Accessed April 7, 2019.

Hyndman, Jennifer. 2001. "The Field as Here and Now, Not There and Then". *Geographical Review* 91 (1/2): 262–272.

Innis, Michelle. December 11, 2014. "Australia Failed to Protect Asylum Seekers, Report Says". *The New York Times.* Available at: https://www.nytimes.com/2014/12/12/world/asia/australia-rioting-papua-new-guinea-manus-island.html?module=inline Accessed April 7, 2019.

Intergovernmental consultations on migration, asylum and refugees (IGC). December 2012. *Report on policies and practices in IGC Participating States.* France: GPS Publishing.

International Air Transport Association (IATA). October 15, 2014. *Inadmissible Persons and Deportees: IATA's Experiences and Concerns.* ICAO Regional Facilitation Seminar. Paris, France. Available at: http://www.icao.int/EURNAT/Other%20Meetings%20Seminars%20and%20Workshops/2014%20FAL%20Seminar%20Paris/Day3%20PPT16%20E.pdf. Accessed March 10, 2016.

International Civil Aviation Organization (ICAO). December 7, 1944. *Convention on International Civil Aviation ("Chicago Convention")* signed at Chicago on December 7, 1944. Available at: http://www.refworld.org/docid/3ddca0dd4.html Accessed December 5, 2014.

International Civil Aviation Organization (ICAO). November 12, 2003. Facilitation Division, Twelfth Session, "FAL/12-WP/6, 12/11/03".

International Civil Aviation Organization (ICAO). July 2005. *Annex 9 to the Convention on International Civil Aviation,* 12th edition, July 2005.[1] Available at: http://www.ifrc.org/docs/IDRL/Chicago%20Convention%20Annex%209.pdf Accessed December 5, 2014.

Iserte, Morgane. 2008. "Enquête en 'zone d'attente réservée' de l'aéroport de Paris-Charles de Gaulle: vers une gestion sécuritaire des 'flux migratoires'" ["Enquiry in Paris-Charles de Gaulle airport's 'reserved waiting zone': towards a securitized management of migratory flows"]. *Cultures & Conflits* 3 (71): 31–53.

Isin, Engin F. and Kim Rygiel. 2007. "Abject Spaces: Frontiers, Zones, Camps". In *Logics of Biopower and the War on Terror,* edited by Elizabeth Dauphinee and Cristina Masters. 181–203. Houndmills, Basingstoke, Hampshire: Palgrave.

Israël, Liora. June 2002. "Deux parcours d'avocats" ["Two lawyers' itineraries"]. In "Immigration : trente ans de combat par le droit". ["Immigration: thirty years of fight through the law"]. *Plein droit* 53–54.

Jackson, Ivor. 1999. *The refugee concept in group situations.* The Hague; London; Boston: Nijhoff.

1 The first page of Annex 9 reads: "This edition incorporates all amendments adopted by the Council prior to 8 March 2005 and supersedes, on November 2005, all previous editions of Annex 9".

Jamet, Constance. January 22, 2010. "Migrants débarqués en Corse: le HCR interpelle la France" ["Disembarked migrants in Corsica: the UNHCR calls on France"]. *Le Figaro.* Available at: http://www.lefigaro.fr/actualite-france/2010/01/22/01016-20100122ARTFIG00500-une-centaine-de-migrants-debarque-sur-une-plage-corse-.php. Accessed August 10, 2016.

Johnson, Heather L. 2011. "Click to Donate: visual images, constructing victims and imagining the female refugee". *Third World Quarterly* 32 (6): 1015–1037.

Johnson, Heather L. 2014. *Borders, Asylum and Global Non-Citizenship: The Other Side of the Fence.* Cambridge: Cambridge University Press.

Journal du droit des jeunes [Journal of youth's law]. 2015. "Centres de rétention administrative: toujours plus d'enfants enfermés, extrait du rapport 2014 sur les centres et locaux de rétention administrative publié par les organisations habilitées à venir en aide aux étrangers retenus" ["Administrative detention centers: always more children locked up, extract from the 2014 report on administrative detention centers published by organizations allowed to assist detained foreigners"]. 5 (345–346): 48–50.

Jupp, James. 2002. *From White Australia to Woomera. The Story of Australian Immigration.* New York: Cambridge University Press.

Karlsen, Elibritt. 2016. *Australia's offshore processing of asylum seekers in Nauru and PNG: a quick guide to statistics and resources.* Parliamentary Library, Research Paper Series, 2016–17.

Khosravi, Shahram. 2010. *"Illegal" Traveller: an auto-ethnography of borders.* Houndsmills, Basingstoke, Hampshire and New York: Palgrave Macmillan.

King, Hugh. 2009. "The extraterritorial human rights obligations of states". *Human Rights Law Review* 9 (4): 521–556.

Klemperer, Victor. 2000. *The language of the Third Reich: LTI-Lingua Tertii Imperii: a Philologist's Notebook.* The Athlone Press.

Kneebone, Susan. 2006. "The Pacific Plan: The Provision of 'Effective Protection'?" *International Journal of Refugee Law* 18 (3–4): 696–721.

Kneebone, Susan. 2010. "Controlling migration by Sea: The Australian Case". In *Extraterritorial Immigration Control, Legal Challenges*, edited by Bernard Ryan and Valsamis Mitsilegas, 347–374. Leiden and Boston: Martinus Nijhoff Publishers.

Kpatinde, Francis. 1995. "(Asylum in Europe)-Welcome to Limbo". *Refugees Magazine* 101.

Labayle, Henri. 1993. "Règlementation et souveraineté des Etats" ["Regulations and State sovereignty"]. In *Frontières du droit, frontières des droits: l'introuvable statut de la "zone internationale"* [Borders of law, borders of rights: the impossible status of the "international zone"], edited by Anafé, 45–61. Paris: L'Harmattan.

Lachaume, Jean-François. 1985 "Jurisprudence française concernant le droit international public. Année 1984" ["French case law regarding international public law. Year 1984"]. *Annuaire français de droit international* 31: 919–961.

Langford, Malcolm et al, ed. 2013. *Global Justice, State Duties: The Extra-territorial Scope of Economic, Social and Cultural Rights in International Law.* Cambridge University Press.

Lauterpacht, Sir Elihu and Daniel Bethlehem. 2003. "The Scope and Content of the Principle of Non-Refoulement: Opinion", In *Refugee Protection in International Law, UNHCR Global Consultations on International Protection,* edited by Erika Feller, Volker Türk and Frances Nicholson, 87–177. Cambridge University Press. Available at: http://www.refworld.org/docid/470a33af0.html Accessed January 28, 2019.

Le Monde, March 14, 2012. "François Hollande s'engage à mettre fin à la rétention des enfants. Le candidat socialiste s'est engagé par écrit à ne plus placer les enfants d'immigrés clandestins en centre de rétention, s'il élu" ["François Hollande commits to end children detention. The Socialist candidate committed in writing to stop detaining illegal migrants should he be elected"]. Available at: https://www.lemonde.fr/election-presidentielle-2012/article/2012/03/14/francois-hollande-s-engage-a-mettre-fin-a-la-retention-des-enfants_1669109_1471069.html Accessed April 22, 2019.

Lipietz, Hélène. November 22, 2012. *Sénat, session ordinaire de 2012–2013, Avis n° 154 présenté au nom de la commission des lois constitutionnelles, de législation, du suffrage universel, du Règlement et d'administration générale (1) sur le projet de loi de finances pour 2013, adopté par l'assemblée nationale, tome XI, immigration, integration et nationalité* [Senate, ordinary session of 2012–2013, Opinion n°154 presented on behalf of the commission of constitutional laws, legislation, universal suffrage, Regulations and general admistration on the 2013 finance bill, adopted by the national assembly, volume XI, immigration, integration and nationality]. Available at: http://www.senat.fr/rap/a12-154-11/a12-154-11.html Accessed September 8, 2016.

Lochak, Danièle. 1992. "Bulletin de jurisprudence française" ["Bulletin of French case law"]. *Journal du droit international* [Journal of international law].

Lord Byron. 1823. *Don Juan.* Penguin Classics 2004.

Lord Mackie of Benshie. September 12, 1991. *Report on the arrival of asylum seekers at European airports.* Report N°6490. Parliamentary Assembly of the Council of Europe.

Macklin, Audrey. 2005. "Disappearing Refugees: Reflections on the Canada-U.S. Safe Third Country Agreement", *Columbia Human Rights Law Review* (36) 2: 101–161.

Makaremi, Chowra. 2007. "Alien confinement in Europe: violence and the Law. The case of Roissy-Charles de Gaulle airport in France". In *Literature of concentration camps,* edited by Colman Hogan and Marta Marín-Dòmine, 39–54. Newcastle : Cambridge Scholar Press.

Makaremi, Chowra. 2008. "Participer en observant. Etudier et assister les étrangers aux frontières" ["Participating while observing. Studying and assisting foreign nationals at borders"]. In *Politiques de l'enquête; épreuves ethnographiques,* [Politics of research; ethnographic proofs] edited by Didier Fassin and Alban Bensa, 165–183. Paris: La Découverte.

Makaremi, Chowra. 2009 a. "Governing Borders in France: From Extra-territorial to Humanitarian Confinement". *Canadian Journal of Law and Society* 24 (3): 411–432.

Makaremi, Chowra. 2009 b. "Violence et refoulement dans la zone d'attente de Roissy" ["Violence and return in Charles de Gaulle's waiting zone"]. In *Enfermés dehors, enquêtes sur le confinement des étrangers,* [Locked outside, enquiries on the confinement of non-citizens] edited by Carolina Kobelinsky and Chowra Makaremi, Paris: Editions du Croquant.

Mares, Peter. August 2011. "Ten years after Tampa". *The Monthly.* Available at: https://www.themonthly.com.au/issue/2011/august/1316394350/peter-mares/comment-ten-years-after-tampa Accessed January 20, 2019.

Martini, Jean-François. 2004. "Mineurs sans famille en zone d'attente", *Revue Hommes et migrations* 1251: 23–31. Available at: http://www.hommes-et-migrations.fr/index.php?/numeros/enfants-sans-frontieres/1334-mineurs-sans-famille-en-zone-d-attente. Accessed 16 September 2015.

Mathew, Penelope. 2002."Australian Refuge Protection in the Wake of the Tampa". *The American Journal of International Law* 96 (3): 661–676.

Mcadam, Jane. 2013. "Australia and Asylum Seekers". *International Journal of Refugee Law* 25 (3): 435–448.

McNevin, Anne. 2007. "The Liberal Paradox and the Politics of Asylum in Australia". *Australian Journal of Political Science* 42 (4): 611-630.

McNevin, Anne. 2014. "Forced Migration in Australia, New Zealand, and the Pacific." In *The Oxford Handbook of Refugee and Forced Migration Studies*, edited by Elena Fiddian-Qasmiyeh et al.

Médecins du Monde. March 6, 2003. *La zone d'attente de Roissy, une zone de non-droit, rapport 2002* [Roissy's waiting zone, a non-right zone, 2002 report]. Available at: http://www.gisti.org/doc/actions/2003/anafe/accablant.html. Accessed January 25, 2016.

Melville, Herman. 1853. *Bartleby, the Scrivener*. Available at: http://www.bartleby.com/129/.

Morin, Edgar and Anne-Brigitte Kern, 1999. *Homeland Earth: A manifesto for the new millennium*. Cresskill, NJ: Hampton Press.

Mountz, Alison. 2010. *Seeking Asylum: Human Smuggling and Bureaucracy at the Border.* Minneapolis: University of Minnesota Press.

Mountz, Alison. 2013. "Shrinking spaces of asylum: vanishing points where geography is used to inhibit and undermine access to asylum". *Australian Journal of Human Rights* 19 (3): 29–50.

NGO letter to the president of the French Constitutional Council. January 28, 1992.

Ocelot, Michel. 1998 "*Kirikou et la sorcière*" (*Kirikou and the witch*).

Office Français de Protection des Réfugiés et Apatrides (OFPRA) [French Office for the Protection of Refugees and Stateless Persons]. April 11, 2012. *Rapport d'activité 2011.* [Activity report 2011]. Available at: https://ofpra.gouv.fr/sites/default/files/atoms/files/rapport_dactivite_2011.pdf. Accessed August 16, 2016.

Office Français de Protection des Réfugiés et Apatrides (OFPRA) [French Office for the Protection of Refugees and Stateless Persons]. April 24, 2013. *Rapport d'activité 2012* [Activity report 2012]. Available at: https://ofpra.gouv.fr/sites/default/files/atoms/files/rapport_dactivite_2012_0.pdf. Accessed August 16, 2016.

Office Français de Protection des Réfugiés et Apatrides (OFPRA) [French Office for the Protection of Refugees and Stateless Persons]. April 12, 2014. *Rapport d'activité 2013* [Activity report 2013]. Available at: https://ofpra.gouv.fr/sites/default/files/atoms/files/rapport_dactivite_2013.pdf. Accessed August 16, 2016.

Office Français de Protection des Réfugiés et Apatrides (OFPRA) [French Office for the Protection of Refugees and Stateless Persons]. April 10, 2015. *Rapport d'activité 2014* [Activity report 2014]. Available at: https://ofpra.gouv.fr/sites/default/files/atoms/files/rapport_dactivite_2014.pdf Accessed August 16, 2016.

Office Français de Protection des Réfugiés et Apatrides (OFPRA) [French Office for the Protection of Refugees and Stateless Persons]. October 17, 2015. "Décision du 9 octobre 2015 fixant la liste des pays d'origine sûrs" ["Decision of October 9, 2015 establishing the list of safe countries of origin"]. *Journal Officiel de la République Française* [Official journal of the French Republic]. Available at: https://ofpra.gouv.fr/sites/default/files/atoms/files/151017_jorf_decision_ca_ofpra_du_9_octobre_2015.pdf. Accessed August 16, 2016.

Office Français de Protection des Réfugiés et Apatrides (OFPRA) [French Office for the Protection of Refugees and Stateless Persons]. May 13, 2016. *Rapport d'activité 2015* [Activity report 2015]. Available at: https://ofpra.gouv.fr/sites/default/files/atoms/files/rapport_dactivite_ofpra_2015_hd.pdf Accessed August 16, 2016.

Office Français de Protection des Réfugiés et Apatrides (OFPRA) [French Office for the Protection of Refugees and Stateless Persons]. April 3, 2017. *Rapport d'activité 2016* [Activity report 2016]. Available at: https://ofpra.gouv.fr/sites/default/files/atoms/files/rapport_dactivite_ofpra_2016_1.pdf Accessed April 11, 2019.

Office Français de Protection des Réfugiés et Apatrides (OFPRA) [French Office for the Protection of Refugees and Stateless Persons]. April 3, 2018. *Rapport d'activité 2017* [Activity report 2017]. Available at: https://ofpra.gouv.fr/sites/default/files/atoms/files/ra_ofpra2017_web_0604.pdf Accessed April 22, 2019.

Ordinance n°45–2658, November 2, 1945. *Ordonnance relative aux conditions d'entrée et de séjour des étrangers en France* [Ordinance regarding conditions of entry and residency of foreign nationals in France]. Available at: https://www.legifrance.gouv.fr/affichTexte.do?cidTexte=LEGITEXT000006069185 Accessed September 12, 2016.

Oxford Online English dictionary. Available at: http://www.oxforddictionaries.com/ Accessed December 7, 2014.

Paik, Naomi. 2016. *Rightlessness, Testimony and Redress in U.S. Prison Camps since World War II.* North Carolina: The University of North Carolina Press.

Palmer, Victoria and Julie Matthews 2006. "Excising Democracy: Ethical irresponsibility, Refugees and Migration Zones". *Social Alternatives* 25 (3) Third Quarter.

Paris'Airports [*Aéroports de Paris*]. 2012. *Guide du client 2012* [Customer guide 2012].

Paris Appeal Court [*Cour d'Appel de Paris*]. December 7, 2004. Ruling.

Paris Appeal Court [*Cour d'Appel de Paris*]. February 21, 2008. Ruling.

Paris Court of First Instance [*Tribunal de Grande Instance de Paris*]. February 26, 1992. First Chamber, Hearing.

Paris Court of First Instance [*Tribunal de Grande Instance de Paris*]. March 25, 1992. Ruling.

Perrigo, Billy. February 1, 2019. "Asylum Seeker Who Wrote Book on WhatsApp from Australian Detention Center Wins Literary Prize". *Time.* Available at: http://time.com/5518468/behrouz-boochani-whatsapp-book-prize/ Accessed April 8, 2019.

Peyrot, Maurice. November 21,1989. "La situation juridique de la zone internationale de l'aéroport de Roissy. Prisonnière au pays de nulle part" ["The legal situation of the international zone of Roissy airport. Prisoner in the nowhere country"]. *Le Monde.*

Phillips, Janet. September 4, 2012. *The "Pacific Solution" revisited: a statistical guide to the asylum seekers caseload on Nauru and Manus Island.* Parliament of Australia, Department of Parliamentary Services.

Phillips, Janet. 2017. *A comparison of Coalition and Labor government asylum policies in Australia since 2001.* Parliament of Australia, Department of Parliamentary Services.

Ramzy, Austin. April 26, 2016. "PNG Finds Australian Offshore Detention Center Illegal". *New York Times.* Available at: https://www.nytimes.com/2016/04/27/world/australia/papua-new-guinea-asylum-seeker.html?module=inline Accessed April 8, 2019.

Reid-Henry, Simon. 2007. "'Exceptional sovereignty?' Guantanamo Bay and the Re-Colonial Present". *Antipode* 39 (4): 627–648.

Roam, Chandra. 2018. "The Uncertain Future of Australia's Pacific Solution". *San Diego International Law Journal* 19 (2). Available at: https://digital.sandiego.edu/cgi/viewcontent.cgi?referer=https://www.google.com/&httpsredir=1&article=1064&context=ilj Accessed February 7, 2019.

Robert, Jacques. 1984. "Consultation".

Rodier, Claire. 2012. *Xénophobie business. A quoi servent les contrôles migratoires?* [Xenophobia business. What is the use of migration controls?] Paris: La Découverte.

Rotman, Charlotte. April 23, 2001. "Les Kurdes naufragés venaient de Syrie, non d'Irak" ["The shipwrecked Kurds came from Syria, not Irak"]. *Libération*, Available at: http://www.liberation.fr/societe/2001/04/23/les-kurdes-naufrages-venaient-de-syrie-non-d-irak_362048. Accessed August 11, 2016.

Ryan, Bernard and Valsamis Mitsilegas, ed. 2010. *Extraterritorial Immigration Control, Legal Challenges*. Leiden and Boston: Martinus Nijhoff Publishers.

Salomon, Margot E. and Ian Seiderman. November 2012. "Human Rights Norms for a Globalized World: The Maastricht Principles on Extraterritorial Obligations of States in the area of Economic, Social and Cultural Rights". *Global Policy* 3 (4): 458–462.

Salter, Mark B. 2007. "Governmentalities of an Airport: Heterotopia and Confession". *International Political Sociology* 1, 49–66.

Schloenhardt, Andreas. 2002. "To Deter, Detain and Deny : Protection of Onshore Asylum Seekers in Australia". *International Journal of Refugee Law* 14 (2/3).

Scholten, Sophie. 2015. *The Privatisation of Immigration Control through Carrier Sanctions. The Role of Private Transport Companies in Dutch and British Immigration Control*. The Netherlands: Brill Nijhoff.

Shachar, Ayelet. 2007. "The Shifting Border of Immigration Regulation". *Stanford Journal of Civil Rights and Civil Liberties* 3.

Simonnot, Dominique and Didier Hassoux. February 21, 2001. "Les clandestins kurdes entrent en France" ["Kurdish illegals enter France"]. *Libération*, Available at: http://www.liberation.fr/evenement/2001/02/21/les-clandestins-kurdes-entrent-en-france_355340 Accessed August 11, 2016.

Stratton, Jon. 2009 "Uncertain lives: migration, the border and neoliberalism in Australia". *Social Identities* 15 (5).

Taylor, Savitri. 2005. "Sovereign power at the border". *Public Law Review* 16 (1): 55–77.

Taylor, Savitri. 2006. "Protection Elsewhere/Nowhere". *International Journal of Refugee Law* 18 (2).

The Guardian. November 10, 2001. "Australia votes on how tightly to close the door". Available at: https://www.theguardian.com/world/2001/nov/10/immigration.uk Accessed January 21, 2019.

The Sydney Morning Herald. July 8, 2003. "Keeping Boat People Away Worth Any Amount, Says PM". Available at: https://www.smh.com.au/politics/federal/keeping-boat-people-away-worth-any-amount-says-pm-20030708-gdh28j.html Accessed February 19, 2019.

The Sydney Morning Herald. "Gillard announces Malaysian Solution". May 7, 2011. Available at:https://www.smh.com.au/national/gillard-announces-malaysian-solution-20110507-1ed0h.html Accessed February 8, 2019.

UNDP. 2018. *Human Development Indices and Indicators: 2018 Statistical Update. Briefing note for countries on the 2018 Statistical Update. Papua New Guinea*. Available at: http://hdr.undp.org/sites/all/themes/hdr_theme/country-notes/PNG.pdf Accessed April 9, 2019.

UN General Assembly. July 28, 1951. *Convention Relating to the Status of Refugees*. United Nations, Treaty Series, vol. 189, p. 137. Available at: http://www.refworld.org/docid/3be01b964.html. Accessed May 23, 2016.

UN General Assembly. January 31, 1967. *Protocol Relating to the Status of Refugees*, United Nations, Treaty Series, vol. 606, p. 267. Available at: http://www.refworld.org/docid/3ae6b3ae4.html. Accessed May 23, 2016.

UN General Assembly. November 20, 1989. *Convention on the Rights of the Child, adopted and opened for signature, ratification and accession by General Assembly resolution 44/25 of 20 November 1989, entry into force 2 September 1990, in accordance with article 49*. Available at: http://www.refworld.org/docid/3ae6b38f0.html. Accessed May 26, 2016.

UNHCR, Executive Committee (Excom). 1989. Conclusion No. 58 "Problem of Refugees and Asylum Seekers who move in an irregular manner from a country in which they had already found protection". Available at: https://www.unhcr.org/excom/exconc/3ae68c4380/problem-refugees-asylum-seekers-move-irregular-manner-country-already-found.html Accessed April 1, 2019.

UNHCR. July 2002. *Resettlement handbook*. Available at: https://reliefweb.int/sites/reliefweb.int/files/resources/597312D96EB2CAB1C1256C61004B0961-hcr-resettlement-jul97.pdf Accessed April 1, 2019.

UNHCR. June 2006. *UNHCR Master Glossary of Terms*. Available at: http://www.unhcr.org/refworld/docid/42ce7d444.html Accessed January 19, 2019.

UNHCR. 2012. *Frequently Asked Questions about Resettlement*. Available at: https://www.unhcr.org/4ac0873d6.html Accessed February 28, 2019.

UNHCR. 2015. *Submission by the United Nations High Commissioner for Refugees for the Office of the High Commissioner for Human Rights' Compilation Report Universal Periodic Review: 2nd Cycle, 23rd Session. The Republic of Nauru*. Available at: https://www.refworld.org/pdfid/563860c54.pdf Accessed January 28, 2019.

UNHCR. December 2016. *Indonesia: fact sheet*. Available at: https://www.unhcr.org/id/wp-content/uploads/sites/42/2017/05/Indonesia-Fact-Sheet-December-2016.pdf Accessed January 17, 2019.

United Nations. Treaty collection. Available at: https://treaties.un.org/Pages/ViewDetailsII.aspx?src=TREATY&mtdsg_no=V-2&chapter=5&Temp=mtdsg2&clang=_en Accessed October 19, 2018.

Vogl, Anthea. 2015. "Over the borderline: a critical inquiry into the geography of territorial excision and the securitisation of the Australian border" *UNSW Law Journal* 38 (1): 114–145.

Volpp, Leti. 2012. "Imaginings of Space in Immigration Law". *Law, Culture and the Humanities:* 1-19.

Waitt, Gordon. 2010. "Doing Foucauldian Discourse Analysis, Revealing Social Realities", in I. Hay (ed.) *Qualitative Methods in Human Geography*, third edition, Melbourne: Oxford University Press, 163-161.

Weber, Leanne. 2006. "The Shifting Frontiers of Migration Control". In *Borders, mobility and technologies of control*, edited by Sharon Pickering, 21–43. Netherlands: Springer.

Weber, Leanne. 2007. "Policing the Virtual Border: Punitive Preemption in Australian Offshore Migration Control". *Social Justice* 34, no. 2 (108), Beyond Transnational Crime, 77–93.

Weissbrodt, David, and Cheryl Heilman. 2011. "Defining Torture and Cruel, Inhuman, and Degrading Treatment". *Law and Inequality* 29 (343). Available at: http://scholarship.law.umn.edu/faculty_articles/366. Accessed September 7, 2016.

Weizman, Eyal. 2005. "On extraterritoriality. Conference lectured at the symposium Archipelago of exception—sovereignties of extraterritoriality", 10–11 November. Available at: http://www.publicspace.org/ca/text-biblioteca/eng/b011-on-extraterritoriality Accessed September 20, 2016.

Wihtol de Wenden, Catherine. 2016. *Migrations, Une nouvelle donne* [Migrations, a new deal]. Paris: Maison des Sciences de l'Homme.

Index

www.ingramcontent.com/pod-product-compliance
Lightning Source LLC
LaVergne TN
LVHW020634300926
849161LV00004B/694
9789004383494